Miss Kobayashi's Dragon Maid

12

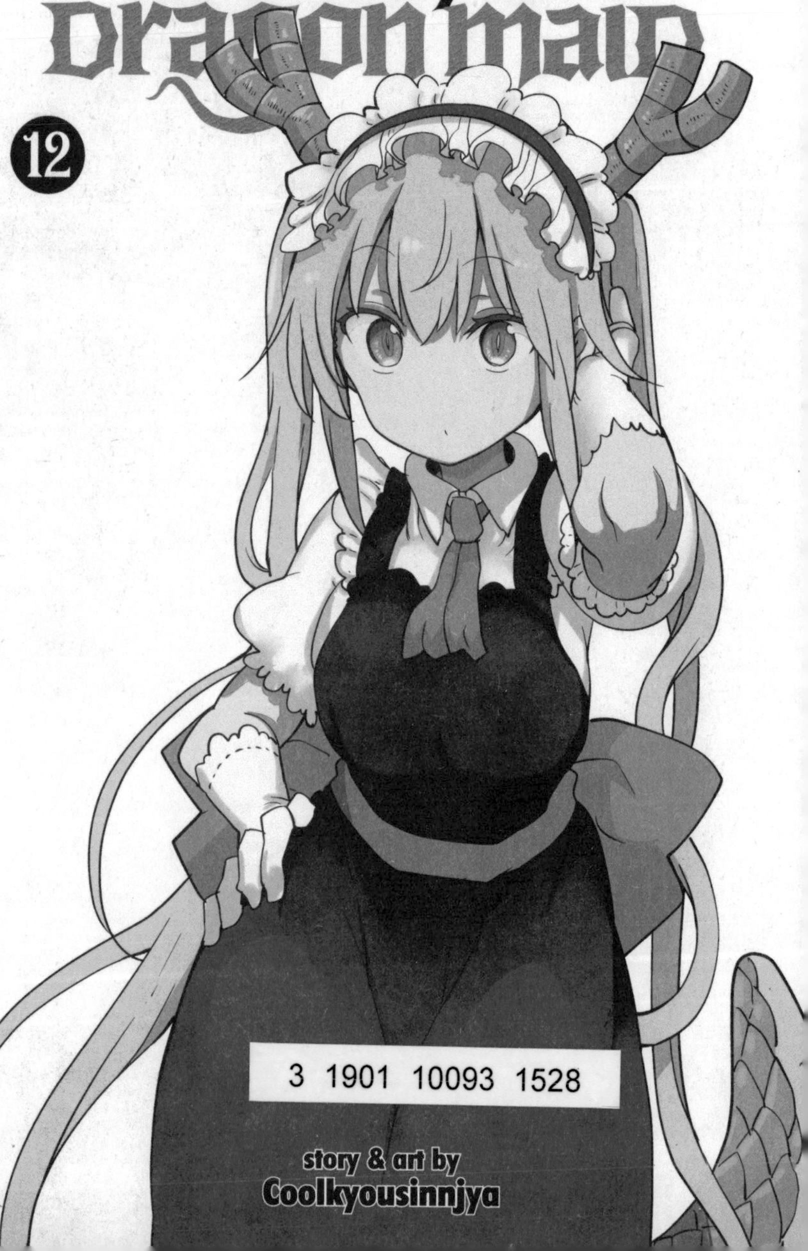

story & art by
Coolkyousinnjya

Miss Kobayashi's
DRAGON MAID

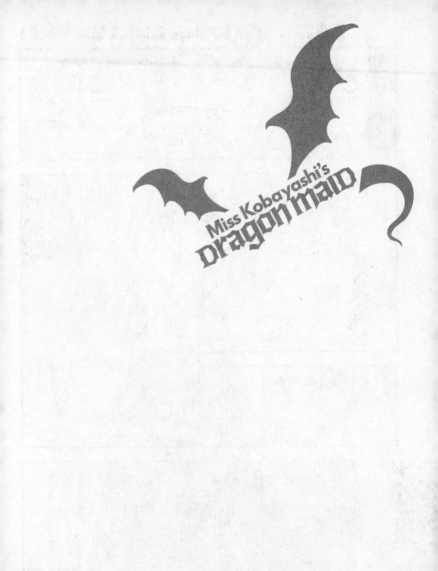

CHAPTER 106: ELMA & MARRIAGE I

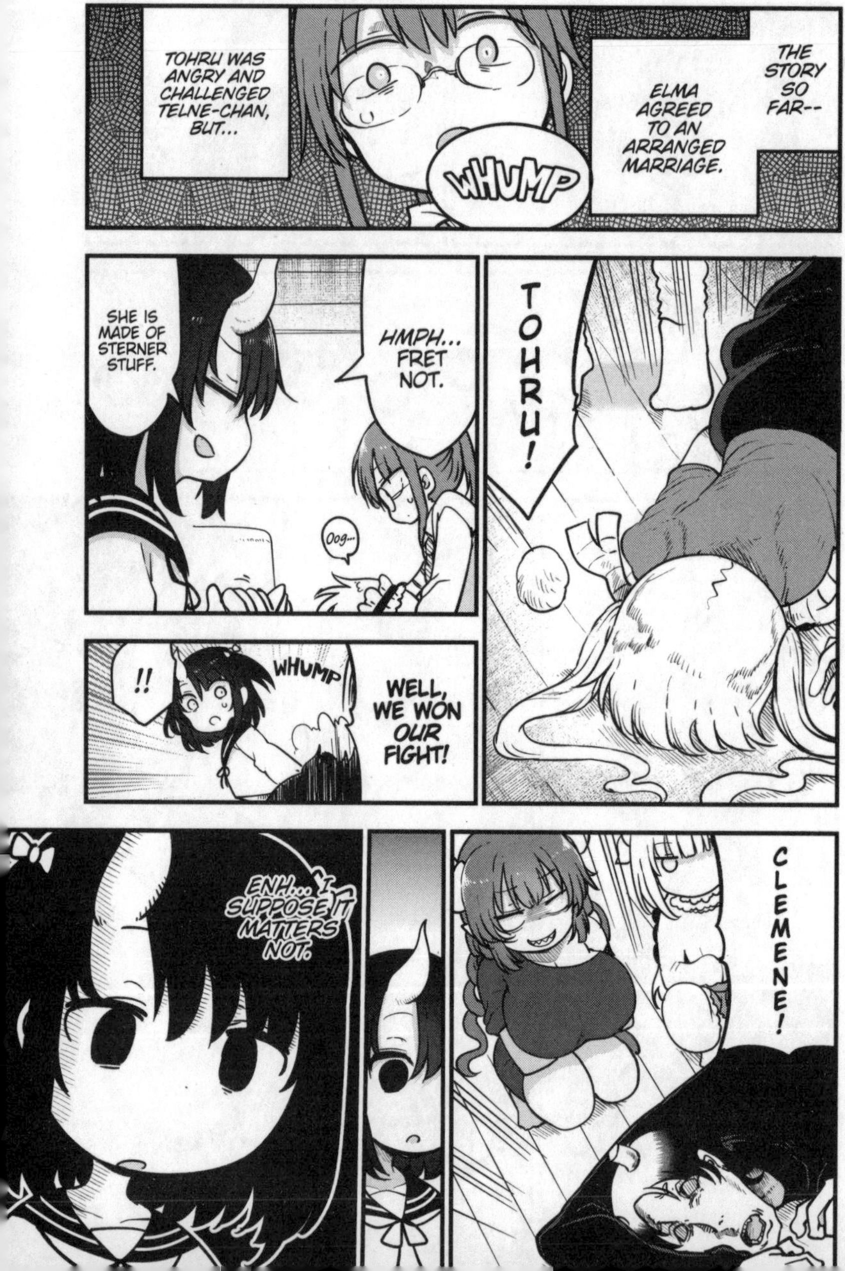
THE STORY SO FAR--
ELMA AGREED TO AN ARRANGED MARRIAGE.
WHUMP
TOHRU WAS ANGRY AND CHALLENGED TELNE-CHAN, BUT...
TOHRU!
HMPH... FRET NOT.
SHE IS MADE OF STERNER STUFF.
Oog...
WELL, WE WON OUR FIGHT!
WHUMP
!!
CLEMENE!
ENH... I SUPPOSE IT MATTERS NOT.

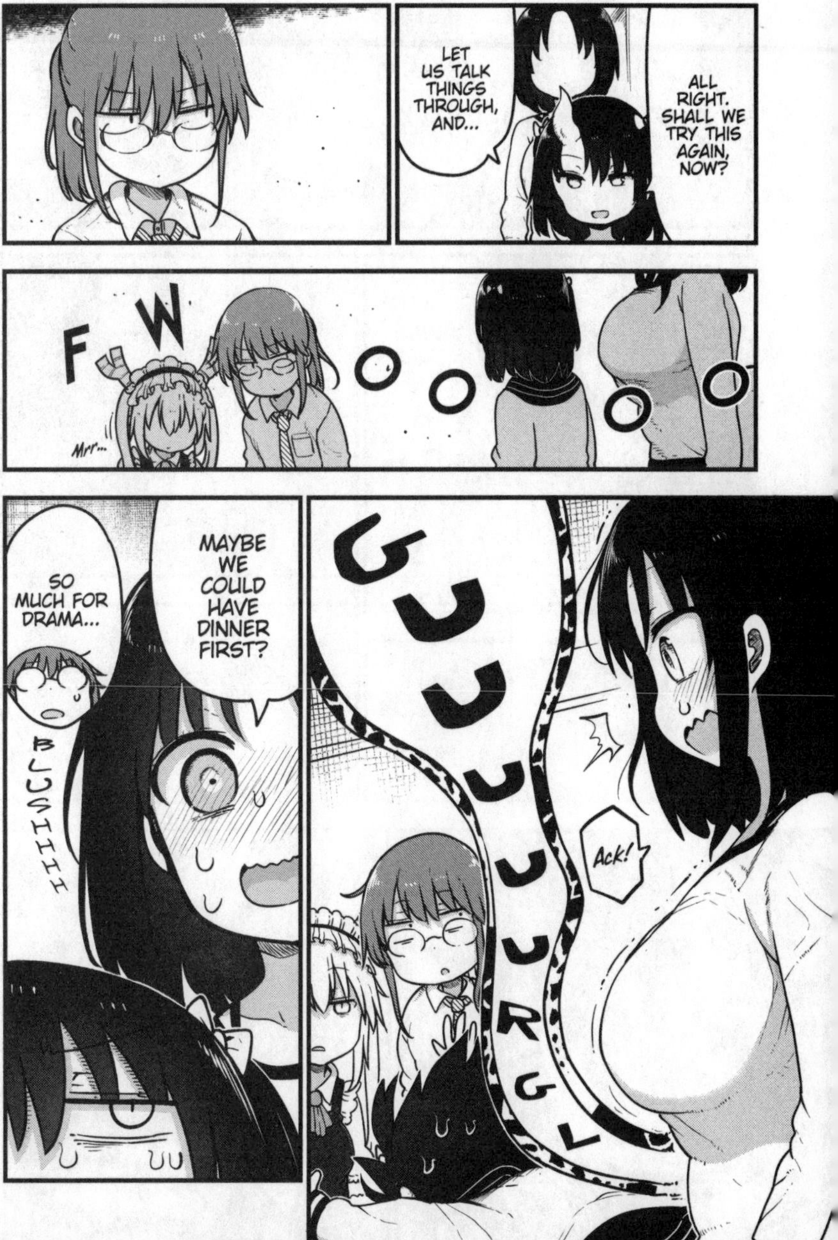
LET US TALK THINGS THROUGH, AND...
ALL RIGHT. SHALL WE TRY THIS AGAIN, NOW?
FWOOOOO
Mrr...
GUUUUURGL
Ack!
MAYBE WE COULD HAVE DINNER FIRST?
SO MUCH FOR DRAMA...
BLUSHHHH

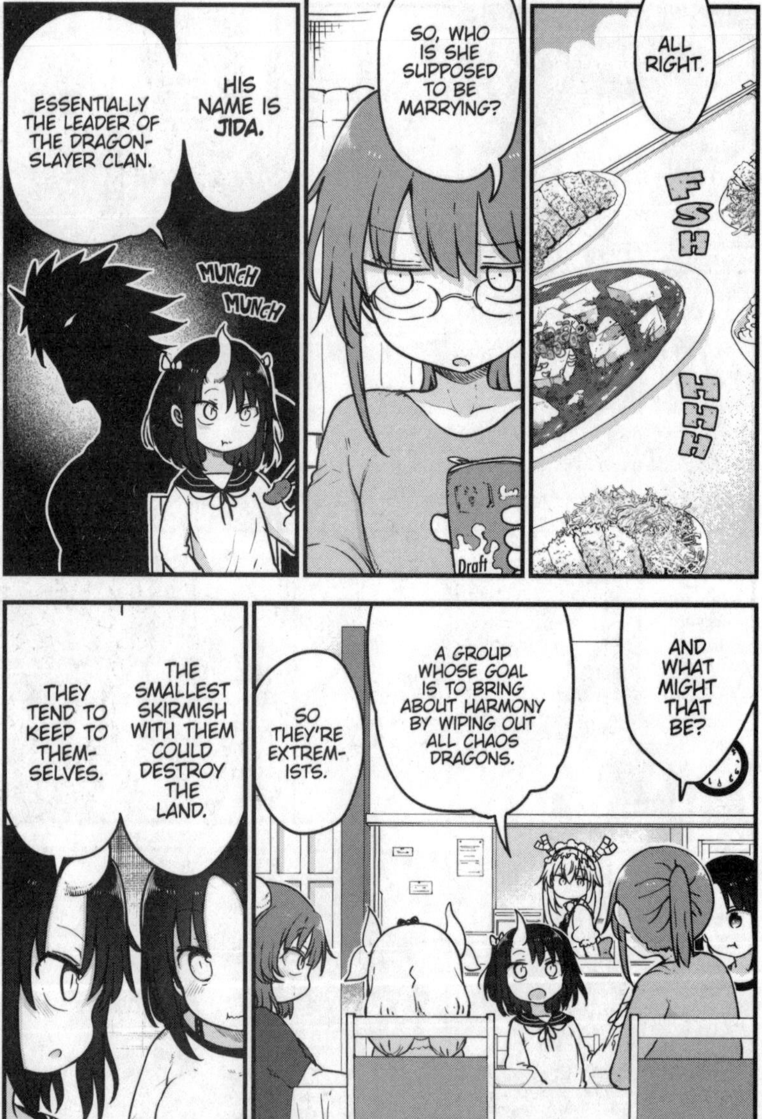
ALL RIGHT.
FSH
HHHH
SO, WHO IS SHE SUPPOSED TO BE MARRYING?
Draft
HIS NAME IS JIDA.
ESSENTIALLY THE LEADER OF THE DRAGON-SLAYER CLAN.
MUNCH MUNCH
AND WHAT MIGHT THAT BE?
A GROUP WHOSE GOAL IS TO BRING ABOUT HARMONY BY WIPING OUT ALL CHAOS DRAGONS.
SO THEY'RE EXTREM-ISTS.
THE SMALLEST SKIRMISH WITH THEM COULD DESTROY THE LAND.
THEY TEND TO KEEP TO THEM-SELVES.

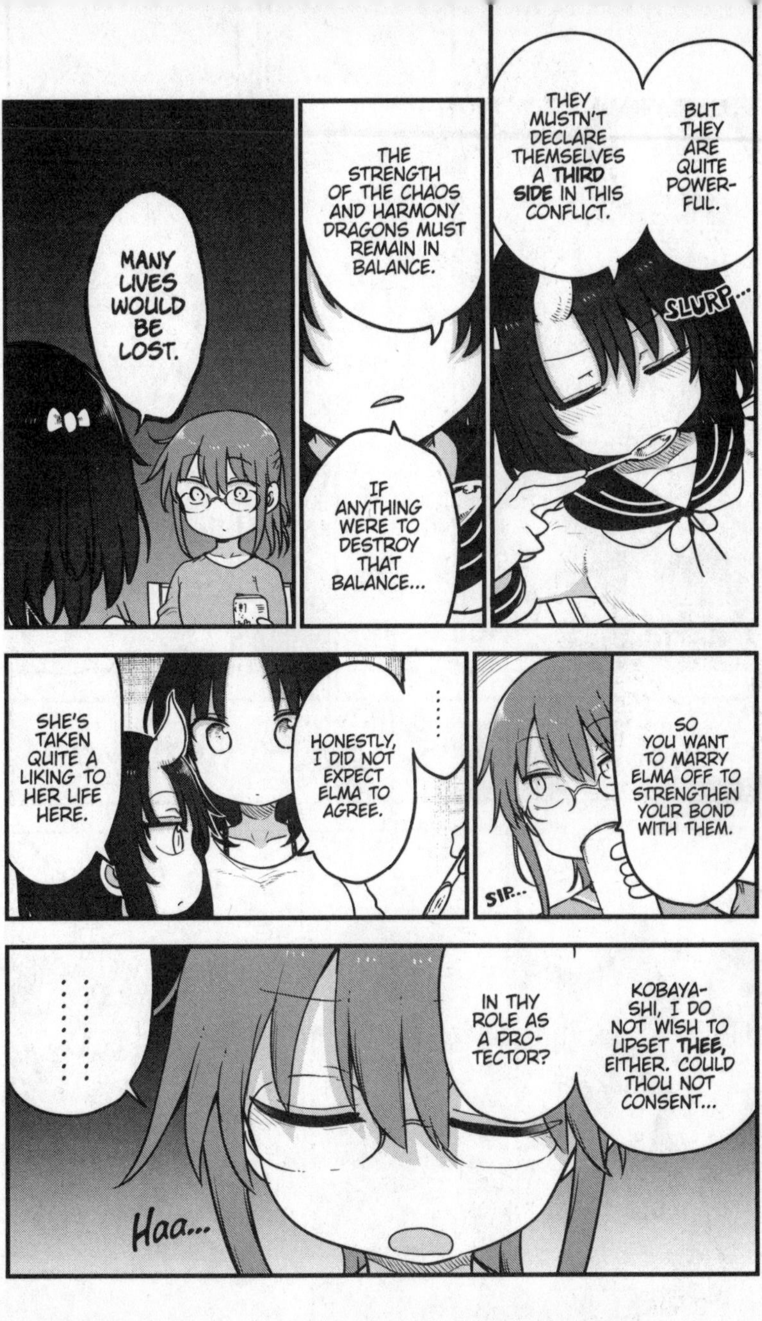
BUT THEY ARE QUITE POWER-FUL.
THEY MUSTN'T DECLARE THEMSELVES A **THIRD SIDE** IN THIS CONFLICT.
SLURP...
THE STRENGTH OF THE CHAOS AND HARMONY DRAGONS MUST REMAIN IN BALANCE.
IF ANYTHING WERE TO DESTROY THAT BALANCE...
MANY LIVES WOULD BE LOST.
SO YOU WANT TO MARRY ELMA OFF TO STRENGTHEN YOUR BOND WITH THEM.
SIP...
......
HONESTLY, I DID NOT EXPECT ELMA TO AGREE.
SHE'S TAKEN QUITE A LIKING TO HER LIFE HERE.
KOBAYA-SHI, I DO NOT WISH TO UPSET **THEE**, EITHER. COULD THOU NOT CONSENT...
IN THY ROLE AS A PRO-TECTOR?
......
Haa...

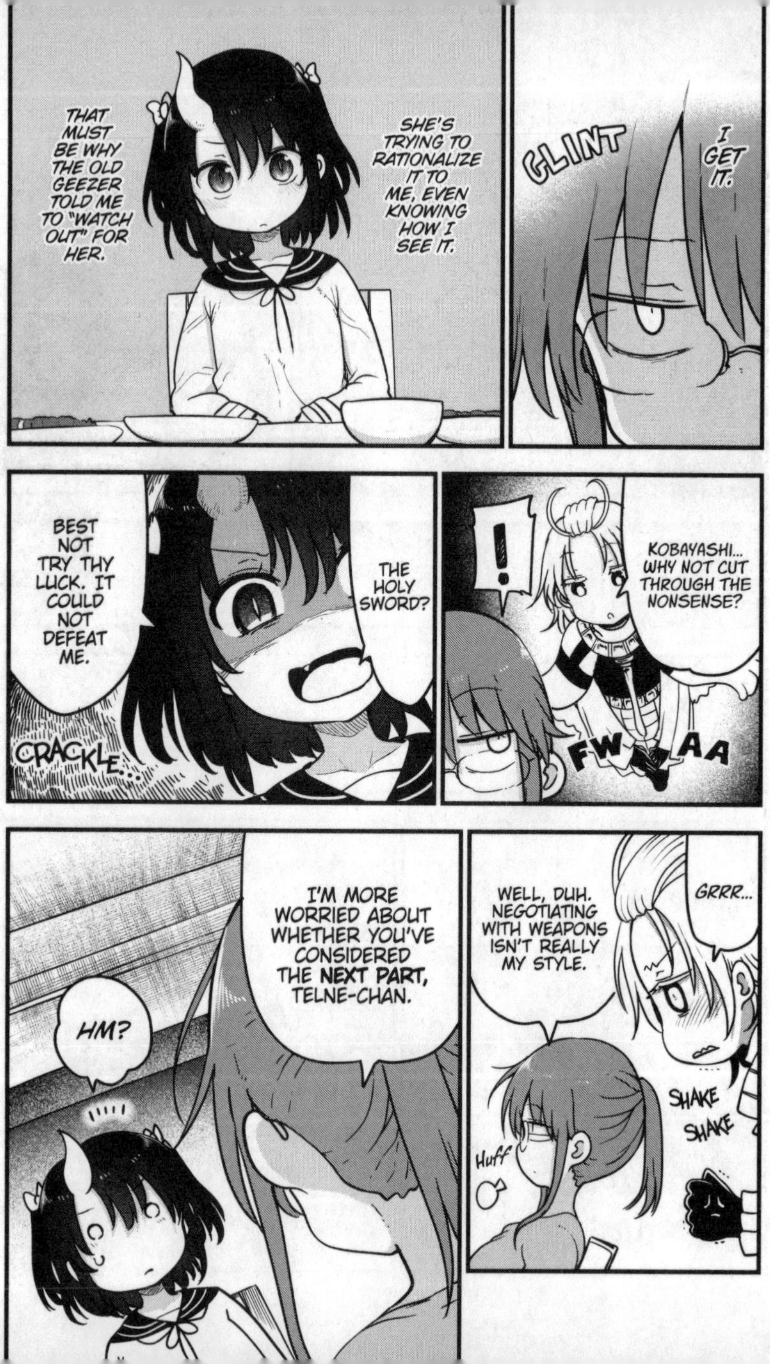

I GET IT.
GLINT
SHE'S TRYING TO RATIONALIZE IT TO ME, EVEN KNOWING HOW I SEE IT.
THAT MUST BE WHY THE OLD GEEZER TOLD ME TO "WATCH OUT" FOR HER.
KOBAYASHI... WHY NOT CUT THROUGH THE NONSENSE?
!
FW AA
THE HOLY SWORD?
BEST NOT TRY THY LUCK. IT COULD NOT DEFEAT ME.
CRACKLE...
GRRR...
WELL, DUH. NEGOTIATING WITH WEAPONS ISN'T REALLY MY STYLE.
SHAKE
SHAKE
Huff
I'M MORE WORRIED ABOUT WHETHER YOU'VE CONSIDERED THE NEXT PART, TELNE-CHAN.
HM?

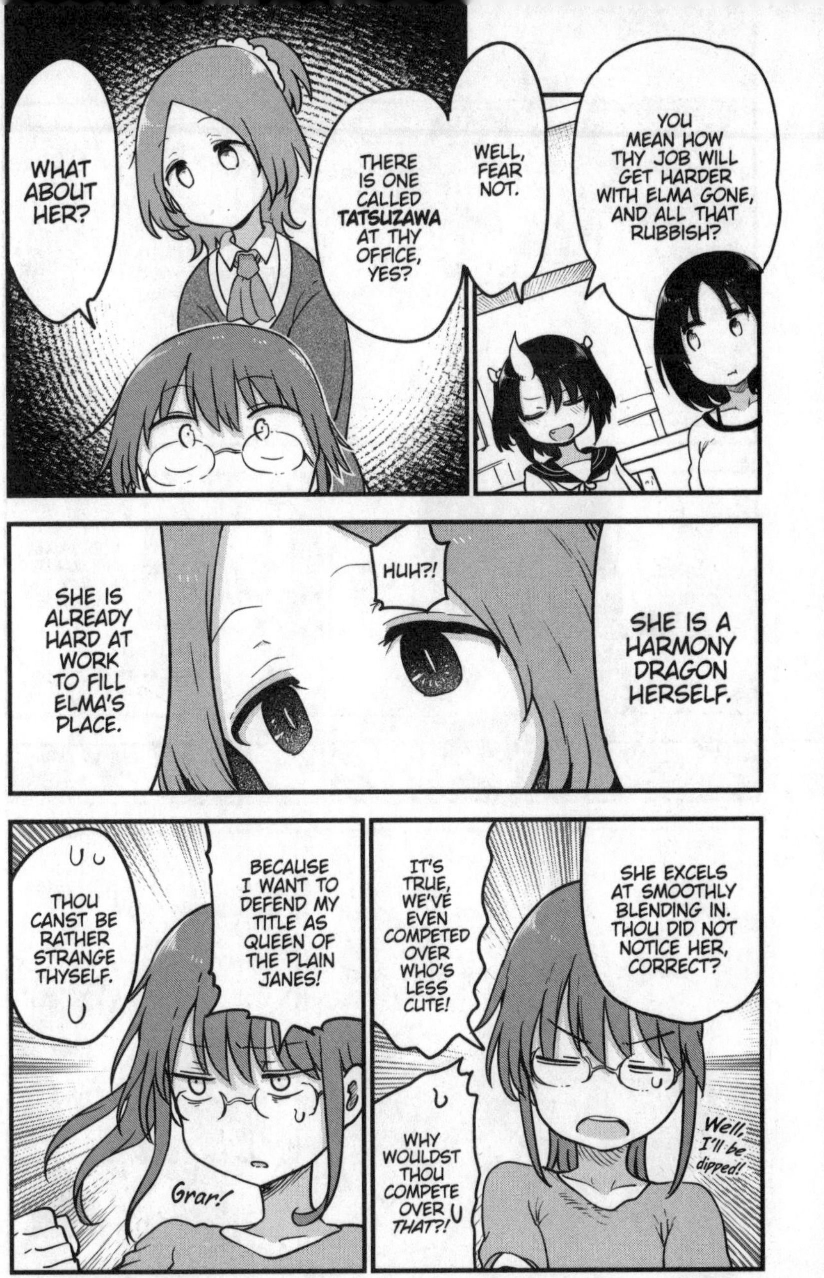
YOU MEAN HOW THY JOB WILL GET HARDER WITH ELMA GONE, AND ALL THAT RUBBISH?
WELL, FEAR NOT.
THERE IS ONE CALLED **TATSUZAWA** AT THY OFFICE, YES?
WHAT ABOUT HER?
HUH?!
SHE IS A HARMONY DRAGON HERSELF.
SHE IS ALREADY HARD AT WORK TO FILL ELMA'S PLACE.
SHE EXCELS AT SMOOTHLY BLENDING IN. THOU DID NOT NOTICE HER, CORRECT?
Well, I'll be dipped!
IT'S TRUE, WE'VE EVEN COMPETED OVER WHO'S LESS CUTE!
WHY WOULDST THOU COMPETE OVER *THAT*?!
BECAUSE I WANT TO DEFEND MY TITLE AS QUEEN OF THE PLAIN JANES!
THOU CANST BE RATHER STRANGE THYSELF.
Grar!

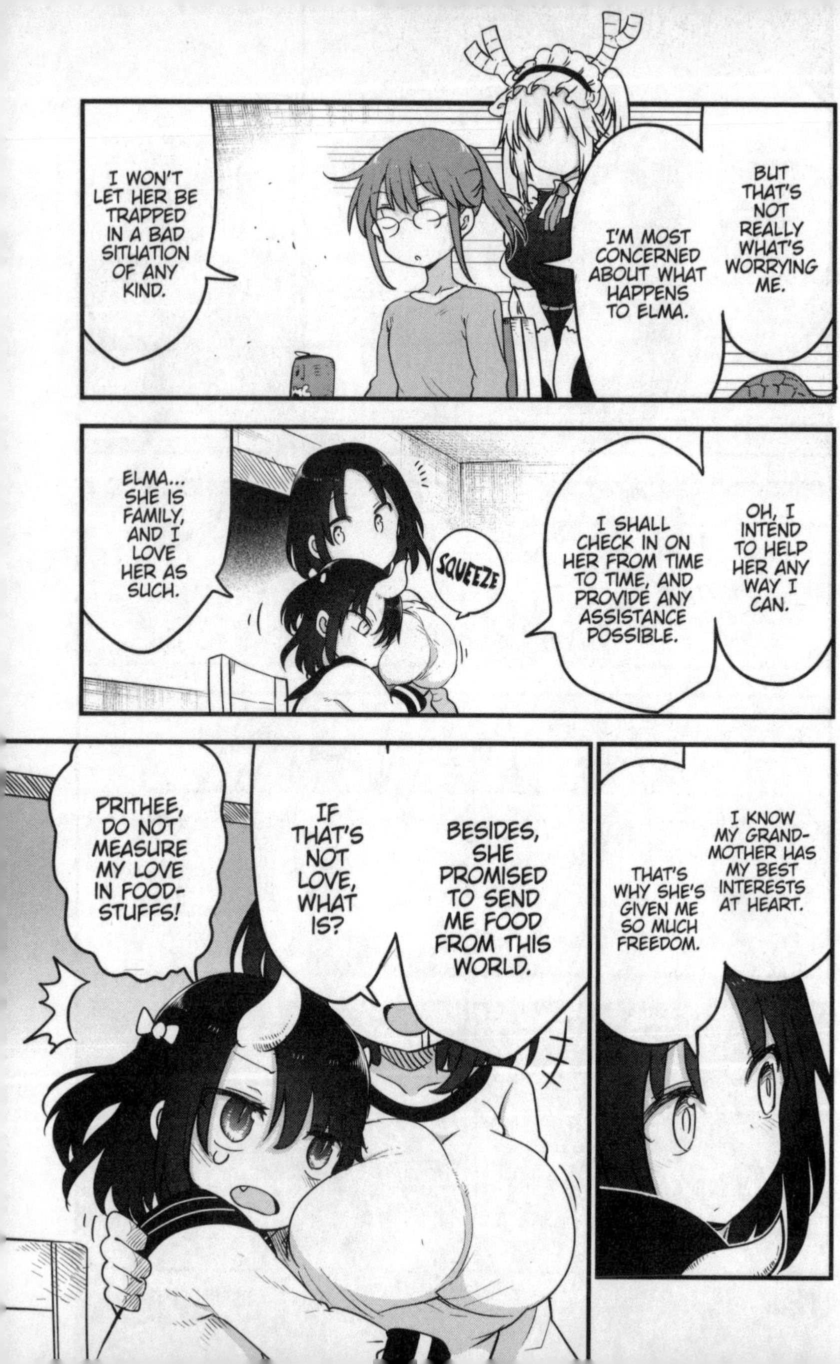
BUT THAT'S NOT REALLY WHAT'S WORRYING ME.
I'M MOST CONCERNED ABOUT WHAT HAPPENS TO ELMA.
I WON'T LET HER BE TRAPPED IN A BAD SITUATION OF ANY KIND.
OH, I INTEND TO HELP HER ANY WAY I CAN.
I SHALL CHECK IN ON HER FROM TIME TO TIME, AND PROVIDE ANY ASSISTANCE POSSIBLE.
SQUEEZE
ELMA... SHE IS FAMILY, AND I LOVE HER AS SUCH.
I KNOW MY GRAND-MOTHER HAS MY BEST INTERESTS AT HEART.
THAT'S WHY SHE'S GIVEN ME SO MUCH FREEDOM.
BESIDES, SHE PROMISED TO SEND ME FOOD FROM THIS WORLD.
IF THAT'S NOT LOVE, WHAT IS?
PRITHEE, DO NOT MEASURE MY LOVE IN FOOD-STUFFS!

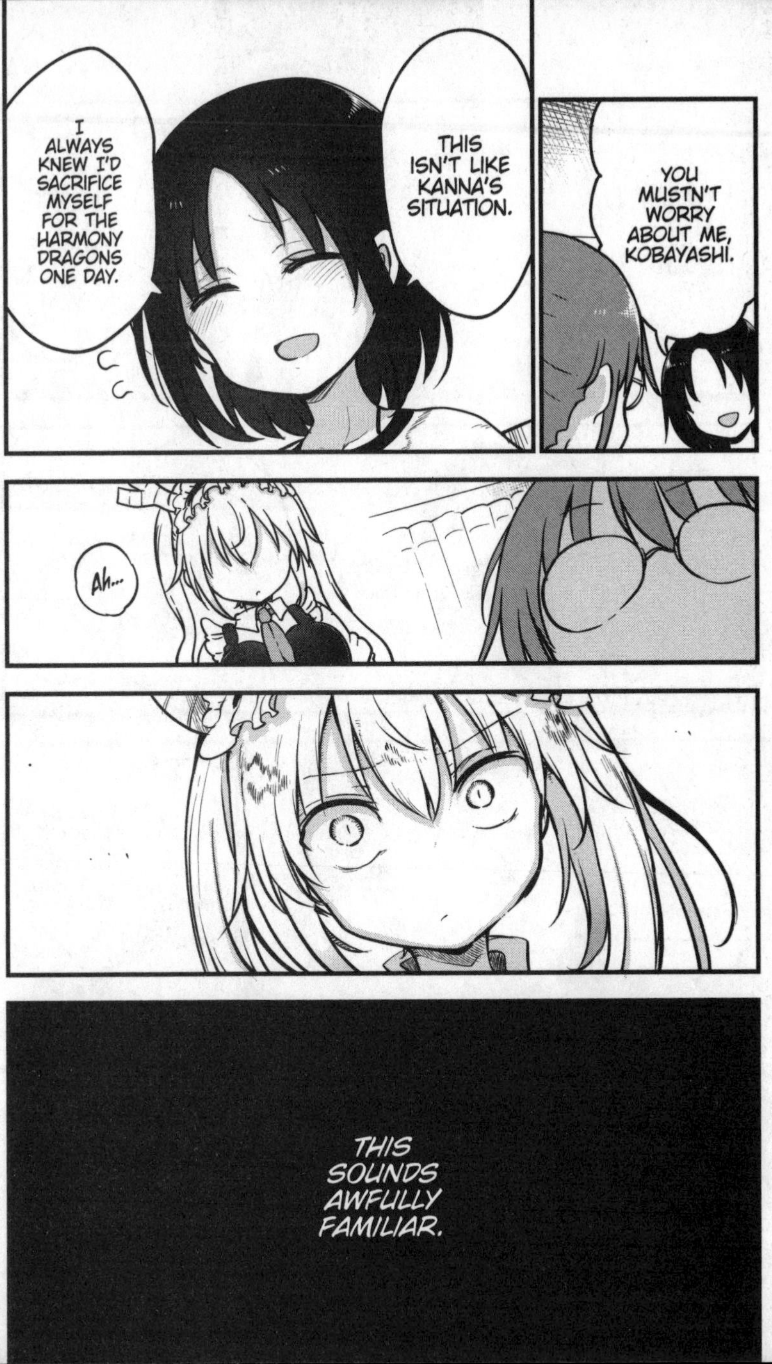
YOU MUSTN'T WORRY ABOUT ME, KOBAYASHI.
THIS ISN'T LIKE KANNA'S SITUATION.
I ALWAYS KNEW I'D SACRIFICE MYSELF FOR THE HARMONY DRAGONS ONE DAY.
Ah...
THIS SOUNDS AWFULLY FAMILIAR.

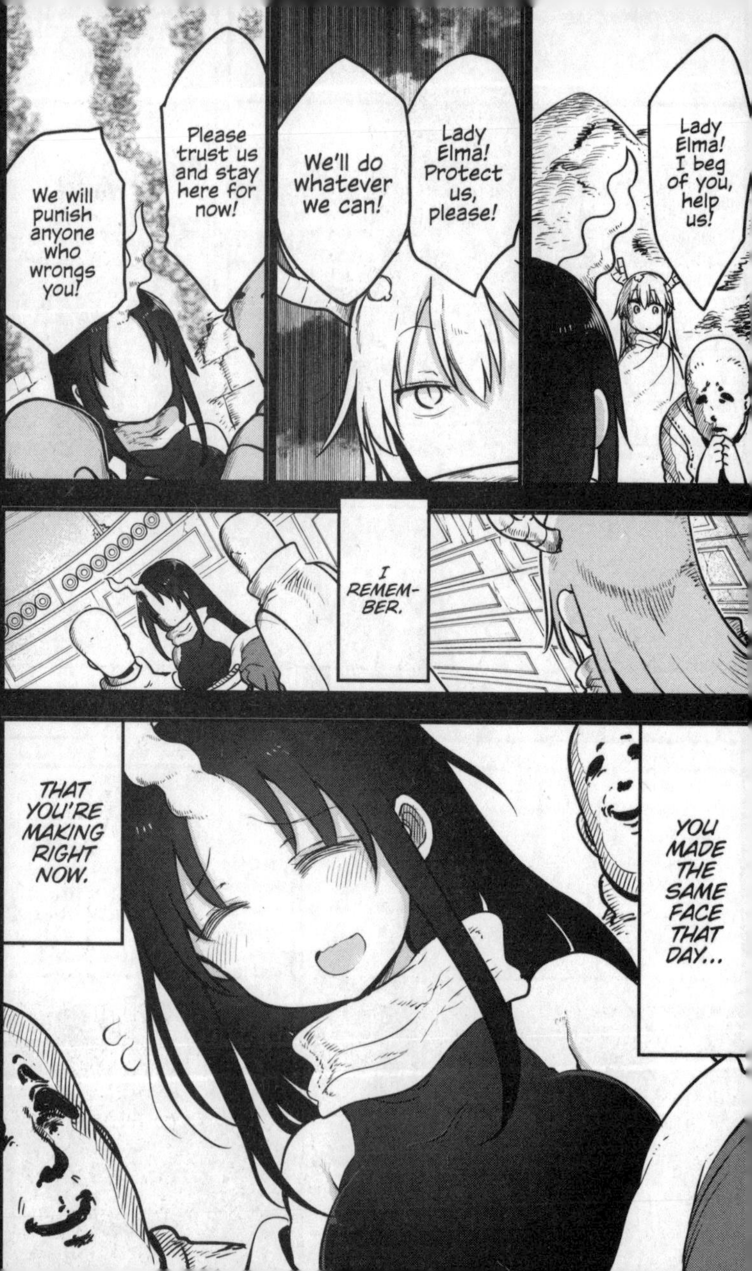
Lady Elma! I beg of you, help us!
Lady Elma! Protect us, please!
We'll do whatever we can!
Please trust us and stay here for now!
We will punish anyone who wrongs you!
I REMEMBER.
YOU MADE THE SAME FACE THAT DAY...
THAT YOU'RE MAKING RIGHT NOW.

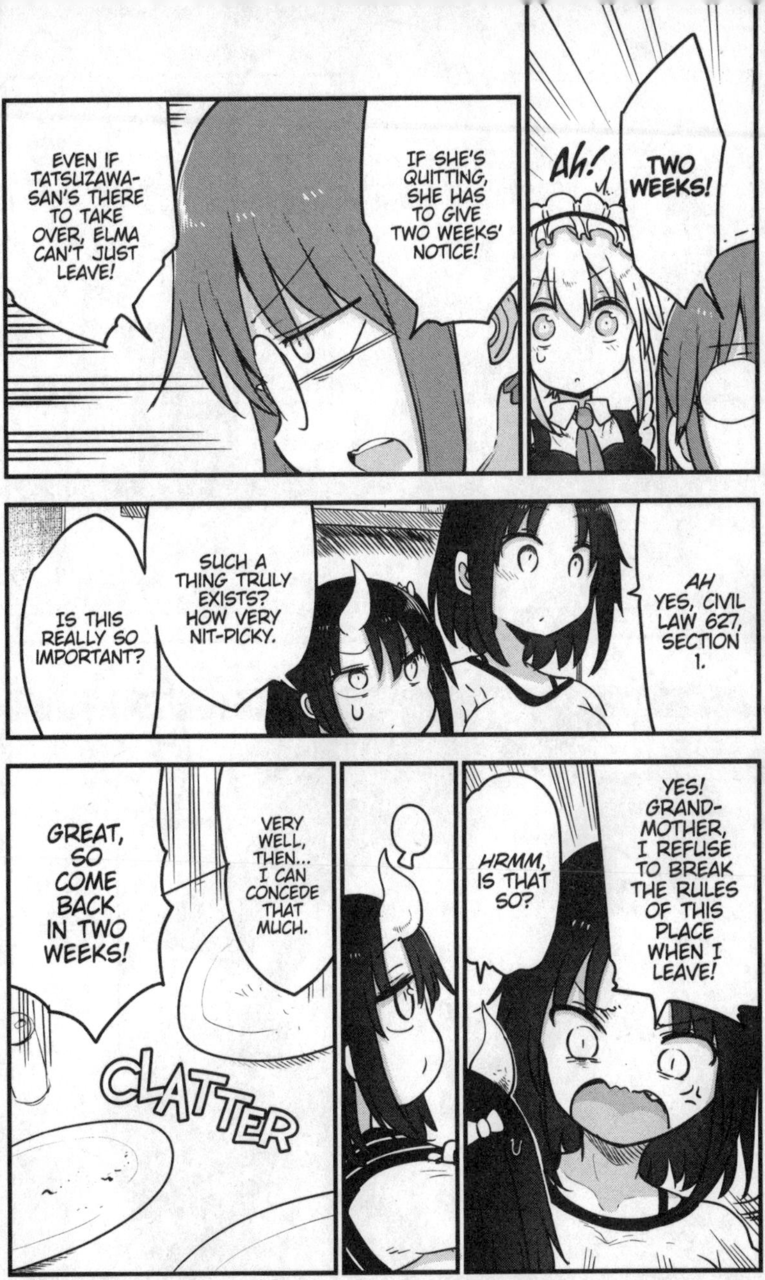
Ah!
TWO WEEKS!
IF SHE'S QUITTING, SHE HAS TO GIVE TWO WEEKS' NOTICE!
EVEN IF TATSUZAWA-SAN'S THERE TO TAKE OVER, ELMA CAN'T JUST LEAVE!
AH YES, CIVIL LAW 627, SECTION 1.
SUCH A THING TRULY EXISTS? HOW VERY NIT-PICKY.
IS THIS REALLY SO IMPORTANT?
YES! GRAND-MOTHER, I REFUSE TO BREAK THE RULES OF THIS PLACE WHEN I LEAVE!
HRMM, IS THAT SO?
VERY WELL, THEN... I CAN CONCEDE THAT MUCH.
GREAT, SO COME BACK IN TWO WEEKS!
CLATTER

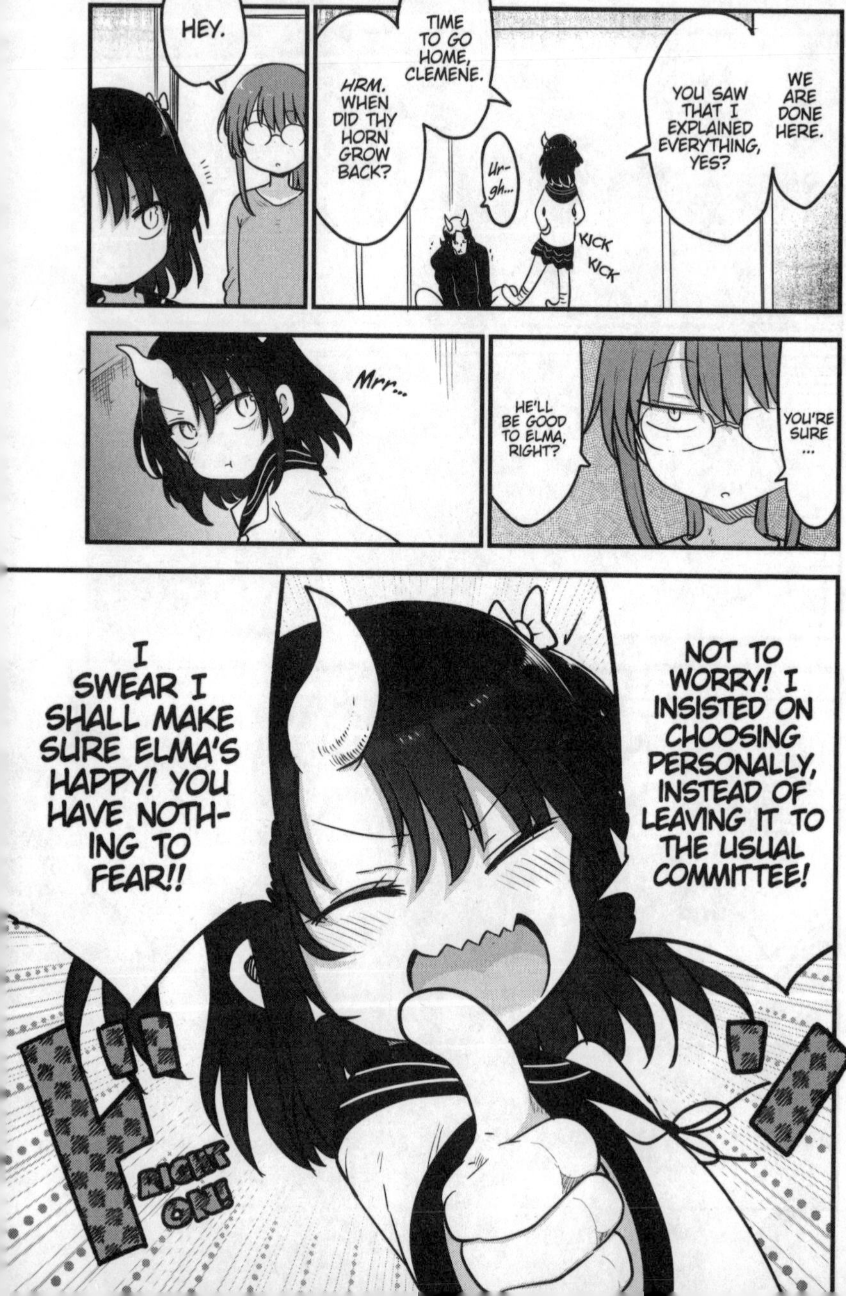
WE ARE DONE HERE.
YOU SAW THAT I EXPLAINED EVERYTHING, YES?
TIME TO GO HOME, CLEMENE.
HRM. WHEN DID THY HORN GROW BACK?
Ur-gh...
KICK KICK
HEY.
YOU'RE SURE ...
HE'LL BE GOOD TO ELMA, RIGHT?
Mrr...
NOT TO WORRY! I INSISTED ON CHOOSING PERSONALLY, INSTEAD OF LEAVING IT TO THE USUAL COMMITTEE!
I SWEAR I SHALL MAKE SURE ELMA'S HAPPY! YOU HAVE NOTHING TO FEAR!!
RIGHT ON!

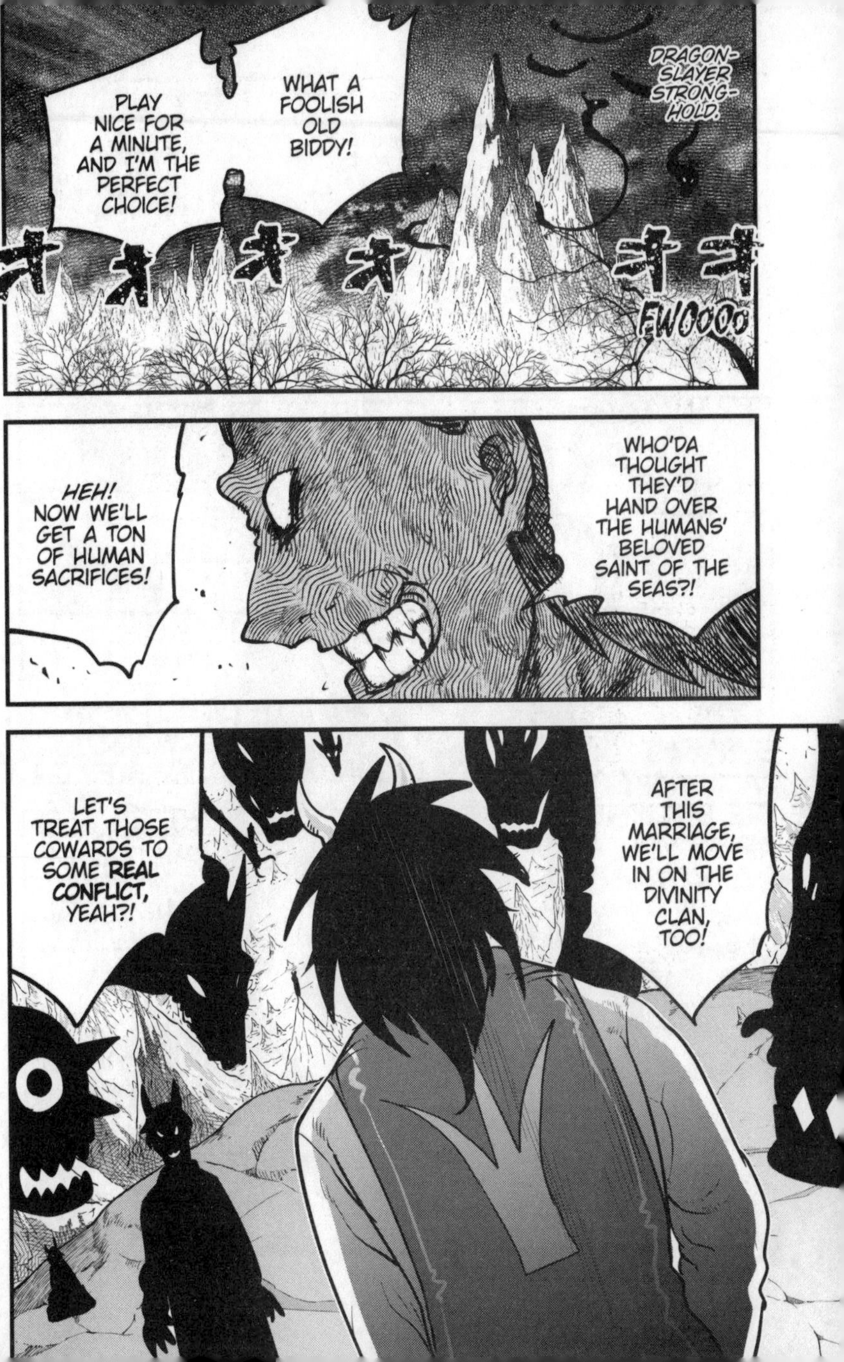
DRAGON-SLAYER STRONGHOLD.
WHAT A FOOLISH OLD BIDDY!
PLAY NICE FOR A MINUTE, AND I'M THE PERFECT CHOICE!
FWOOOO
WHO'DA THOUGHT THEY'D HAND OVER THE HUMANS' BELOVED SAINT OF THE SEAS?!
HEH! NOW WE'LL GET A TON OF HUMAN SACRIFICES!
AFTER THIS MARRIAGE, WE'LL MOVE IN ON THE DIVINITY CLAN, TOO!
LET'S TREAT THOSE COWARDS TO SOME **REAL CONFLICT**, YEAH?!

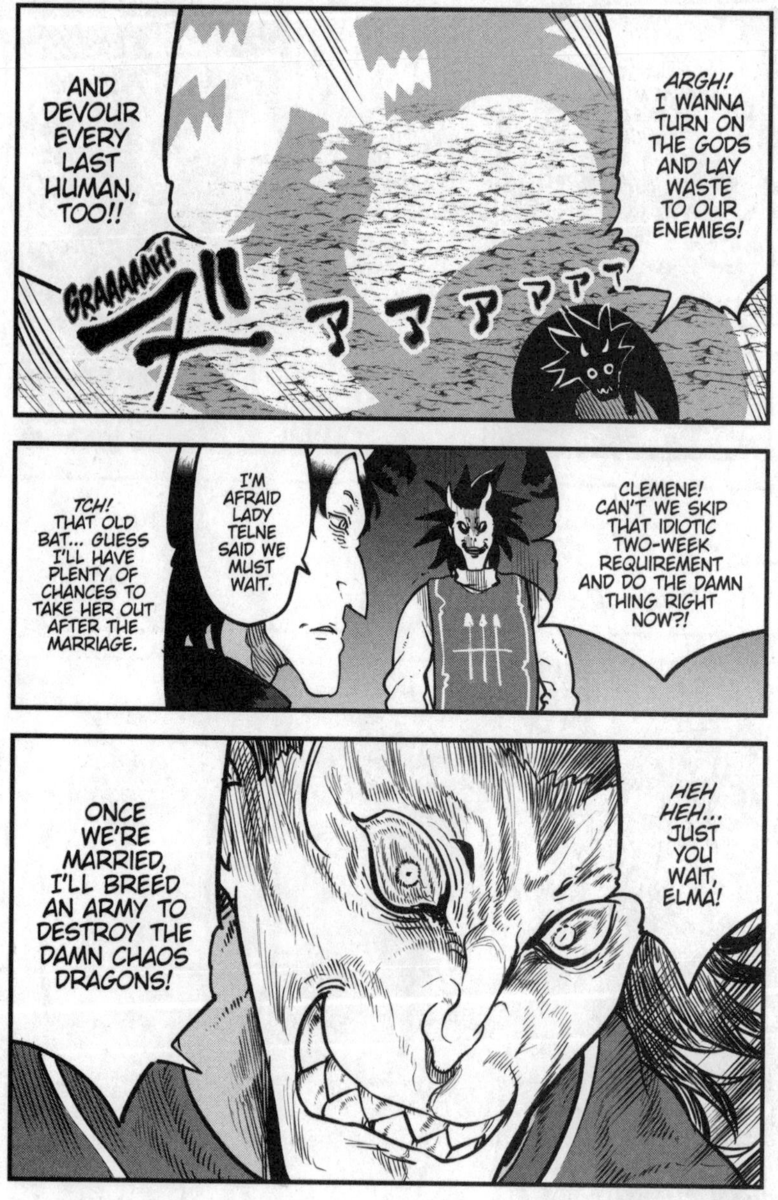
ARGH! I WANNA TURN ON THE GODS AND LAY WASTE TO OUR ENEMIES!
AND DEVOUR EVERY LAST HUMAN, TOO!!
GRAAAAAH!
CLEMENE! CAN'T WE SKIP THAT IDIOTIC TWO-WEEK REQUIREMENT AND DO THE DAMN THING RIGHT NOW?!
I'M AFRAID LADY TELNE SAID WE MUST WAIT.
TCH! THAT OLD BAT... GUESS I'LL HAVE PLENTY OF CHANCES TO TAKE HER OUT AFTER THE MARRIAGE.
HEH HEH... JUST YOU WAIT, ELMA!
ONCE WE'RE MARRIED, I'LL BREED AN ARMY TO DESTROY THE DAMN CHAOS DRAGONS!

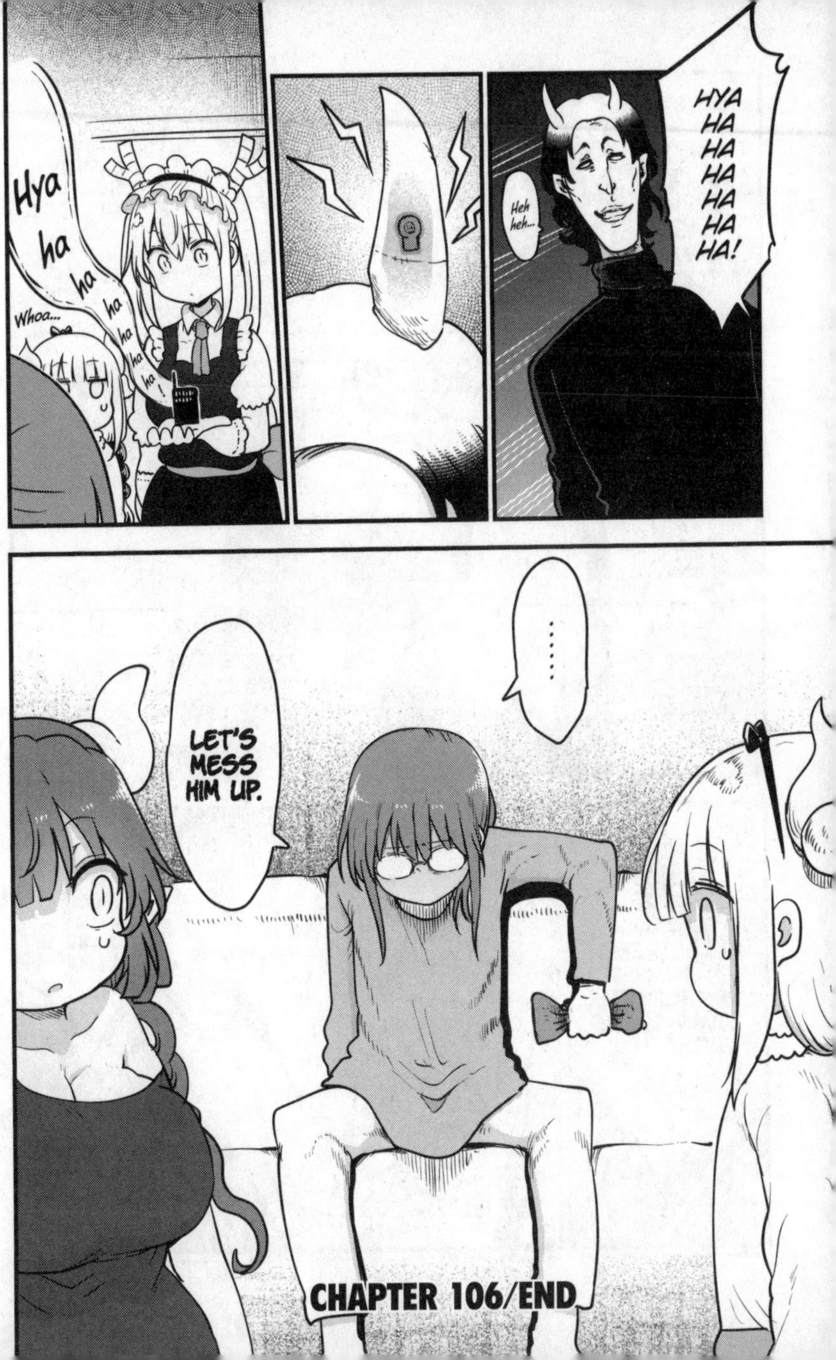
HYA HA HA HA HA HA HA!
Heh heh...
Hya ha ha ha ha ha ha!
Whoa...
......
LET'S MESS HIM UP.
CHAPTER 106/END

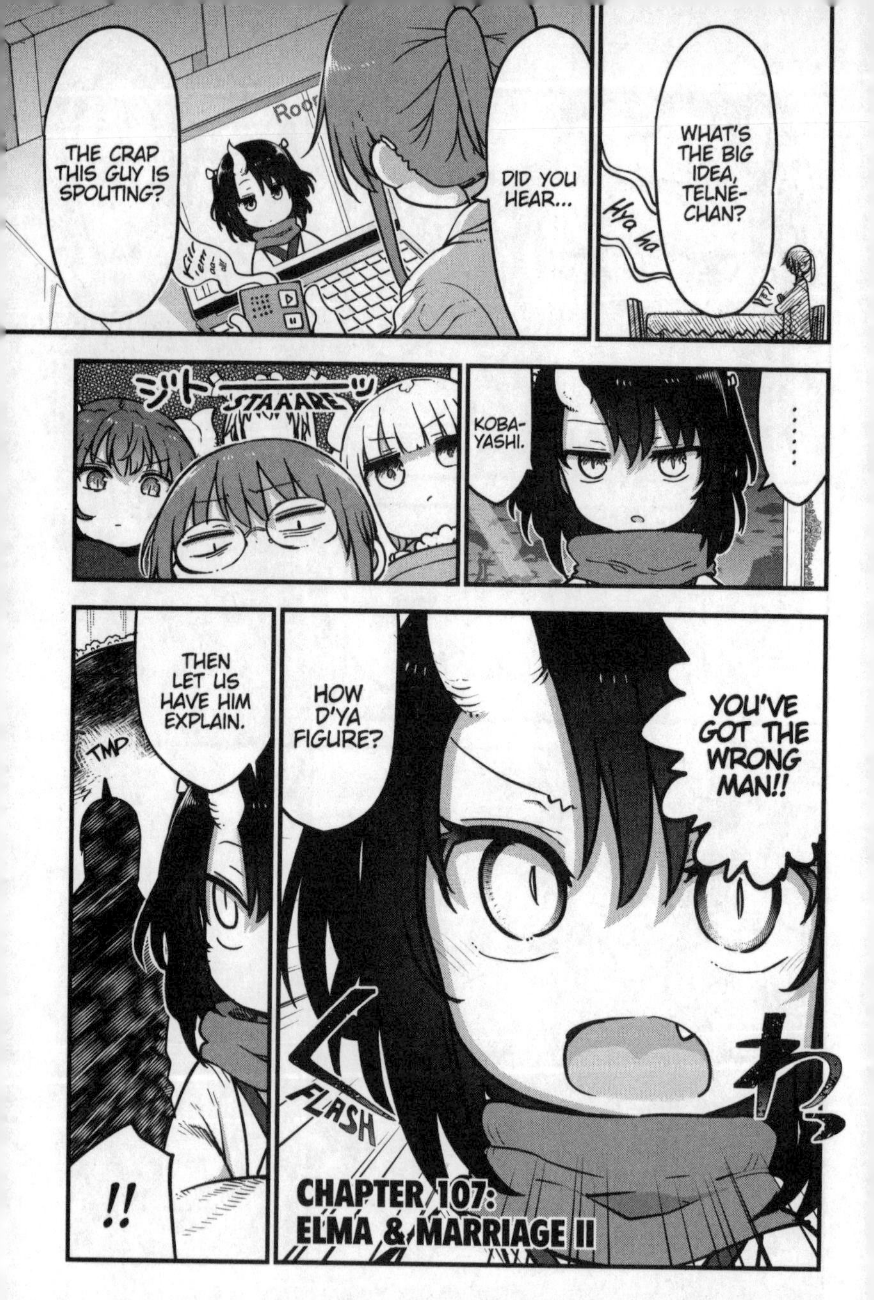
WHAT'S THE BIG IDEA, TELNE-CHAN?
Hya ha
DID YOU HEAR...
THE CRAP THIS GUY IS SPOUTING?
Kill 'em aa-all
......
KOBA-YASHI.
STAAARE
YOU'VE GOT THE WRONG MAN!!
FLASH
HOW D'YA FIGURE?
THEN LET US HAVE HIM EXPLAIN.
TMP
!!
CHAPTER 107: ELMA & MARRIAGE II

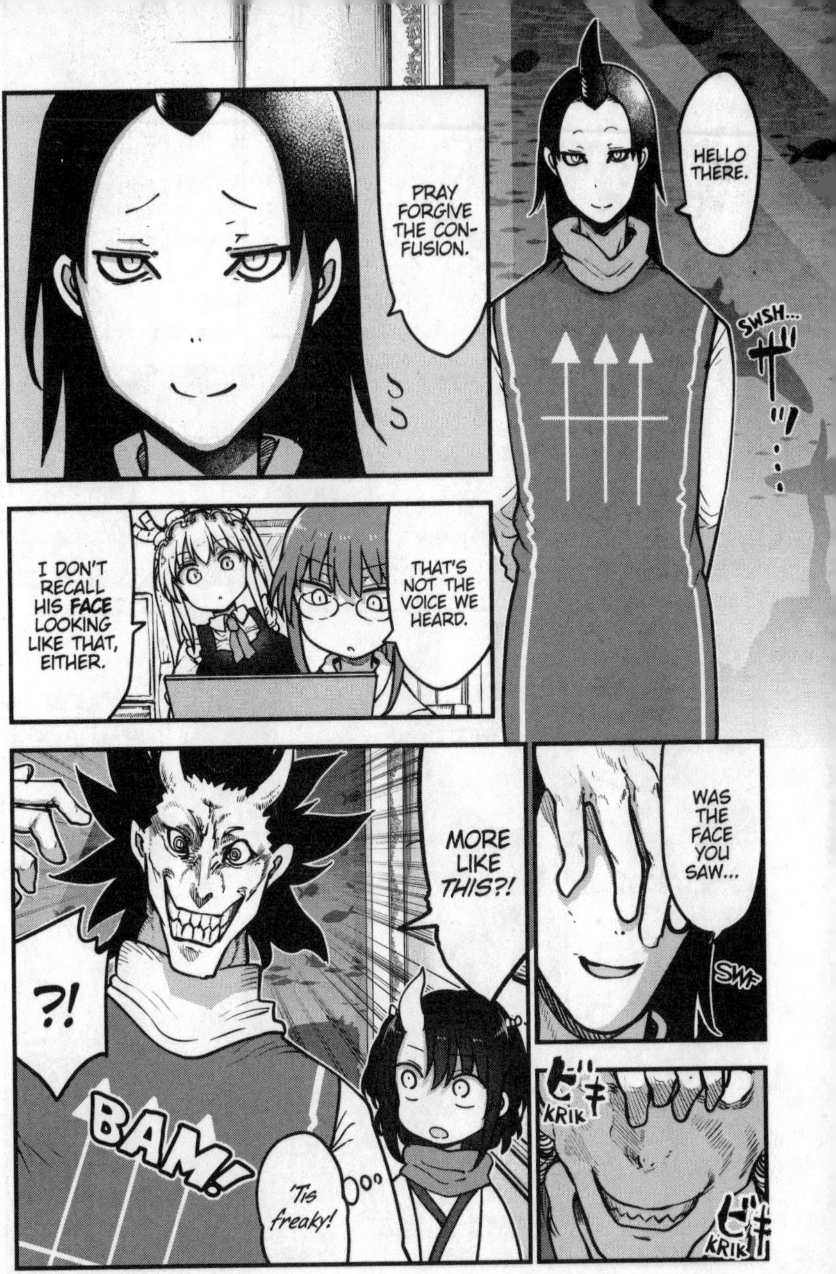
HELLO THERE.
SWSH...
PRAY FORGIVE THE CON-FUSION.
THAT'S NOT THE VOICE WE HEARD.
I DON'T RECALL HIS **FACE** LOOKING LIKE THAT, EITHER.
WAS THE FACE YOU SAW...
SWF
KRIK
KRIK
MORE LIKE *THIS?!*
?!
BAM!
'Tis freaky!

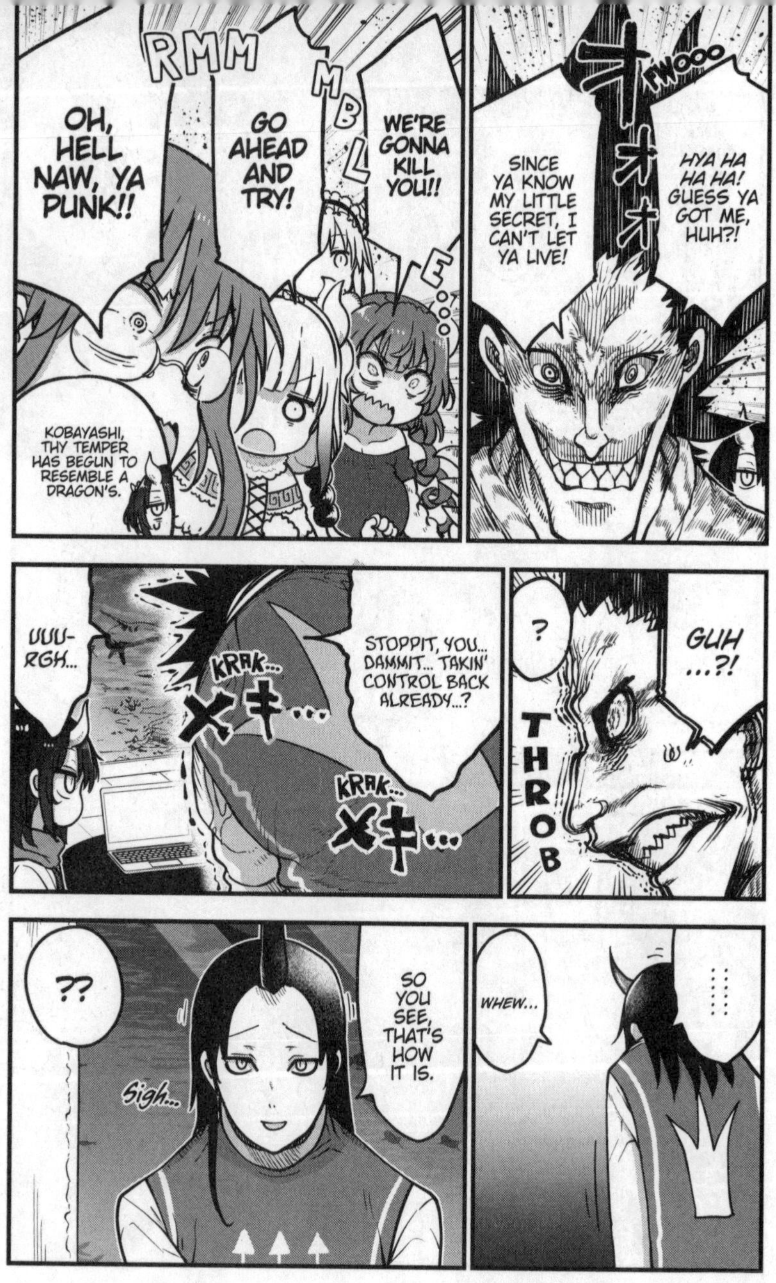
FWOOO
HYA HA HA HA! GUESS YA GOT ME, HUH?!
SINCE YA KNOW MY LITTLE SECRET, I CAN'T LET YA LIVE!
RMMMBLE
WE'RE GONNA KILL YOU!!
GO AHEAD AND TRY!
OH, HELL NAW, YA PUNK!!
KOBAYASHI, THY TEMPER HAS BEGUN TO RESEMBLE A DRAGON'S.
GUH ...?!
?
THROB
STOPPIT, YOU... DAMMIT... TAKIN' CONTROL BACK ALREADY...?
KRAK... メキ...
KRAK... メキ...
UUU-RGH...
......
WHEW...
SO YOU SEE, THAT'S HOW IT IS.
Sigh...
??

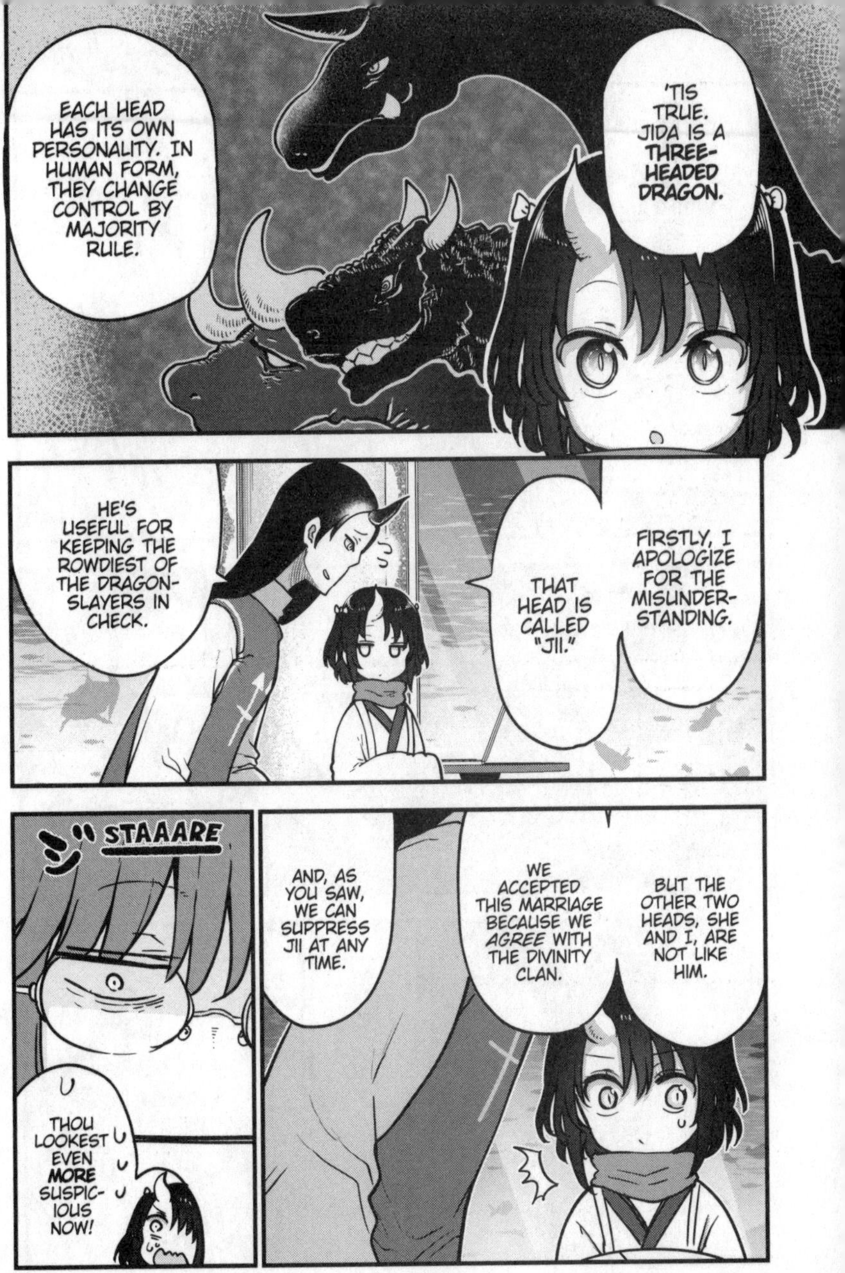
'TIS TRUE. JIDA IS A THREE-HEADED DRAGON.
EACH HEAD HAS ITS OWN PERSONALITY. IN HUMAN FORM, THEY CHANGE CONTROL BY MAJORITY RULE.
FIRSTLY, I APOLOGIZE FOR THE MISUNDERSTANDING.
THAT HEAD IS CALLED "JII."
HE'S USEFUL FOR KEEPING THE ROWDIEST OF THE DRAGON-SLAYERS IN CHECK.
BUT THE OTHER TWO HEADS, SHE AND I, ARE NOT LIKE HIM.
WE ACCEPTED THIS MARRIAGE BECAUSE WE *AGREE* WITH THE DIVINITY CLAN.
AND, AS YOU SAW, WE CAN SUPPRESS JII AT ANY TIME.
STAAARE
THOU LOOKEST EVEN **MORE** SUSPICIOUS NOW!

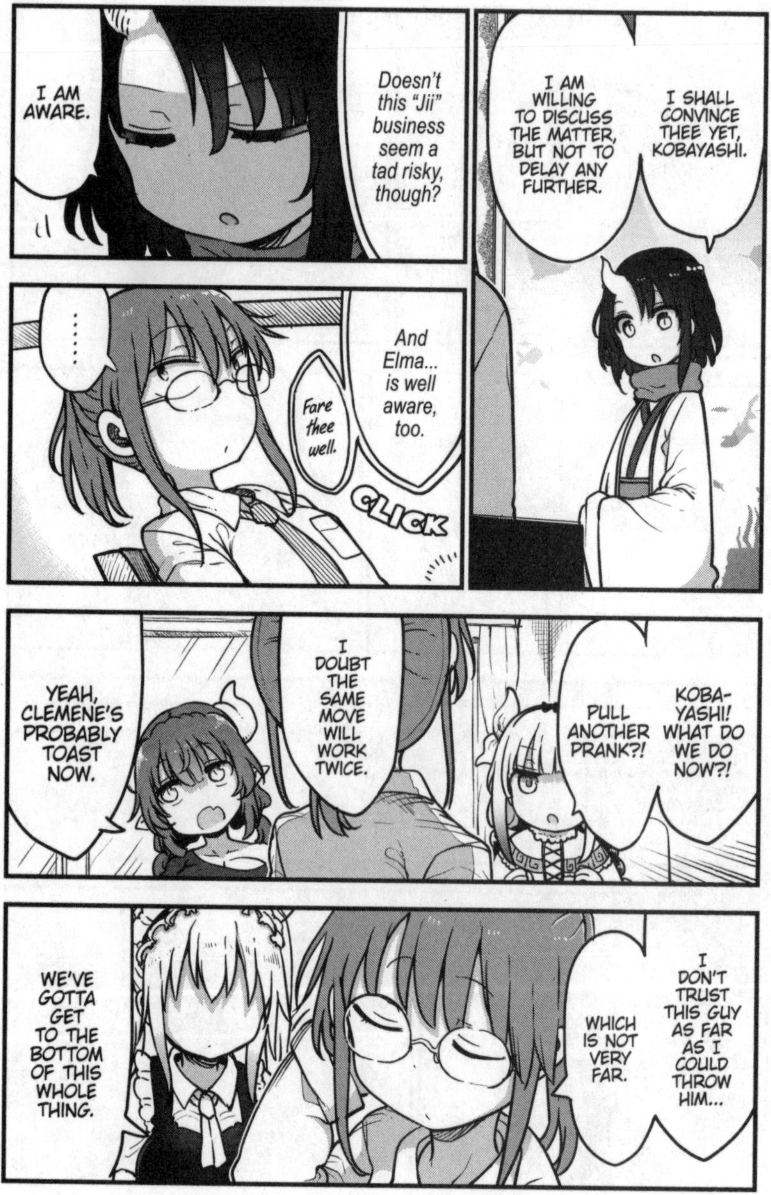
I SHALL CONVINCE THEE YET, KOBAYASHI.
I AM WILLING TO DISCUSS THE MATTER, BUT NOT TO DELAY ANY FURTHER.
Doesn't this "Jii" business seem a tad risky, though?
I AM AWARE.
And Elma... is well aware, too.
Fare thee well.
CLICK
......
KOBAYASHI! WHAT DO WE DO NOW?!
PULL ANOTHER PRANK?!
I DOUBT THE SAME MOVE WILL WORK TWICE.
YEAH, CLEMENE'S PROBABLY TOAST NOW.
I DON'T TRUST THIS GUY AS FAR AS I COULD THROW HIM...
WHICH IS NOT VERY FAR.
WE'VE GOTTA GET TO THE BOTTOM OF THIS WHOLE THING.

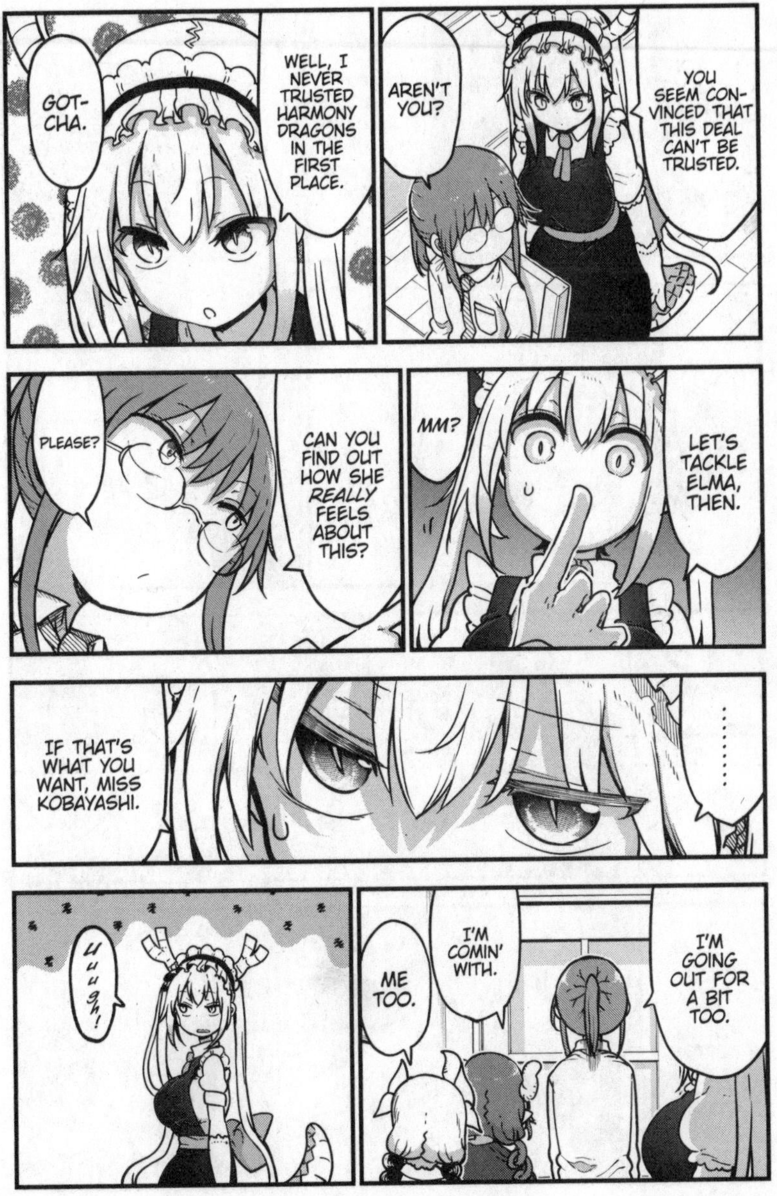
YOU SEEM CON-VINCED THAT THIS DEAL CAN'T BE TRUSTED.
AREN'T YOU?
WELL, I NEVER TRUSTED HARMONY DRAGONS IN THE FIRST PLACE.
GOT-CHA.
LET'S TACKLE ELMA, THEN.
MM?
CAN YOU FIND OUT HOW SHE *REALLY* FEELS ABOUT THIS?
PLEASE?
......
IF THAT'S WHAT YOU WANT, MISS KOBAYASHI.
I'M GOING OUT FOR A BIT TOO.
I'M COMIN' WITH.
ME TOO.
Uuugh!

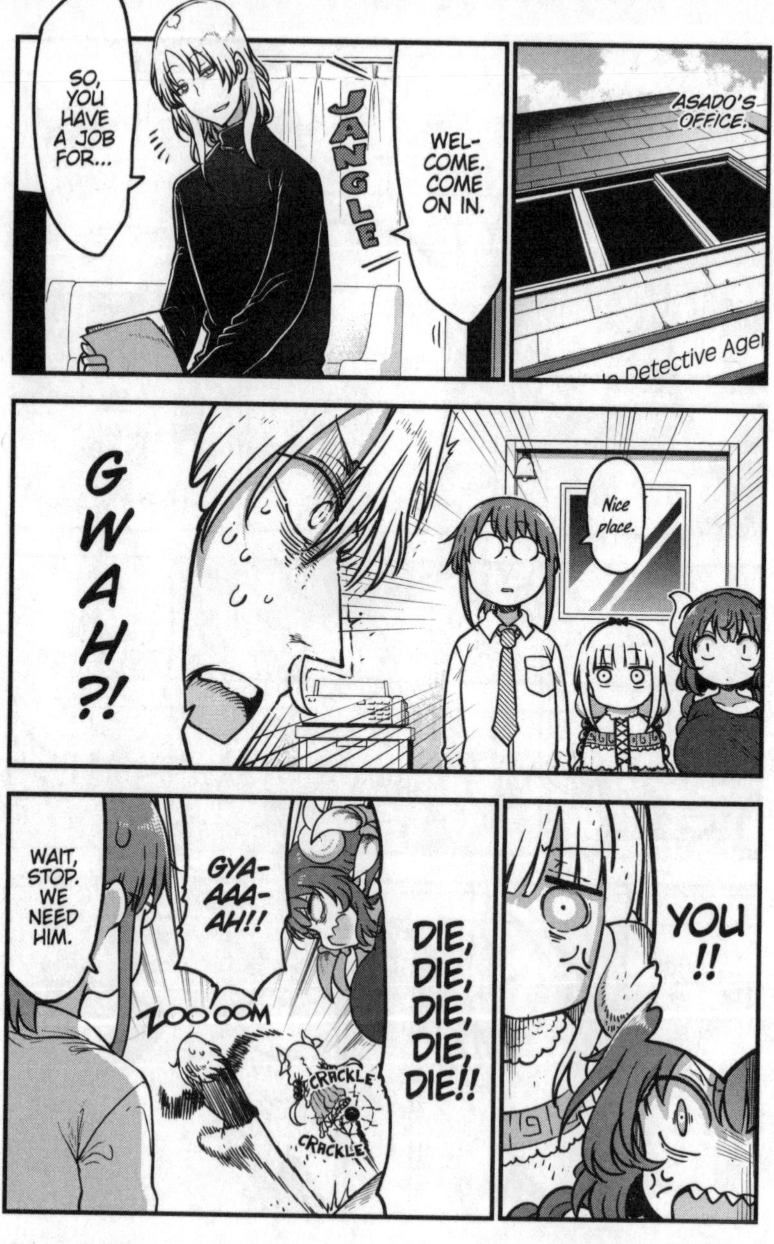
ASADO'S OFFICE.
Detective Agen
WEL-COME. COME ON IN.
JANGLE
SO, YOU HAVE A JOB FOR...
Nice place.
GWAH?!
YOU!!
DIE, DIE, DIE, DIE, DIE!!
GYA-AAA-AH!!
ZOOOOM
CRACKLE
CRACKLE
WAIT, STOP. WE NEED HIM.

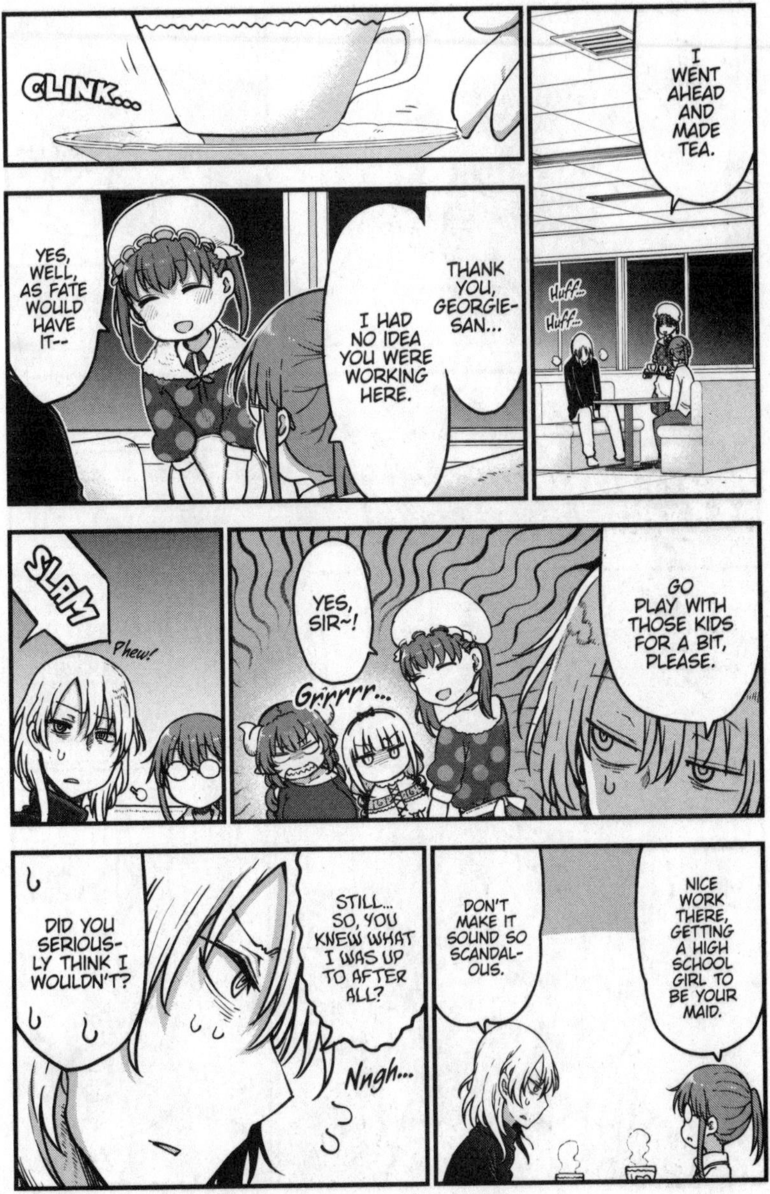
I WENT AHEAD AND MADE TEA.
Huff... Huff...
CLINK...
THANK YOU, GEORGIE-SAN...
I HAD NO IDEA YOU WERE WORKING HERE.
YES, WELL, AS FATE WOULD HAVE IT--
GO PLAY WITH THOSE KIDS FOR A BIT, PLEASE.
YES, SIR~!
Grrrrr...
SLAM
Phew!
NICE WORK THERE, GETTING A HIGH SCHOOL GIRL TO BE YOUR MAID.
DON'T MAKE IT SOUND SO SCANDAL-OUS.
STILL... SO, YOU KNEW WHAT I WAS UP TO AFTER ALL?
Nngh...
DID YOU SERIOUS-LY THINK I WOULDN'T?

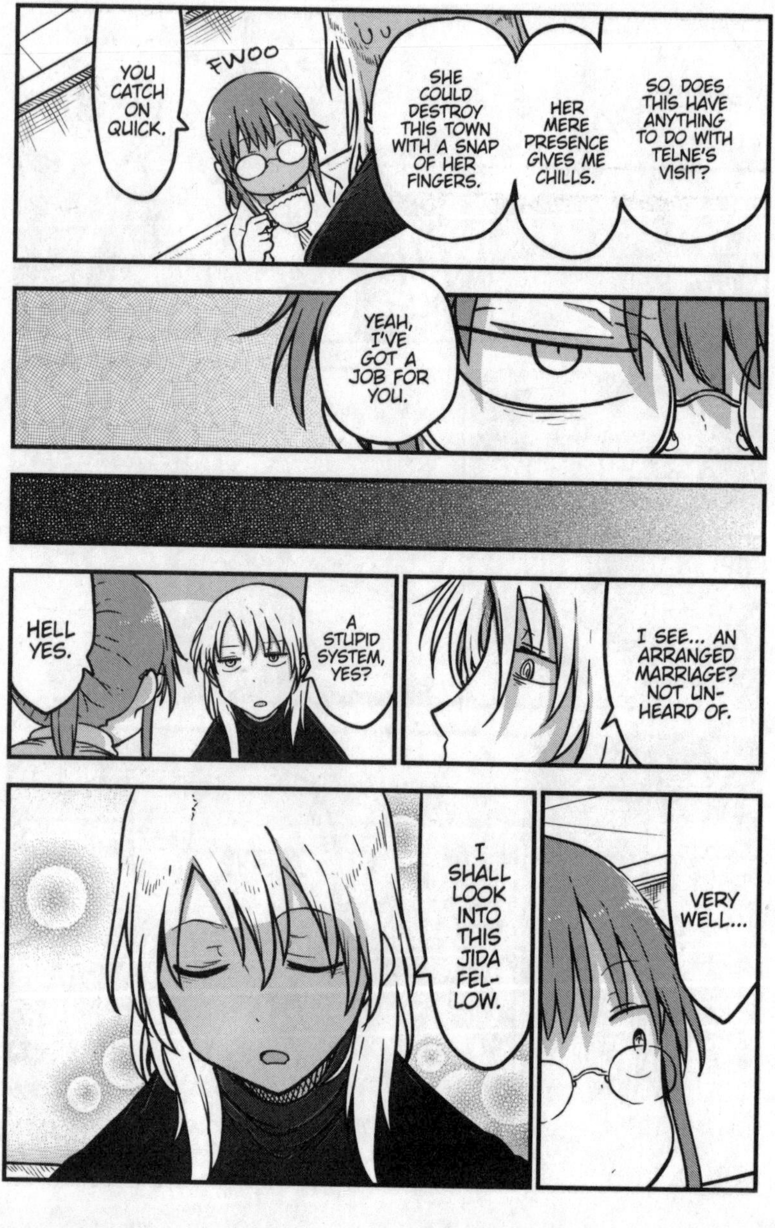
SO, DOES THIS HAVE ANYTHING TO DO WITH TELNE'S VISIT?
HER MERE PRESENCE GIVES ME CHILLS.
SHE COULD DESTROY THIS TOWN WITH A SNAP OF HER FINGERS.
FWOO
YOU CATCH ON QUICK.
YEAH, I'VE GOT A JOB FOR YOU.
I SEE... AN ARRANGED MARRIAGE? NOT UN-HEARD OF.
A STUPID SYSTEM, YES?
HELL YES.
VERY WELL...
I SHALL LOOK INTO THIS JIDA FEL-LOW.

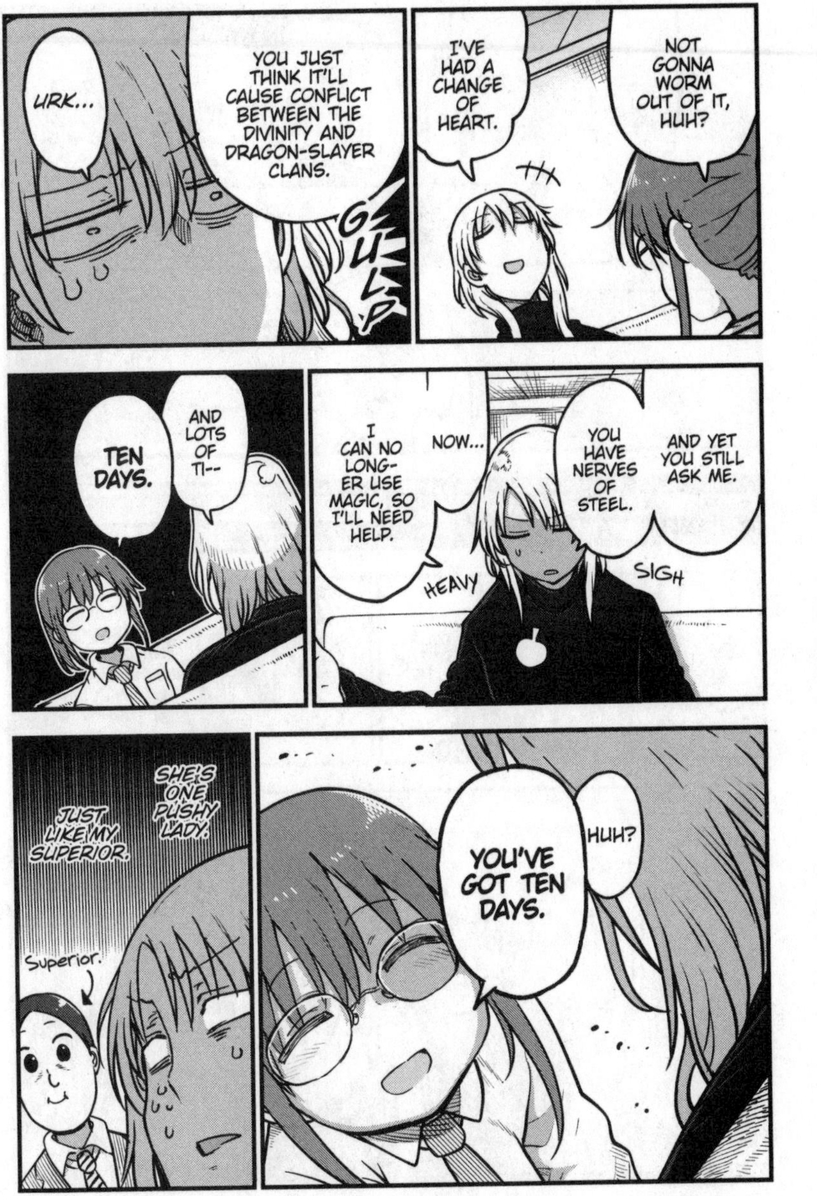
NOT GONNA WORM OUT OF IT, HUH?
I'VE HAD A CHANGE OF HEART.
YOU JUST THINK IT'LL CAUSE CONFLICT BETWEEN THE DIVINITY AND DRAGON-SLAYER CLANS.
URK...
GULP
AND YET YOU STILL ASK ME.
YOU HAVE NERVES OF STEEL.
SIGH
NOW...
I CAN NO LONGER USE MAGIC, SO I'LL NEED HELP.
HEAVY
AND LOTS OF TI--
TEN DAYS.
HUH?
YOU'VE GOT TEN DAYS.
SHE'S ONE PUSHY LADY.
JUST LIKE MY SUPERIOR.
Superior.

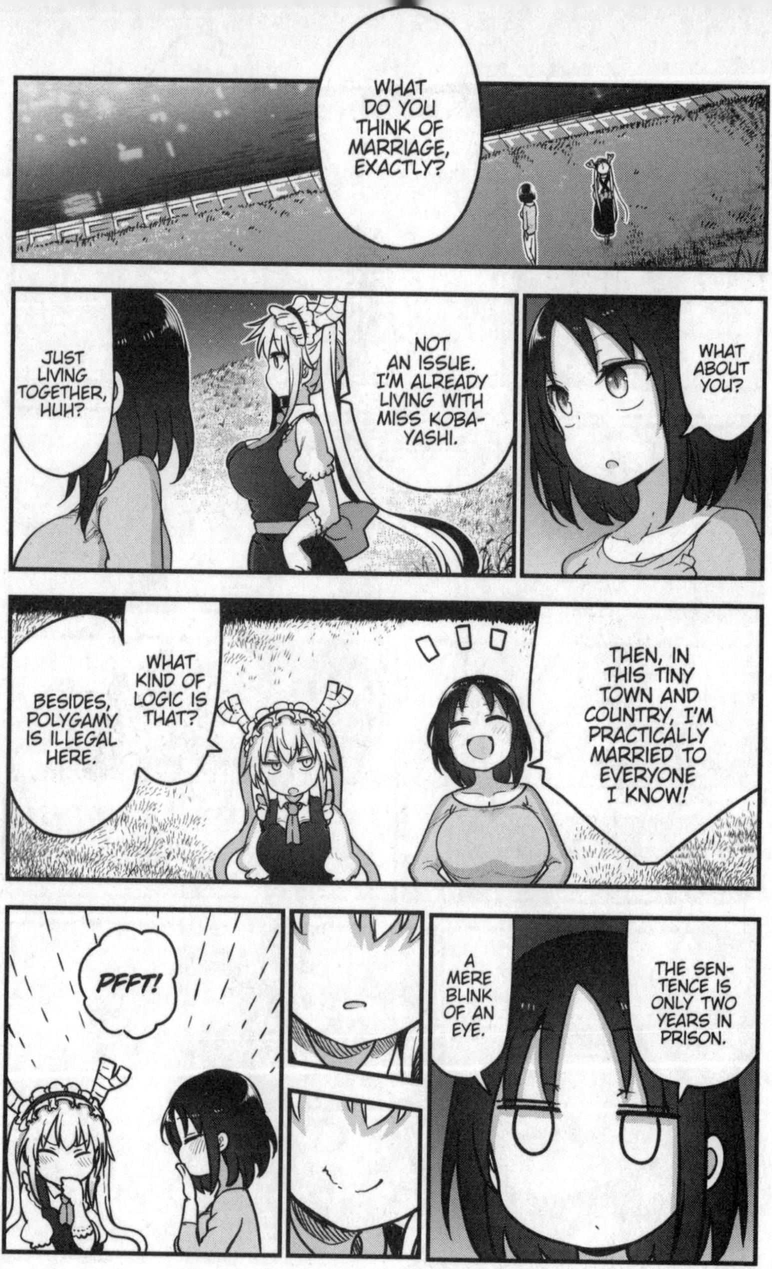
WHAT DO YOU THINK OF MARRIAGE, EXACTLY?
WHAT ABOUT YOU?
NOT AN ISSUE. I'M ALREADY LIVING WITH MISS KOBA-YASHI.
JUST LIVING TOGETHER, HUH?
THEN, IN THIS TINY TOWN AND COUNTRY, I'M PRACTICALLY MARRIED TO EVERYONE I KNOW!
WHAT KIND OF LOGIC IS THAT?
BESIDES, POLYGAMY IS ILLEGAL HERE.
THE SEN-TENCE IS ONLY TWO YEARS IN PRISON.
A MERE BLINK OF AN EYE.
PFFT!

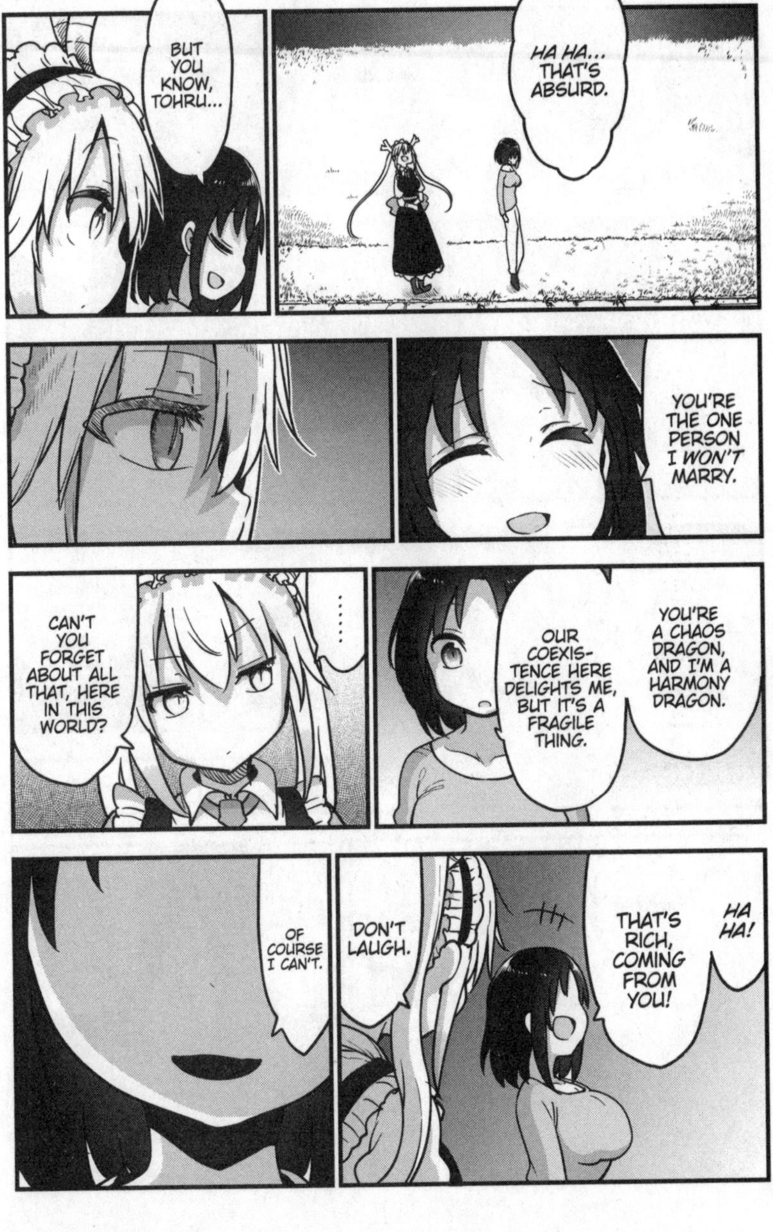
HA HA... THAT'S ABSURD.
BUT YOU KNOW, TOHRU...
YOU'RE THE ONE PERSON I *WON'T* MARRY.
YOU'RE A CHAOS DRAGON, AND I'M A HARMONY DRAGON.
OUR COEXIS-TENCE HERE DELIGHTS ME, BUT IT'S A FRAGILE THING.
......
CAN'T YOU FORGET ABOUT ALL THAT, HERE IN THIS WORLD?
HA HA!
THAT'S RICH, COMING FROM YOU!
DON'T LAUGH.
OF COURSE I CAN'T.

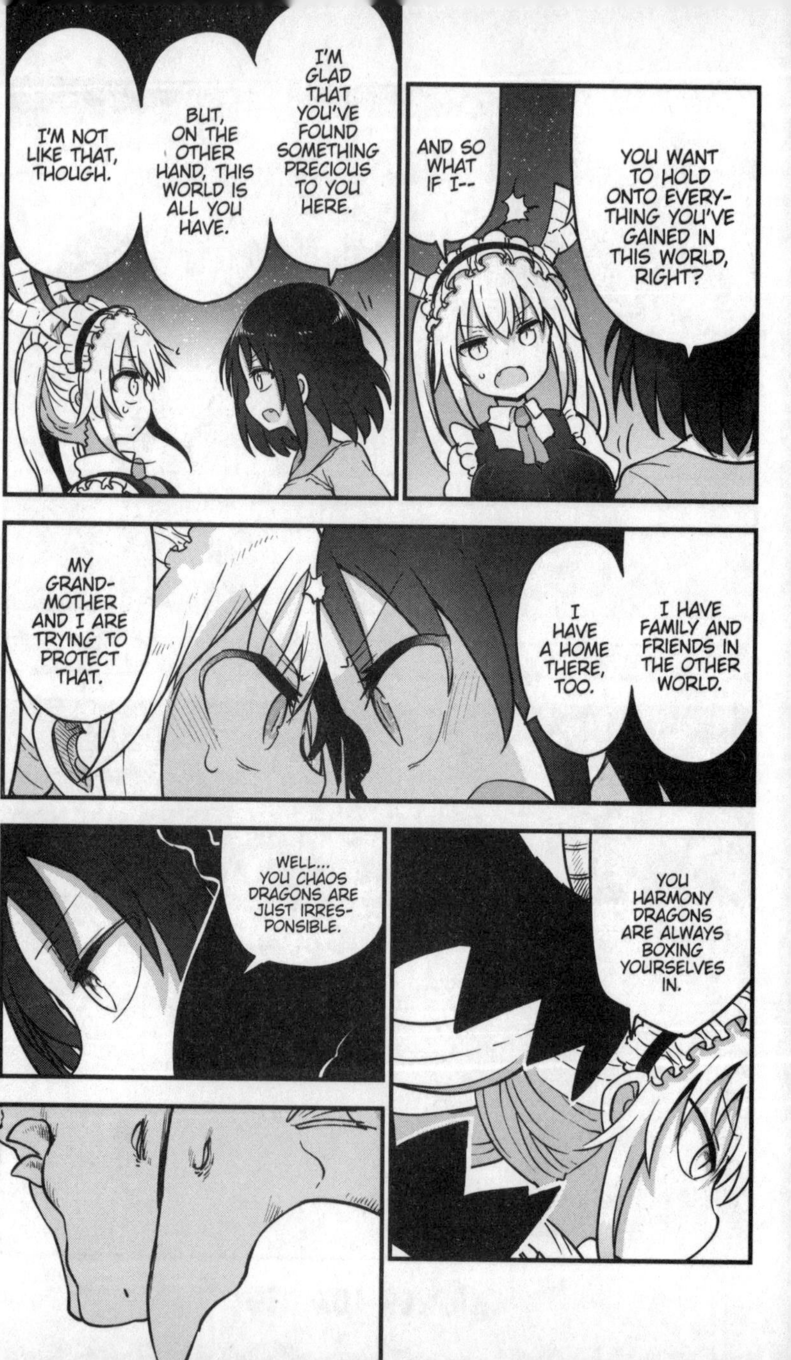
YOU WANT TO HOLD ONTO EVERY-THING YOU'VE GAINED IN THIS WORLD, RIGHT?
AND SO WHAT IF I--
I'M GLAD THAT YOU'VE FOUND SOMETHING PRECIOUS TO YOU HERE.
BUT, ON THE OTHER HAND, THIS WORLD IS ALL YOU HAVE.
I'M NOT LIKE THAT, THOUGH.
I HAVE FAMILY AND FRIENDS IN THE OTHER WORLD.
I HAVE A HOME THERE, TOO.
MY GRAND-MOTHER AND I ARE TRYING TO PROTECT THAT.
YOU HARMONY DRAGONS ARE ALWAYS BOXING YOURSELVES IN.
WELL... YOU CHAOS DRAGONS ARE JUST IRRES-PONSIBLE.

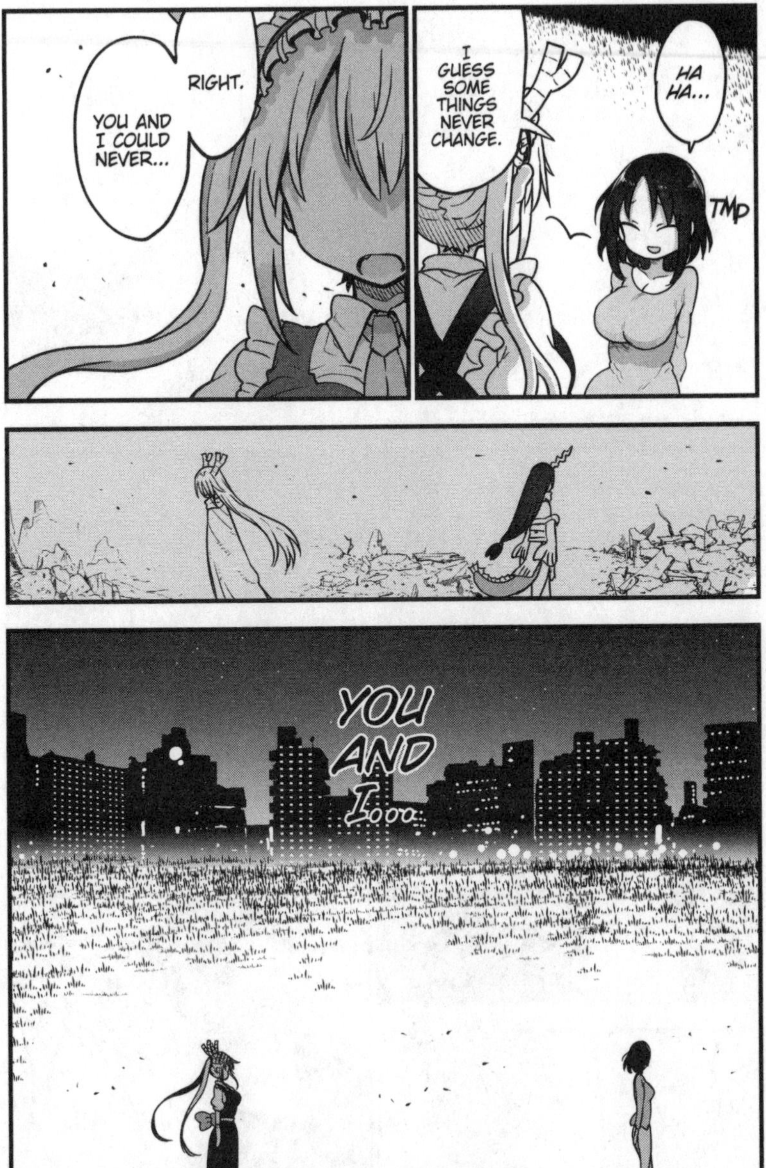
HA HA...
I GUESS SOME THINGS NEVER CHANGE.
TMP
RIGHT.
YOU AND I COULD NEVER...
YOU AND I...

CHAPTER 107/END

Miss Kobayashi's Dragon Maid

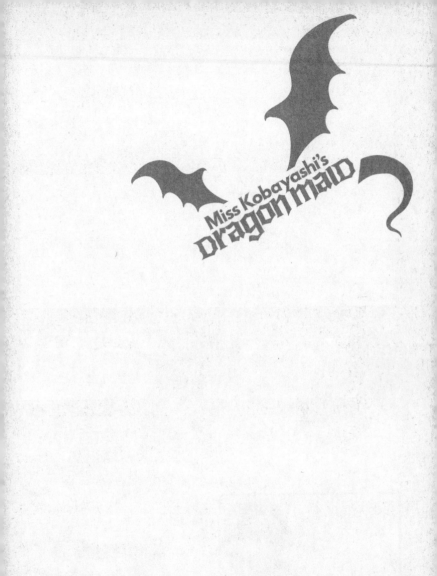

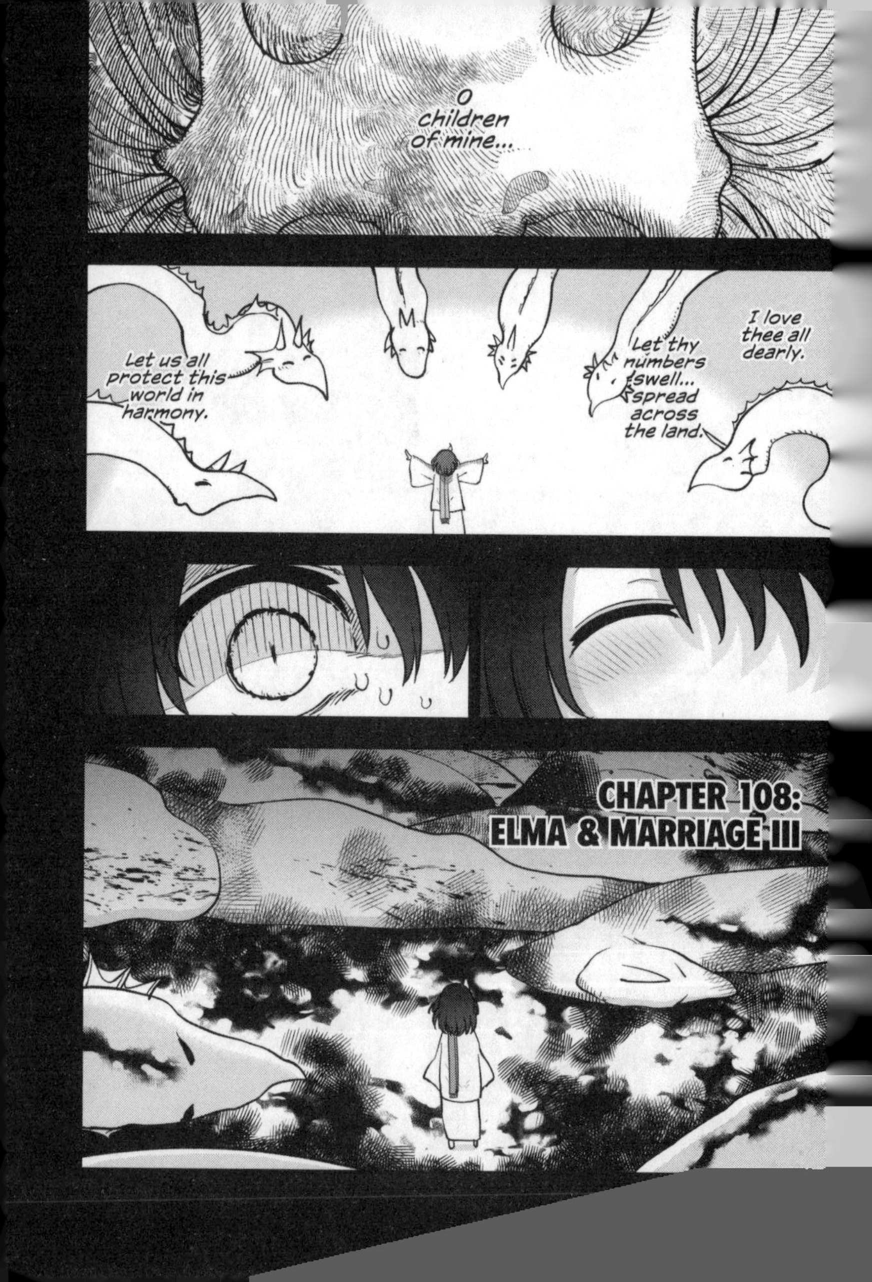
O children of mine...
I love thee all dearly.
Let thy numbers swell... spread across the land.
Let us all protect this world in harmony.
CHAPTER 108: ELMA & MARRIAGE III

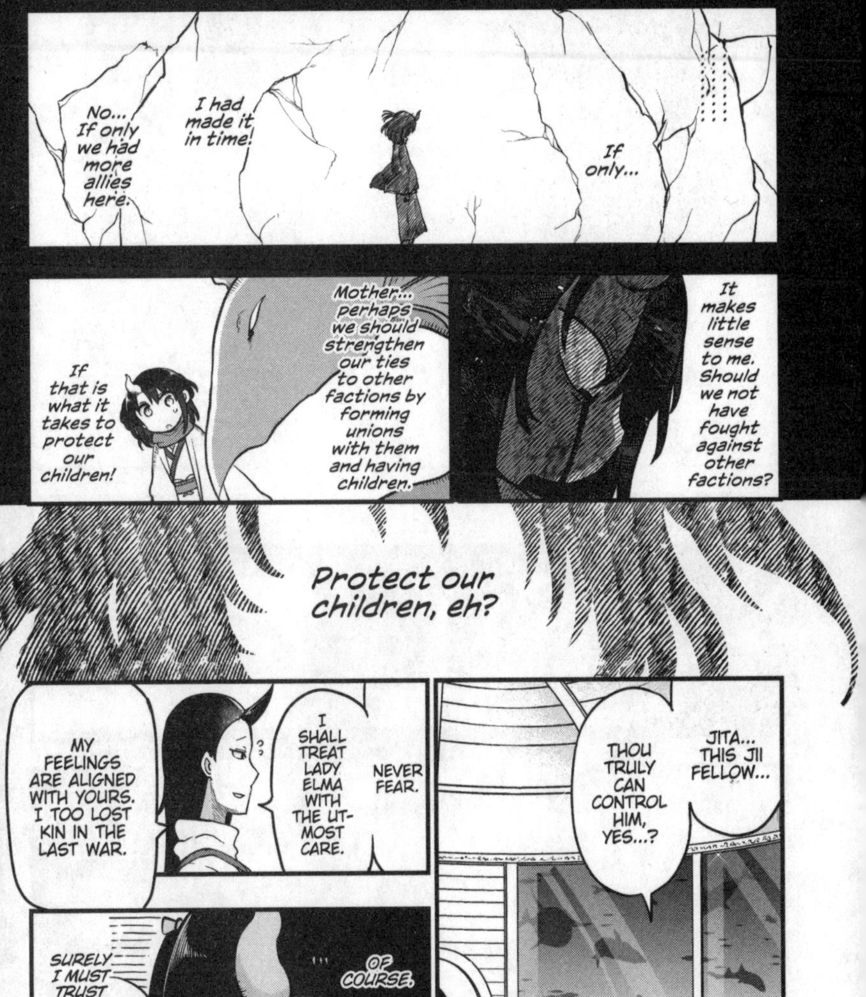
If only...
I had made it in time!
No... If only we had more allies here.
It makes little sense to me. Should we not have fought against other factions?
Mother... perhaps we should strengthen our ties to other factions by forming unions with them and having children.
If that is what it takes to protect our children!
Protect our children, eh?
JITA... THIS JII FELLOW...
THOU TRULY CAN CONTROL HIM, YES...?
NEVER FEAR.
I SHALL TREAT LADY ELMA WITH THE UT-MOST CARE.
MY FEELINGS ARE ALIGNED WITH YOURS. I TOO LOST KIN IN THE LAST WAR.
OF COURSE.
HE HAS ENDURED THE VERY SAME PAIN.
SURELY I MUST TRUST HIM.

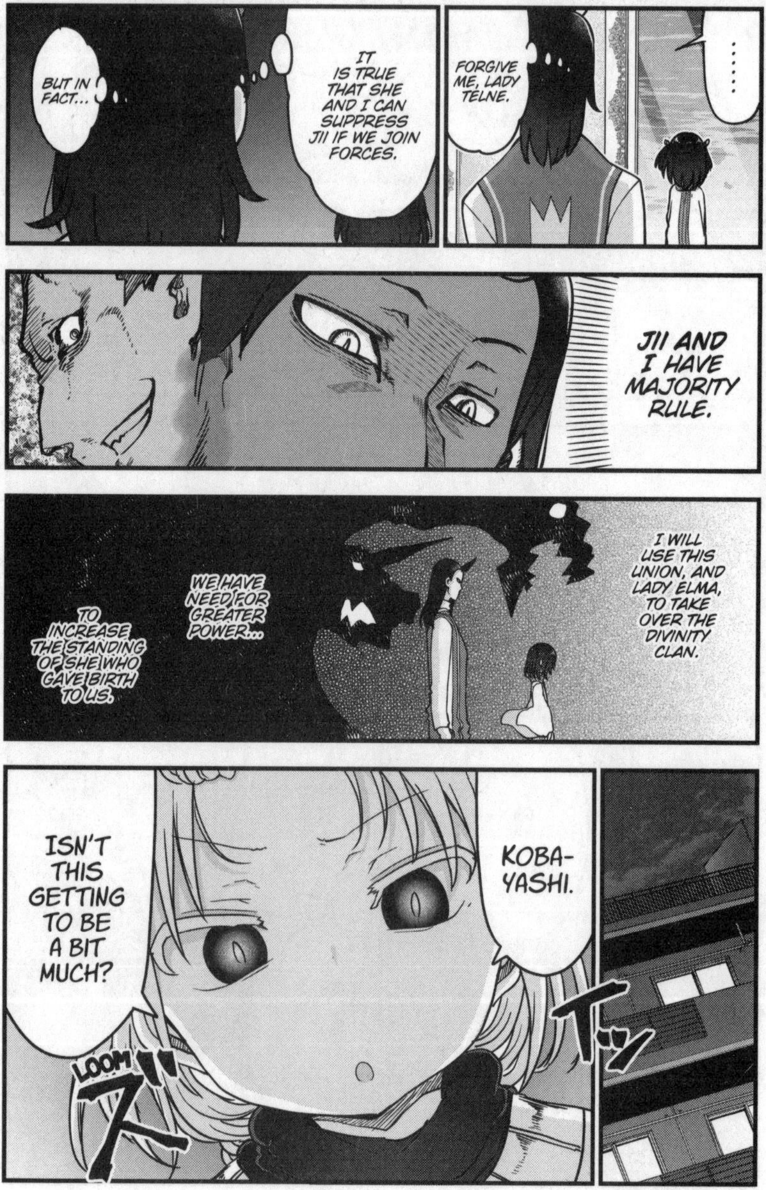
……
FORGIVE ME, LADY TELNE.
IT IS TRUE THAT SHE AND I CAN SUPPRESS JII IF WE JOIN FORCES.
BUT IN FACT…
JII AND I HAVE MAJORITY RULE.
I WILL USE THIS UNION, AND LADY ELMA, TO TAKE OVER THE DIVINITY CLAN.
WE HAVE NEED FOR GREATER POWER…
TO INCREASE THE STANDING OF SHE WHO GAVE BIRTH TO US.
KOBA-YASHI.
ISN'T THIS GETTING TO BE A BIT MUCH?
LOOM

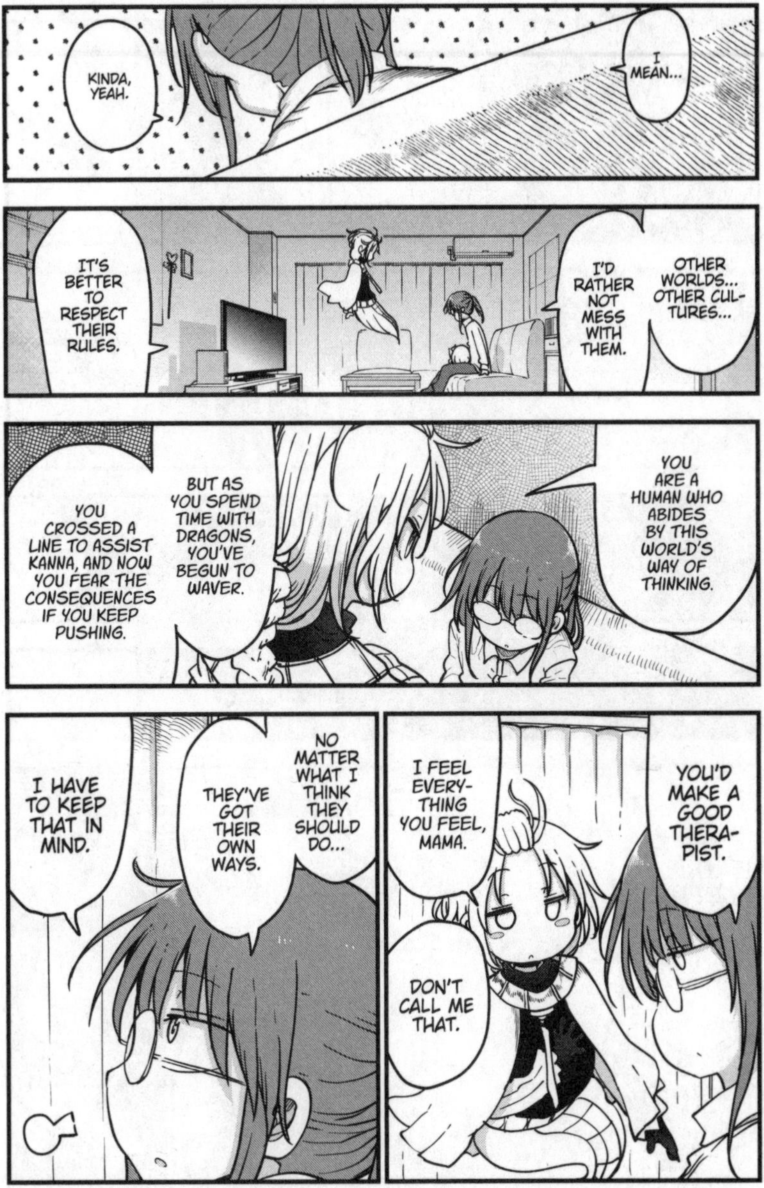
I MEAN...
KINDA, YEAH.
OTHER WORLDS... OTHER CULTURES...
I'D RATHER NOT MESS WITH THEM.
IT'S BETTER TO RESPECT THEIR RULES.
YOU ARE A HUMAN WHO ABIDES BY THIS WORLD'S WAY OF THINKING.
BUT AS YOU SPEND TIME WITH DRAGONS, YOU'VE BEGUN TO WAVER.
YOU CROSSED A LINE TO ASSIST KANNA, AND NOW YOU FEAR THE CONSEQUENCES IF YOU KEEP PUSHING.
YOU'D MAKE A GOOD THERAPIST.
I FEEL EVERYTHING YOU FEEL, MAMA.
DON'T CALL ME THAT.
NO MATTER WHAT I THINK THEY SHOULD DO...
THEY'VE GOT THEIR OWN WAYS.
I HAVE TO KEEP THAT IN MIND.

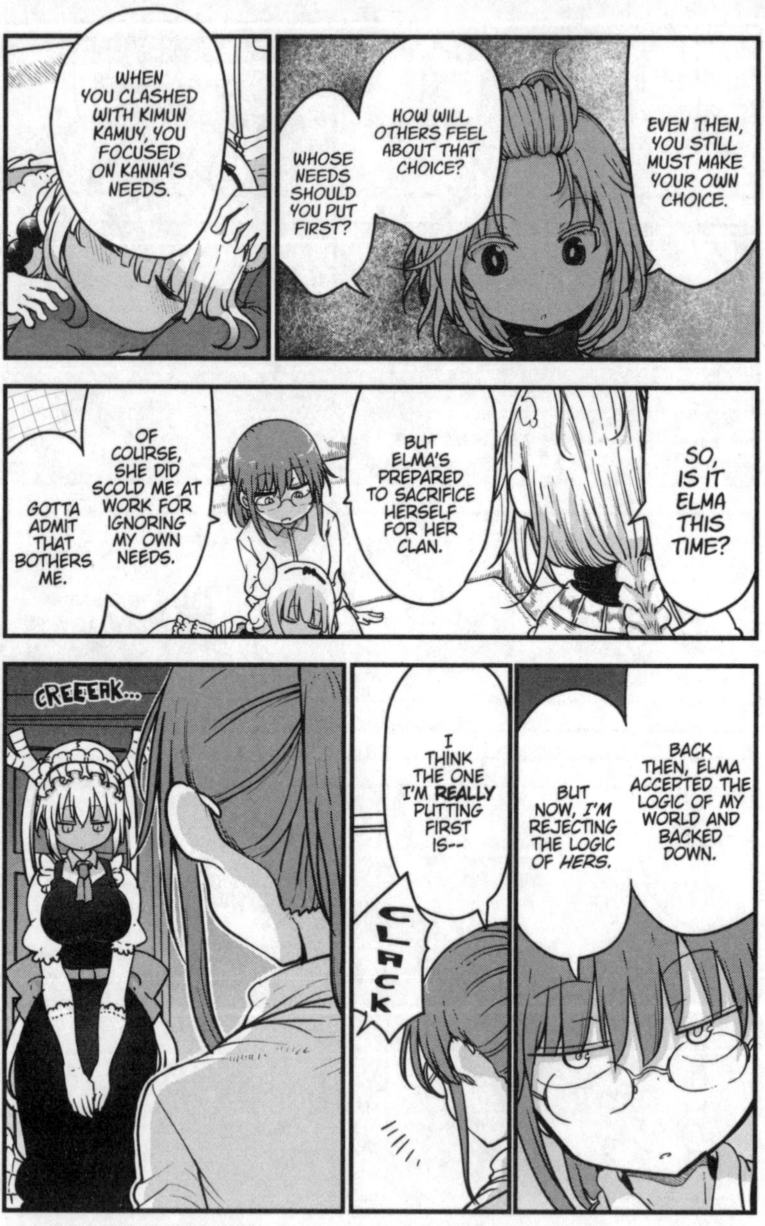
EVEN THEN, YOU STILL MUST MAKE YOUR OWN CHOICE.
HOW WILL OTHERS FEEL ABOUT THAT CHOICE?
WHOSE NEEDS SHOULD YOU PUT FIRST?
WHEN YOU CLASHED WITH KIMUN KAMUY, YOU FOCUSED ON KANNA'S NEEDS.
SO, IS IT ELMA THIS TIME?
BUT ELMA'S PREPARED TO SACRIFICE HERSELF FOR HER CLAN.
OF COURSE, SHE DID SCOLD ME AT WORK FOR IGNORING MY OWN NEEDS.
GOTTA ADMIT THAT BOTHERS ME.
BACK THEN, ELMA ACCEPTED THE LOGIC OF MY WORLD AND BACKED DOWN.
BUT NOW, *I'M* REJECTING THE LOGIC OF *HERS*.
I THINK THE ONE I'M **REALLY** PUTTING FIRST IS--
CLACK
CREEEAK...

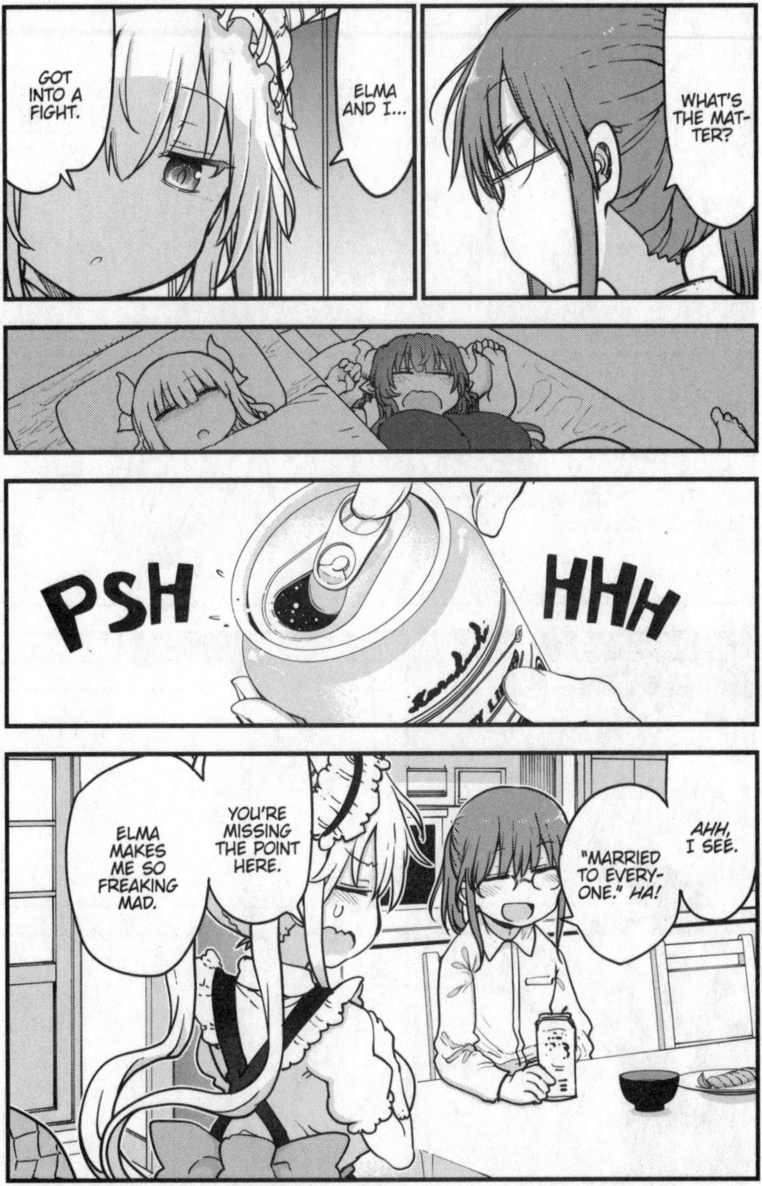
WHAT'S THE MAT-TER?
ELMA AND I...
GOT INTO A FIGHT.
PSH HHH
AHH, I SEE.
"MARRIED TO EVERY-ONE." HA!
YOU'RE MISSING THE POINT HERE.
ELMA MAKES ME SO FREAKING MAD.

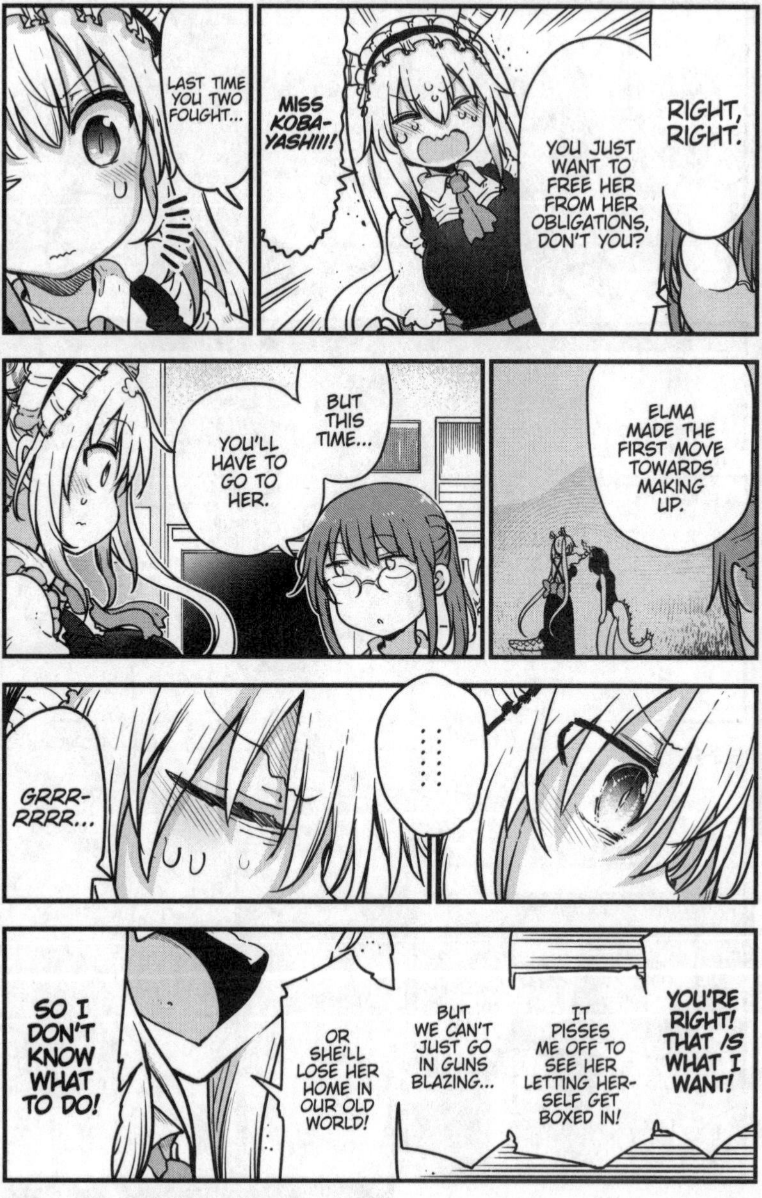
RIGHT, RIGHT.
YOU JUST WANT TO FREE HER FROM HER OBLIGATIONS, DON'T YOU?
MISS KOBA-YASHIIII!
LAST TIME YOU TWO FOUGHT...
ELMA MADE THE FIRST MOVE TOWARDS MAKING UP.
BUT THIS TIME...
YOU'LL HAVE TO GO TO HER.
......
GRRRR-RRRR...
YOU'RE RIGHT! THAT IS WHAT I WANT!
IT PISSES ME OFF TO SEE HER LETTING HER-SELF GET BOXED IN!
BUT WE CAN'T JUST GO IN GUNS BLAZING...
OR SHE'LL LOSE HER HOME IN OUR OLD WORLD!
SO I DON'T KNOW WHAT TO DO!

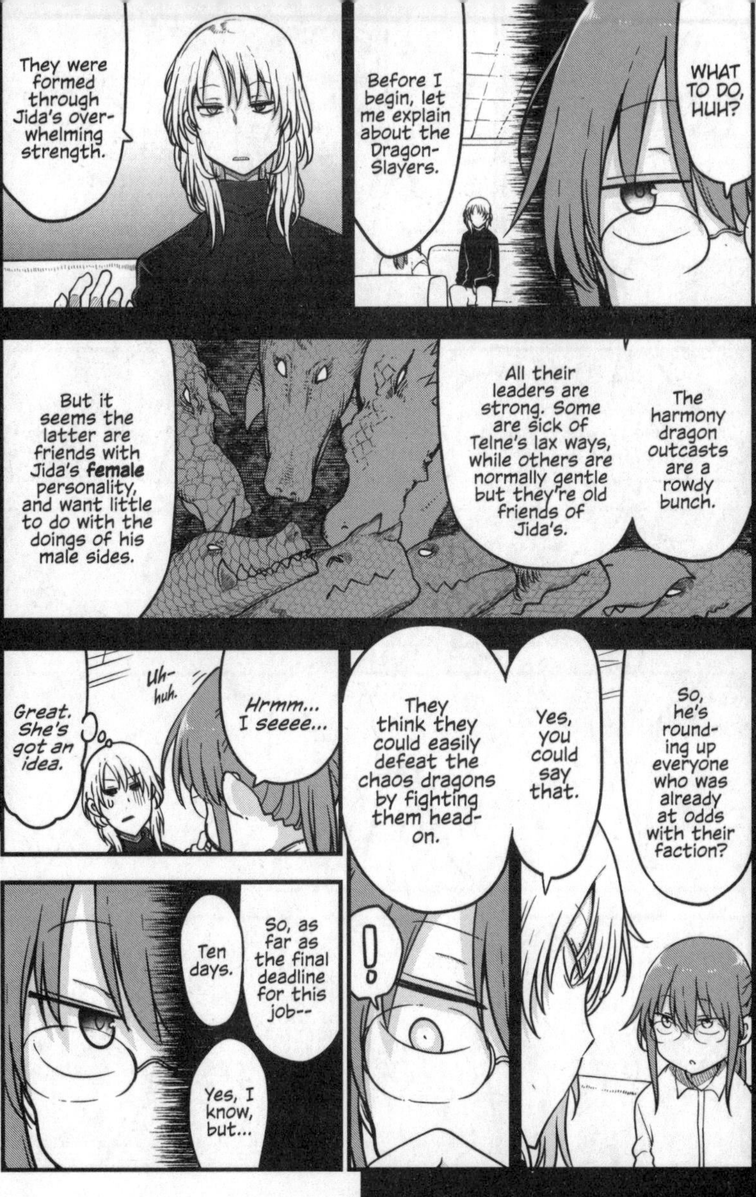
WHAT TO DO, HUH?
Before I begin, let me explain about the Dragon-Slayers.
They were formed through Jida's over-whelming strength.
The harmony dragon outcasts are a rowdy bunch.
All their leaders are strong. Some are sick of Telne's lax ways, while others are normally gentle but they're old friends of Jida's.
But it seems the latter are friends with Jida's **female** personality, and want little to do with the doings of his male sides.
So, he's round-ing up everyone who was already at odds with their faction?
Yes, you could say that.
They think they could easily defeat the chaos dragons by fighting them head-on.
!
Hrmm... I seeee...
Uh-huh.
Great. She's got an idea.
So, as far as the final deadline for this job--
Ten days.
Yes, I know, but...

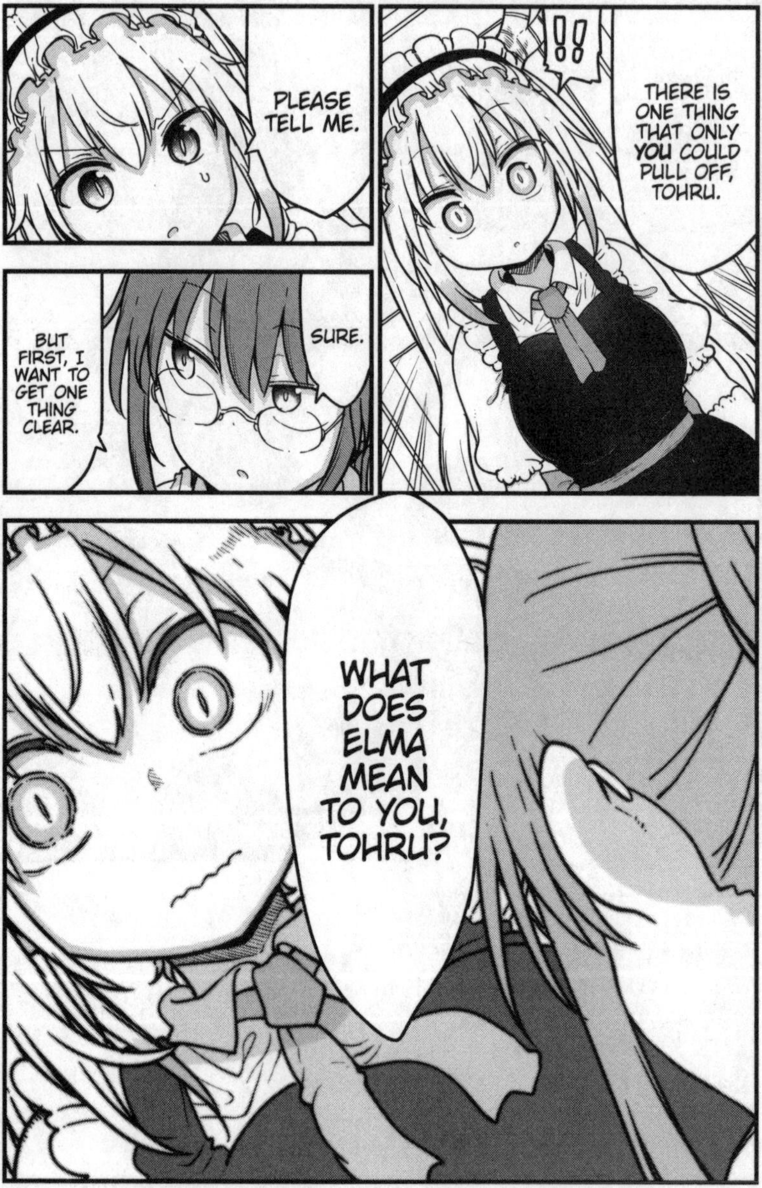
!!
THERE IS ONE THING THAT ONLY YOU COULD PULL OFF, TOHRU.
PLEASE TELL ME.
SURE.
BUT FIRST, I WANT TO GET ONE THING CLEAR.
WHAT DOES ELMA MEAN TO YOU, TOHRU?

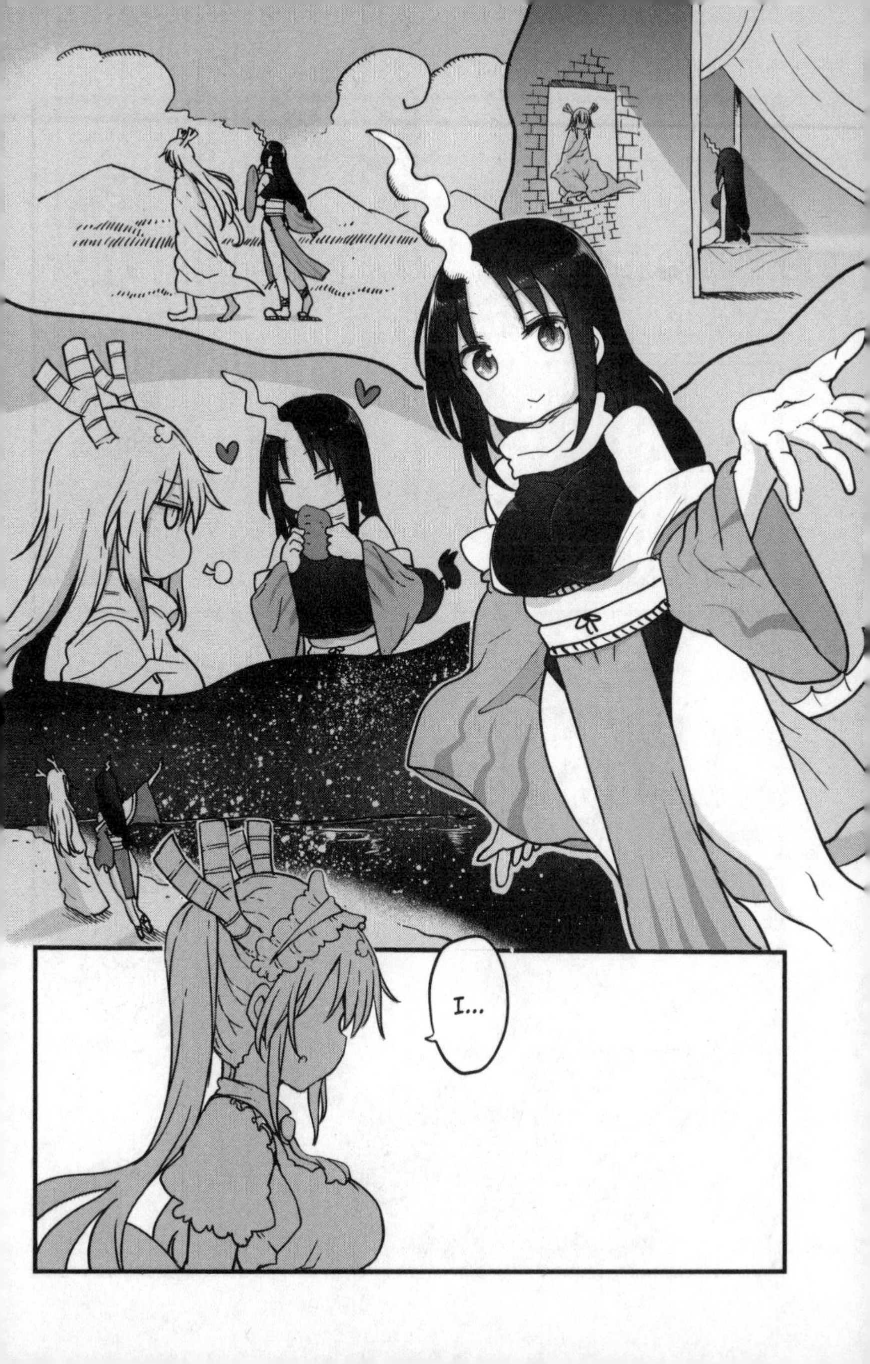
I...

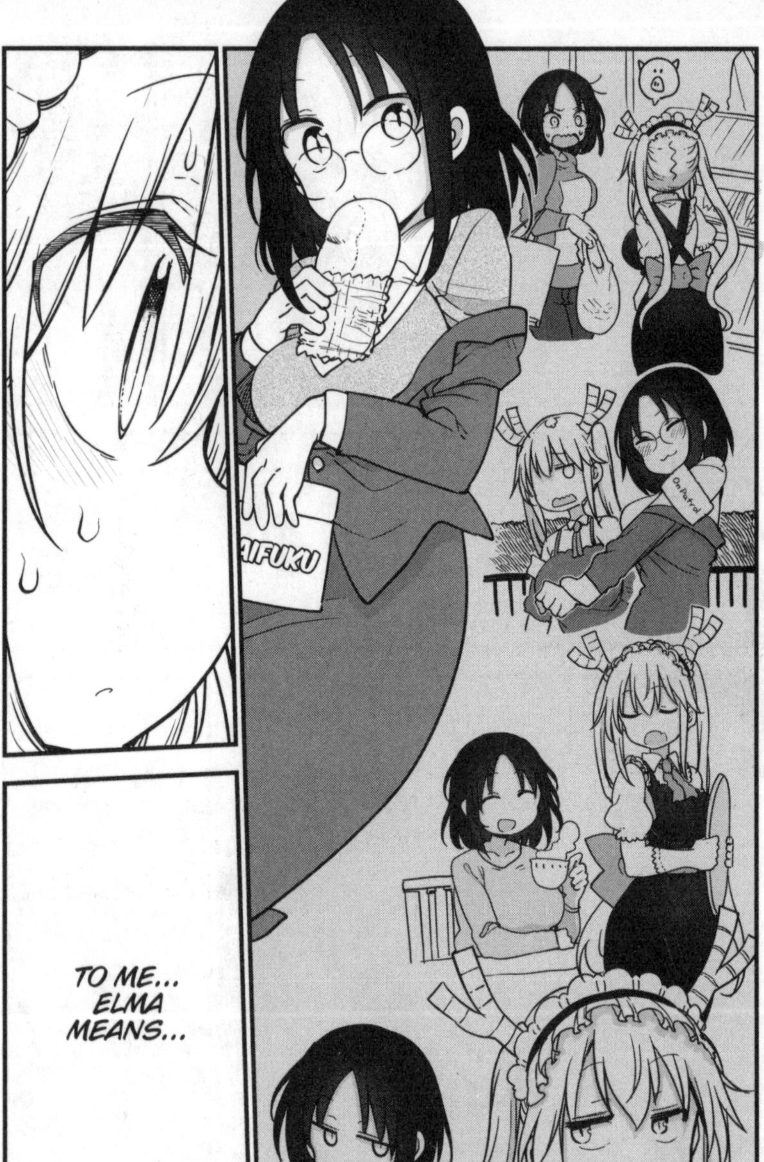
AIFUKU
On Patrol
TO ME... ELMA MEANS...

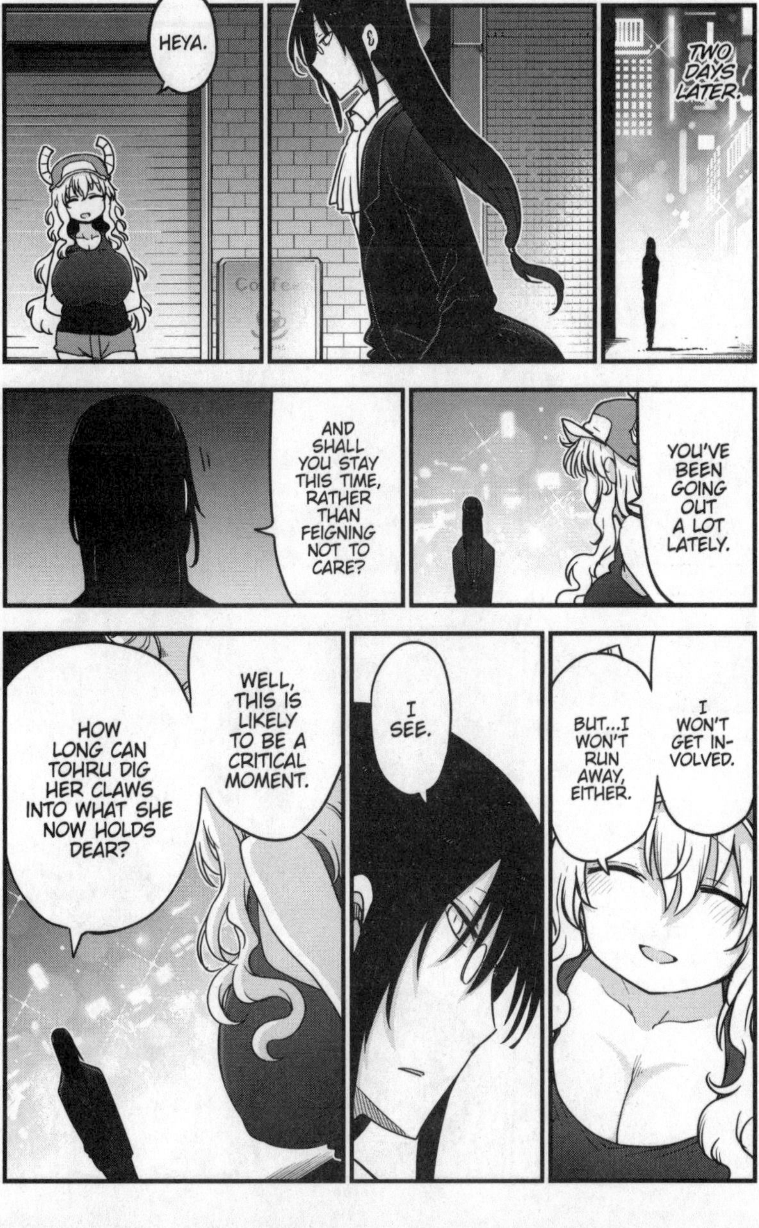
TWO DAYS LATER.
HEYA.
YOU'VE BEEN GOING OUT A LOT LATELY.
AND SHALL YOU STAY THIS TIME, RATHER THAN FEIGNING NOT TO CARE?
I WON'T GET INVOLVED.
BUT...I WON'T RUN AWAY, EITHER.
I SEE.
WELL, THIS IS LIKELY TO BE A CRITICAL MOMENT.
HOW LONG CAN TOHRU DIG HER CLAWS INTO WHAT SHE NOW HOLDS DEAR?

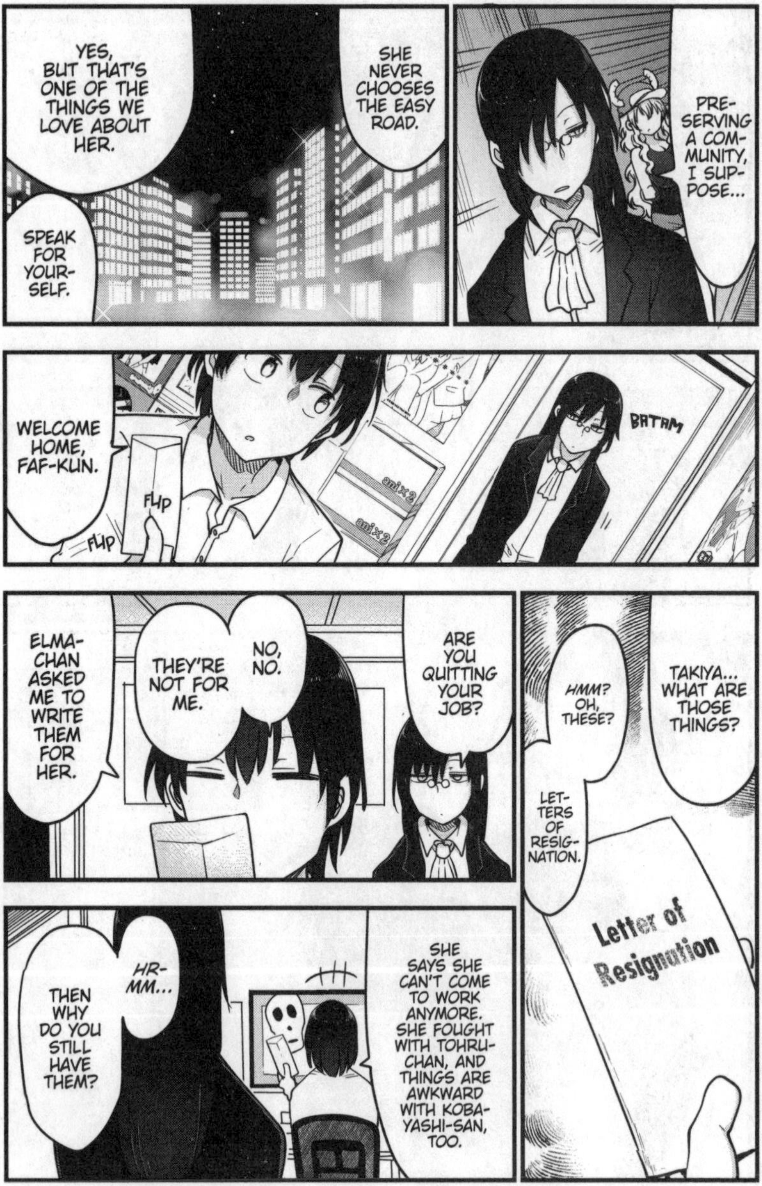
PRESERVING A COMMUNITY, I SUPPOSE...
SHE NEVER CHOOSES THE EASY ROAD.
YES, BUT THAT'S ONE OF THE THINGS WE LOVE ABOUT HER.
SPEAK FOR YOURSELF.
BATAM
WELCOME HOME, FAF-KUN.
FLIP
FLIP
TAKIYA... WHAT ARE THOSE THINGS?
HMM? OH, THESE?
LETTERS OF RESIGNATION.
Letter of Resignation
ARE YOU QUITTING YOUR JOB?
NO, NO.
THEY'RE NOT FOR ME.
ELMA-CHAN ASKED ME TO WRITE THEM FOR HER.
SHE SAYS SHE CAN'T COME TO WORK ANYMORE. SHE FOUGHT WITH TOHRU-CHAN, AND THINGS ARE AWKWARD WITH KOBAYASHI-SAN, TOO.
HR-MM...
THEN WHY DO YOU STILL HAVE THEM?

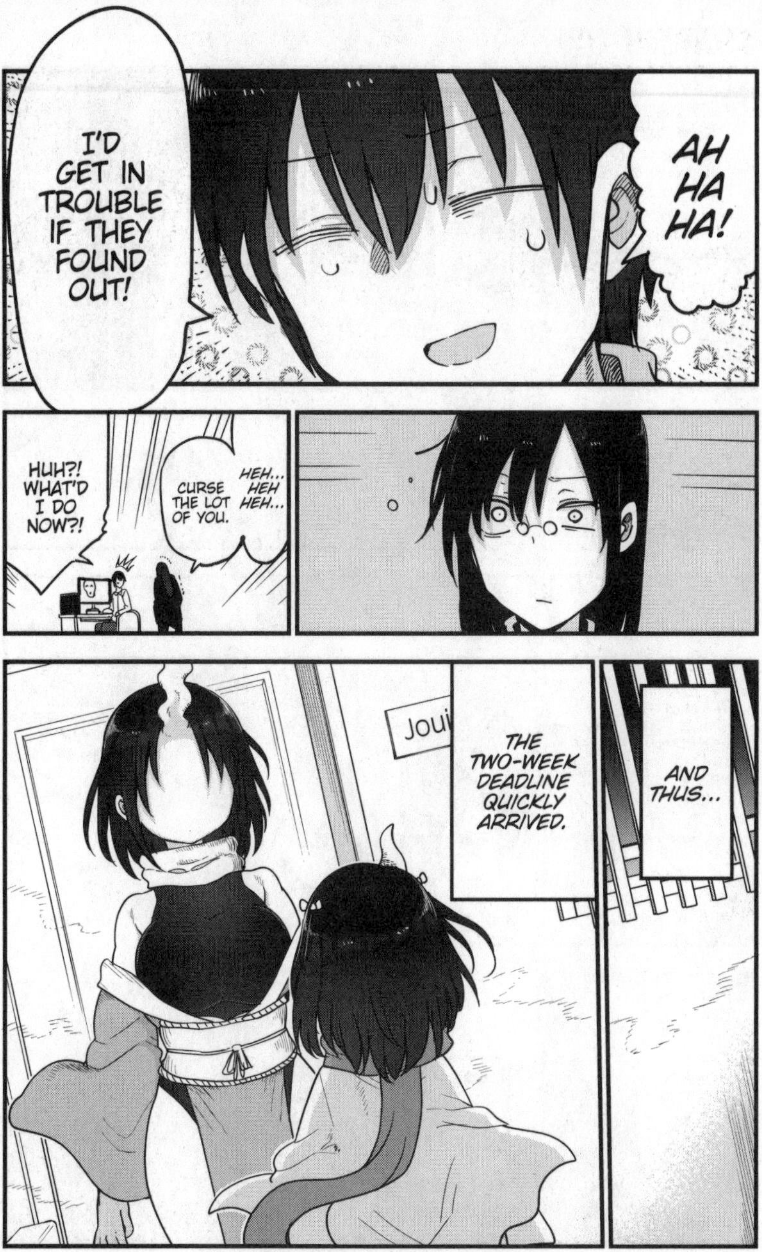
AH HA HA!
I'D GET IN TROUBLE IF THEY FOUND OUT!
HEH... HEH HEH...
CURSE THE LOT OF YOU.
HUH?! WHAT'D I DO NOW?!
AND THUS...
THE TWO-WEEK DEADLINE QUICKLY ARRIVED.

CHAPTER 108/END

CHAPTER 109

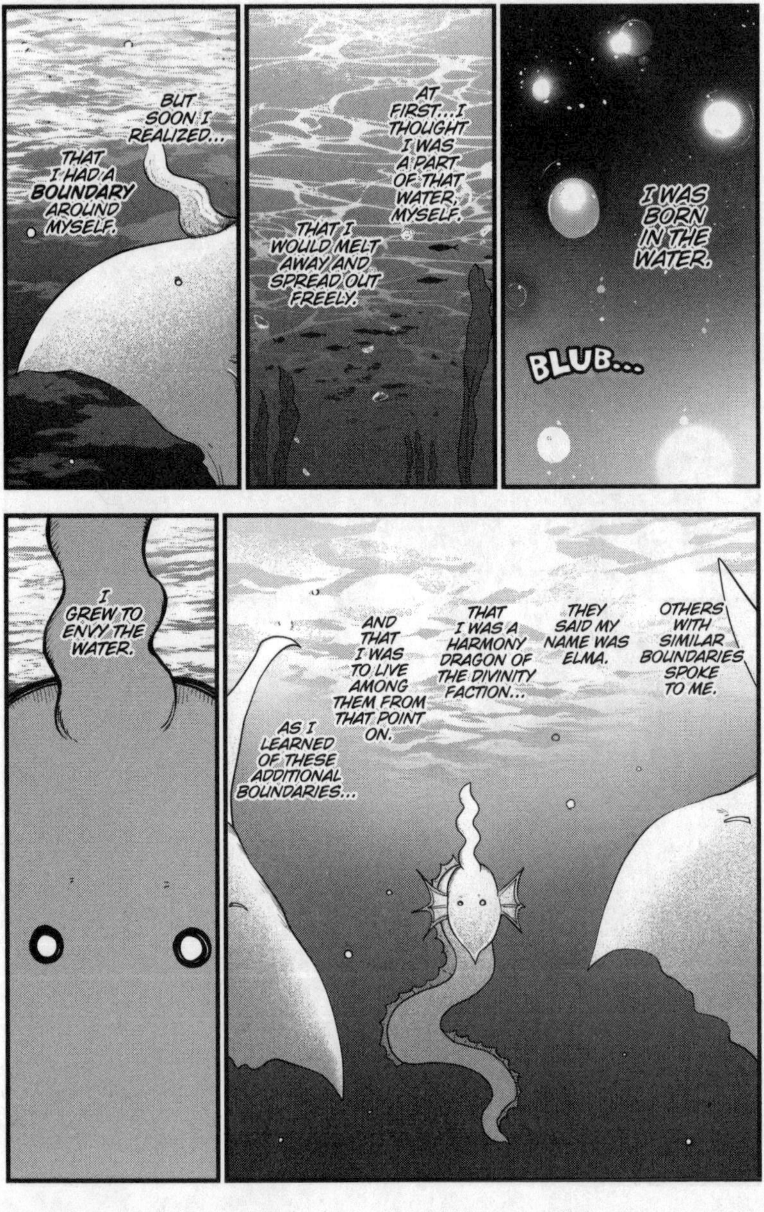
I WAS BORN IN THE WATER.
BLUB...
AT FIRST... I THOUGHT I WAS A PART OF THAT WATER, MYSELF.
THAT I WOULD MELT AWAY AND SPREAD OUT FREELY.
BUT SOON I REALIZED...
THAT I HAD A BOUNDARY AROUND MYSELF.
OTHERS WITH SIMILAR BOUNDARIES SPOKE TO ME.
THEY SAID MY NAME WAS ELMA.
THAT I WAS A HARMONY DRAGON OF THE DIVINITY FACTION...
AND THAT I WAS TO LIVE AMONG THEM FROM THAT POINT ON.
AS I LEARNED OF THESE ADDITIONAL BOUNDARIES...
I GREW TO ENVY THE WATER.

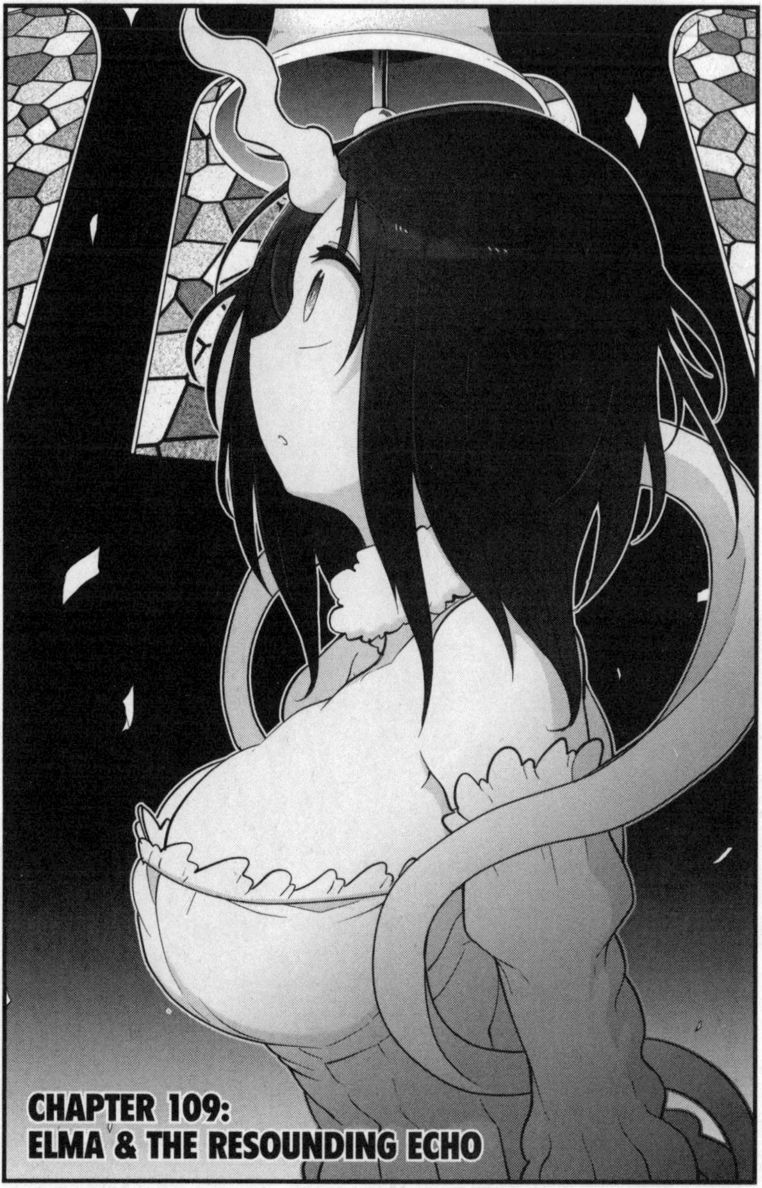
CHAPTER 109:
ELMA & THE RESOUNDING ECHO

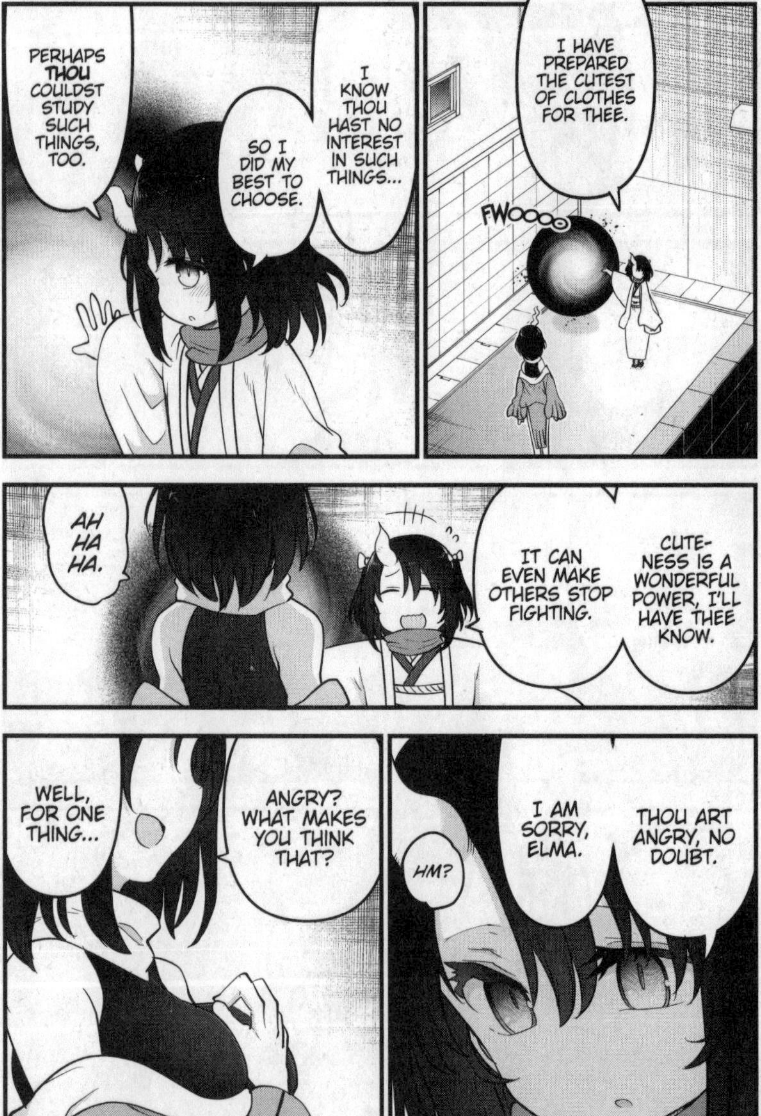
I HAVE PREPARED THE CUTEST OF CLOTHES FOR THEE.
FWOOOOO
I KNOW THOU HAST NO INTEREST IN SUCH THINGS...
SO I DID MY BEST TO CHOOSE.
PERHAPS THOU COULDST STUDY SUCH THINGS, TOO.
CUTENESS IS A WONDERFUL POWER, I'LL HAVE THEE KNOW.
IT CAN EVEN MAKE OTHERS STOP FIGHTING.
AH HA HA.
THOU ART ANGRY, NO DOUBT.
I AM SORRY, ELMA.
HM?
ANGRY? WHAT MAKES YOU THINK THAT?
WELL, FOR ONE THING...

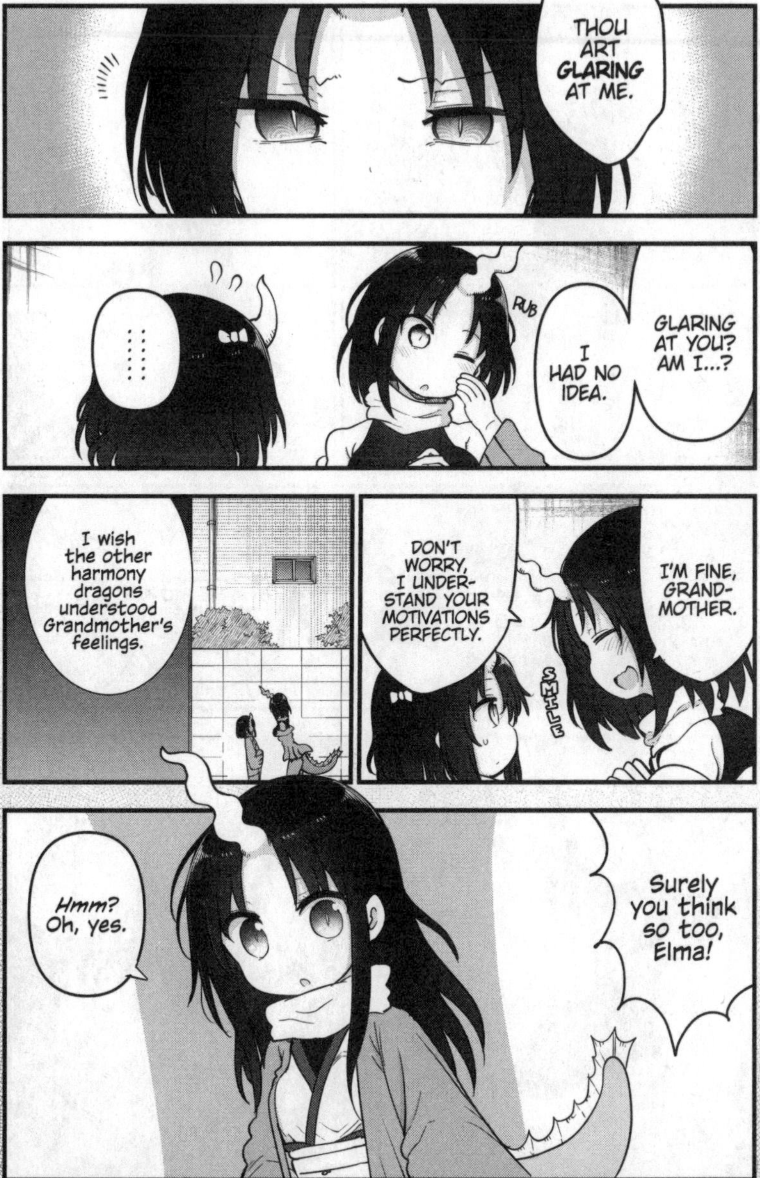
THOU ART GLARING AT ME.
GLARING AT YOU? AM I...?
I HAD NO IDEA.
RUB
......
I'M FINE, GRAND-MOTHER.
DON'T WORRY, I UNDER-STAND YOUR MOTIVATIONS PERFECTLY.
SMILE
I wish the other harmony dragons understood Grandmother's feelings.
Surely you think so too, Elma!
Hmm? Oh, yes.

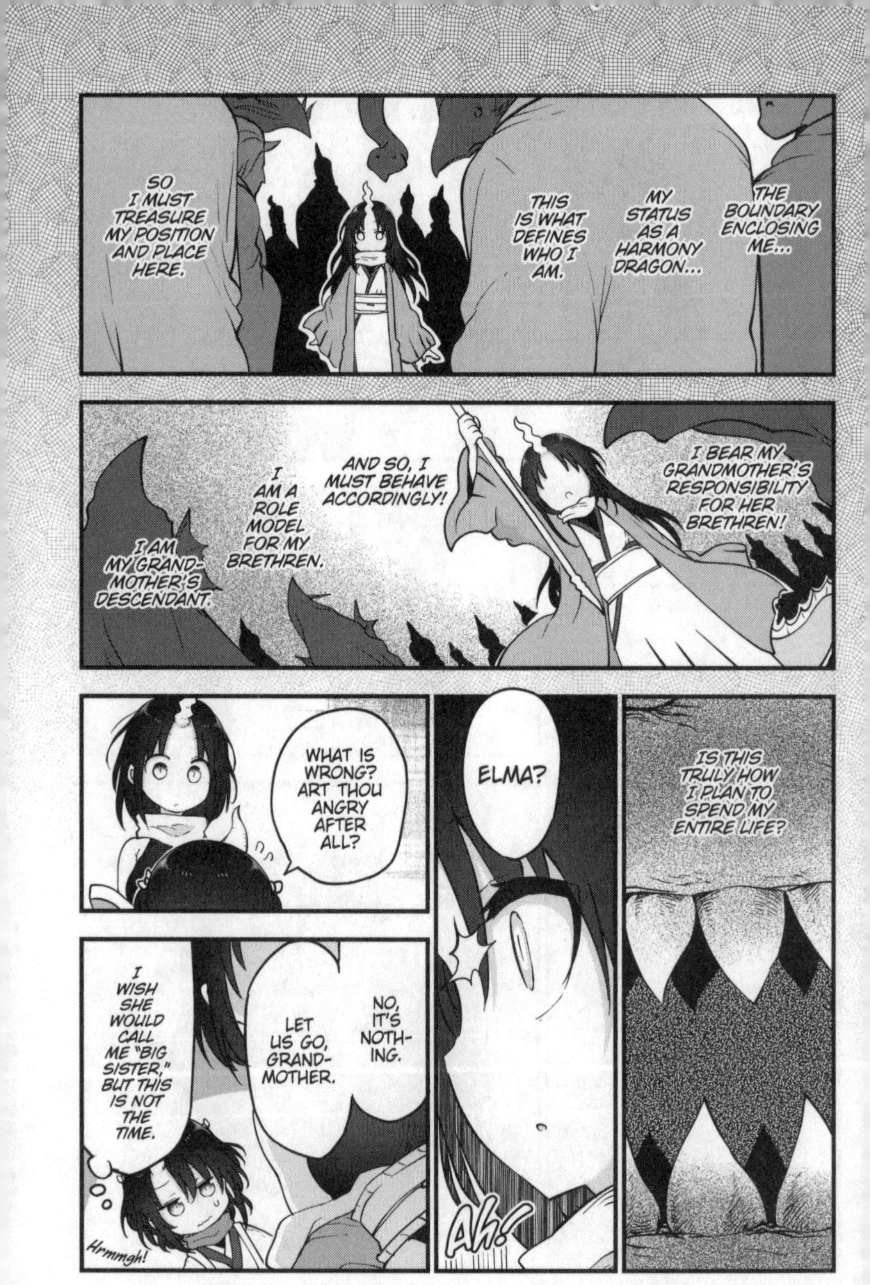
THE BOUNDARY ENCLOSING ME...
MY STATUS AS A HARMONY DRAGON...
THIS IS WHAT DEFINES WHO I AM.
SO I MUST TREASURE MY POSITION AND PLACE HERE.
I BEAR MY GRANDMOTHER'S RESPONSIBILITY FOR HER BRETHREN!
AND SO, I MUST BEHAVE ACCORDINGLY!
I AM A ROLE MODEL FOR MY BRETHREN.
I AM MY GRAND-MOTHER'S DESCENDANT.
IS THIS TRULY HOW I PLAN TO SPEND MY ENTIRE LIFE?
ELMA?
Ah!
WHAT IS WRONG? ART THOU ANGRY AFTER ALL?
NO, IT'S NOTH-ING.
LET US GO, GRAND-MOTHER.
I WISH SHE WOULD CALL ME "BIG SISTER," BUT THIS IS NOT THE TIME.
Hrmmgh!

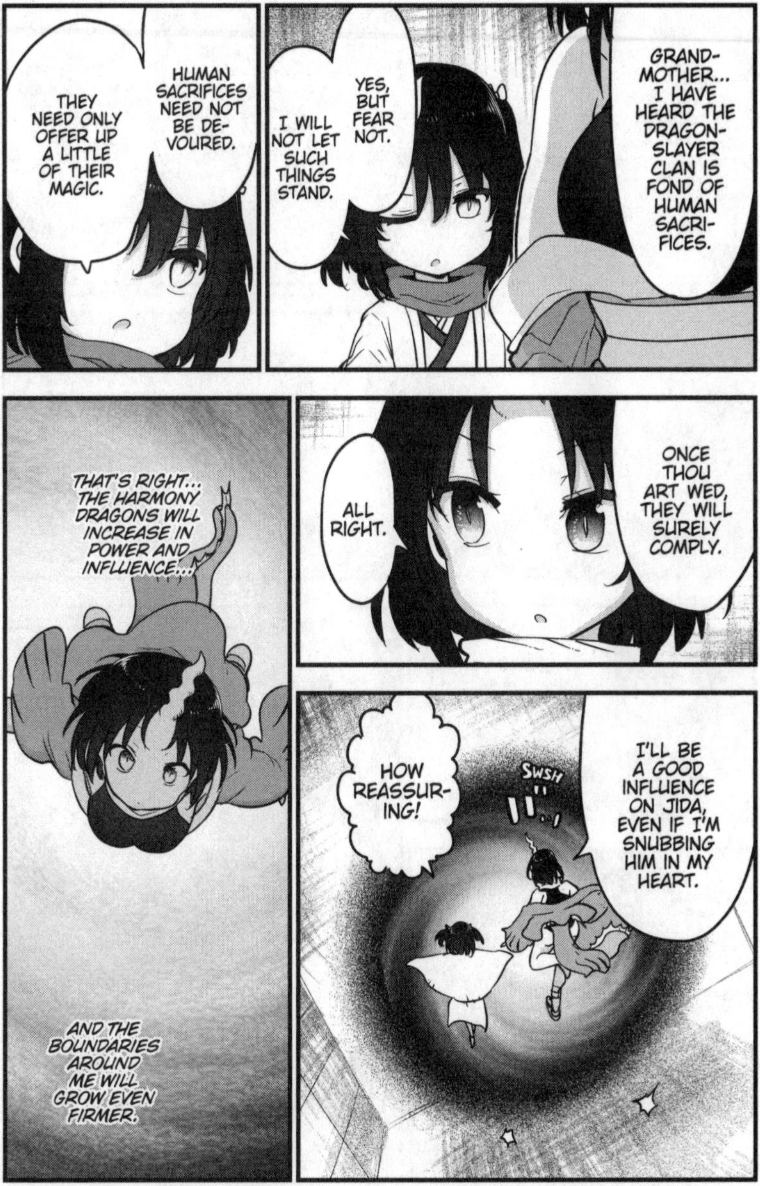
GRAND-MOTHER... I HAVE HEARD THE DRAGON-SLAYER CLAN IS FOND OF HUMAN SACRI-FICES.
YES, BUT FEAR NOT.
I WILL NOT LET SUCH THINGS STAND.
HUMAN SACRIFICES NEED NOT BE DE-VOURED.
THEY NEED ONLY OFFER UP A LITTLE OF THEIR MAGIC.
ONCE THOU ART WED, THEY WILL SURELY COMPLY.
ALL RIGHT.
I'LL BE A GOOD INFLUENCE ON JIDA, EVEN IF I'M SNUBBING HIM IN MY HEART.
SWSH
HOW REASSUR-ING!
THAT'S RIGHT... THE HARMONY DRAGONS WILL INCREASE IN POWER AND INFLUENCE...
AND THE BOUNDARIES AROUND ME WILL GROW EVEN FIRMER.

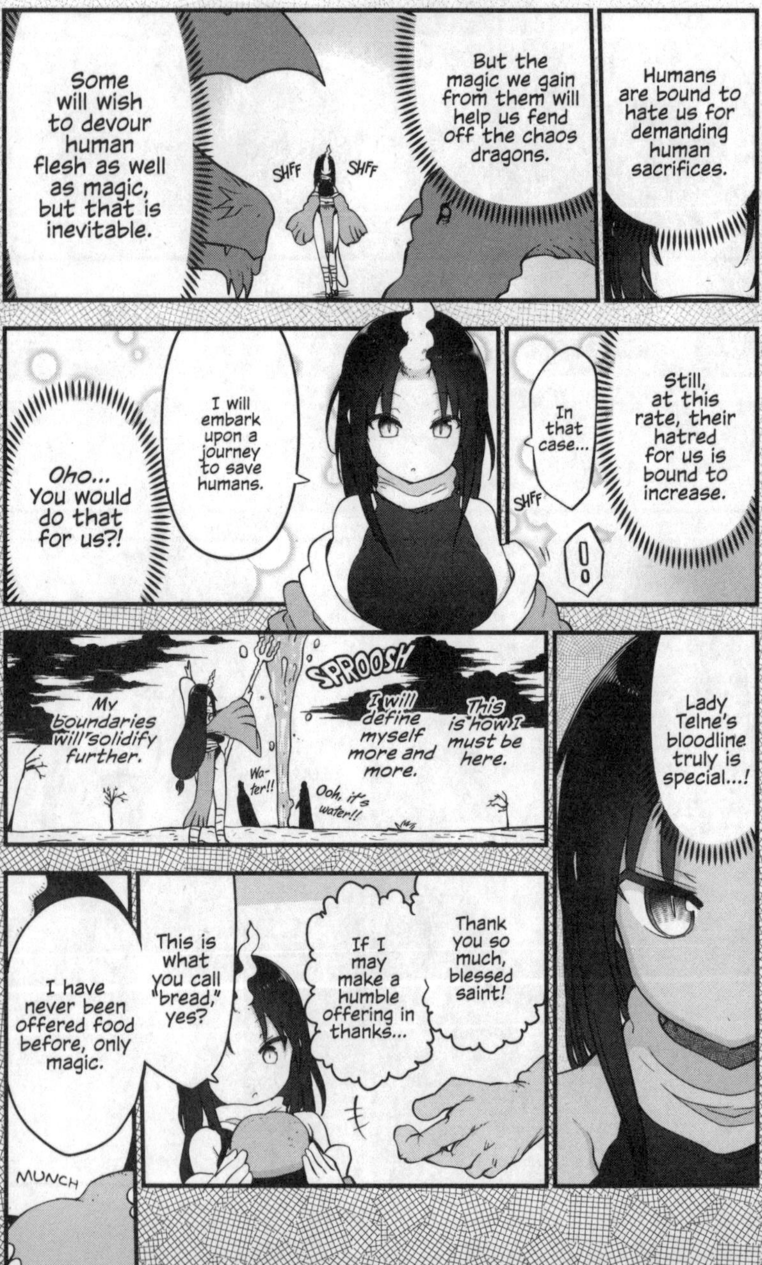
Humans are bound to hate us for demanding human sacrifices.
But the magic we gain from them will help us fend off the chaos dragons.
SHFF
SHFF
Some will wish to devour human flesh as well as magic, but that is inevitable.
Still, at this rate, their hatred for us is bound to increase.
In that case...
SHFF
!
I will embark upon a journey to save humans.
Oho... You would do that for us?!
Lady Telne's bloodline truly is special...!
SPROOSH
This is how I must be here.
I will define myself more and more.
My boundaries will solidify further.
Water!!
Ooh, it's water!!
Thank you so much, blessed saint!
If I may make a humble offering in thanks...
This is what you call "bread," yes?
I have never been offered food before, only magic.
MUNCH

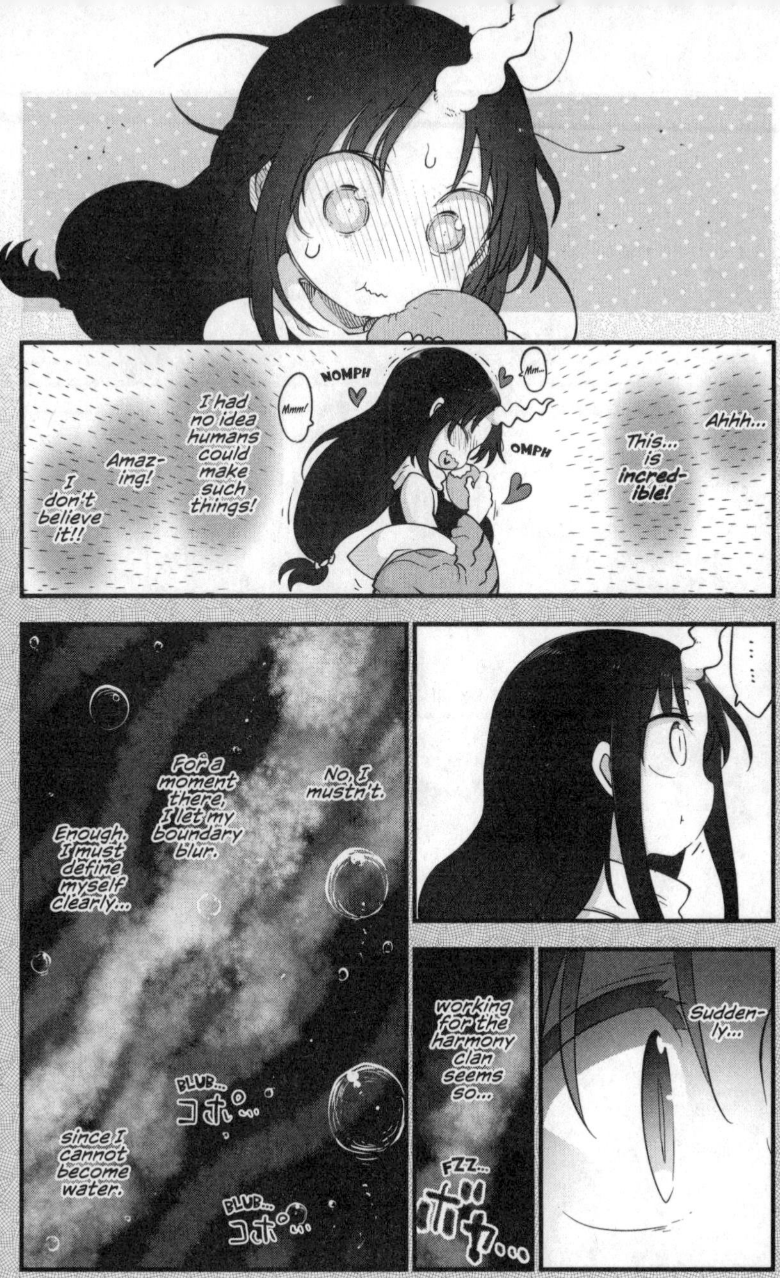
Ahhh...
This... is incred-ible!
Mm...
OMPH
NOMPH
Mmm!
I had no idea humans could make such things!
Amaz-ing!
I don't believe it!!
......
Sudden-ly...
working for the harmony clan seems so...
FZZ...
ボヤ...
No, I mustn't.
For a moment there, I let my boundary blur.
Enough. I must define myself clearly...
BLUB...
コポ...
since I cannot become water.
BLUB...
コポ...

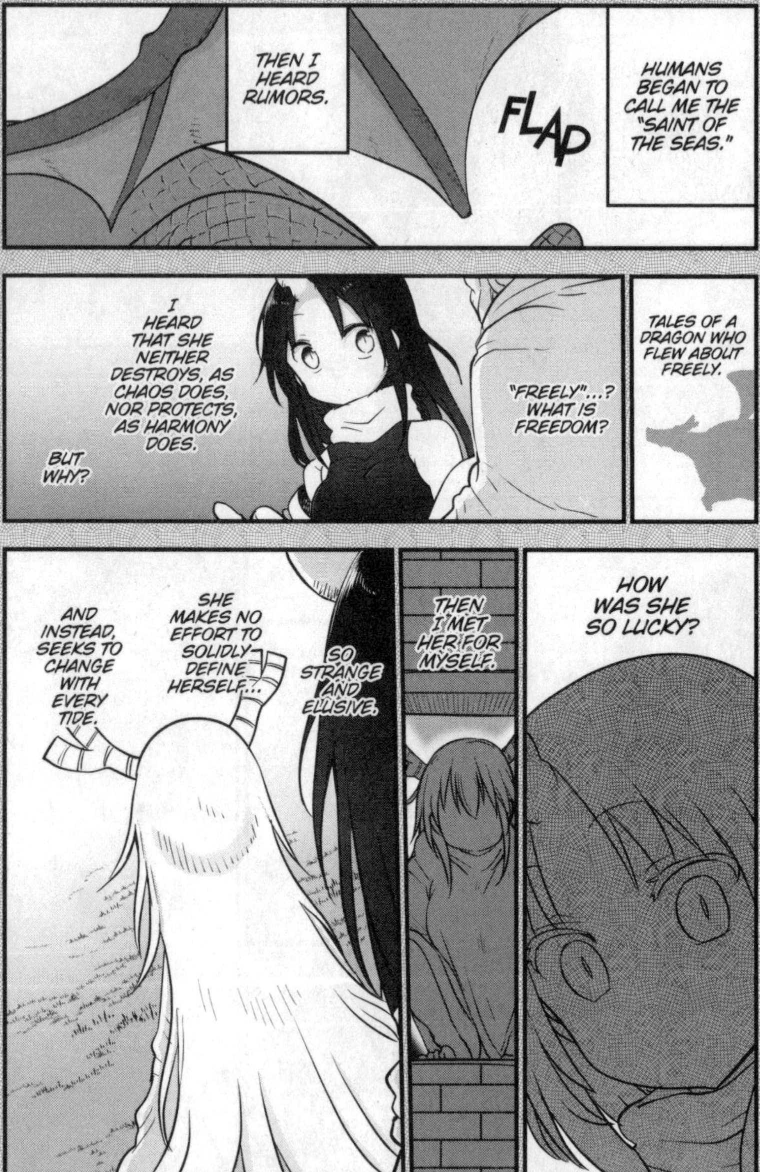
HUMANS BEGAN TO CALL ME THE "SAINT OF THE SEAS."
FLAP
THEN I HEARD RUMORS.
TALES OF A DRAGON WHO FLEW ABOUT FREELY.
"FREELY"...? WHAT IS FREEDOM?
I HEARD THAT SHE NEITHER DESTROYS, AS CHAOS DOES, NOR PROTECTS, AS HARMONY DOES.
BUT WHY?
HOW WAS SHE SO LUCKY?
THEN I MET HER FOR MYSELF.
SO STRANGE AND ELLUSIVE.
SHE MAKES NO EFFORT TO SOLIDLY DEFINE HERSELF...
AND INSTEAD, SEEKS TO CHANGE WITH EVERY TIDE.

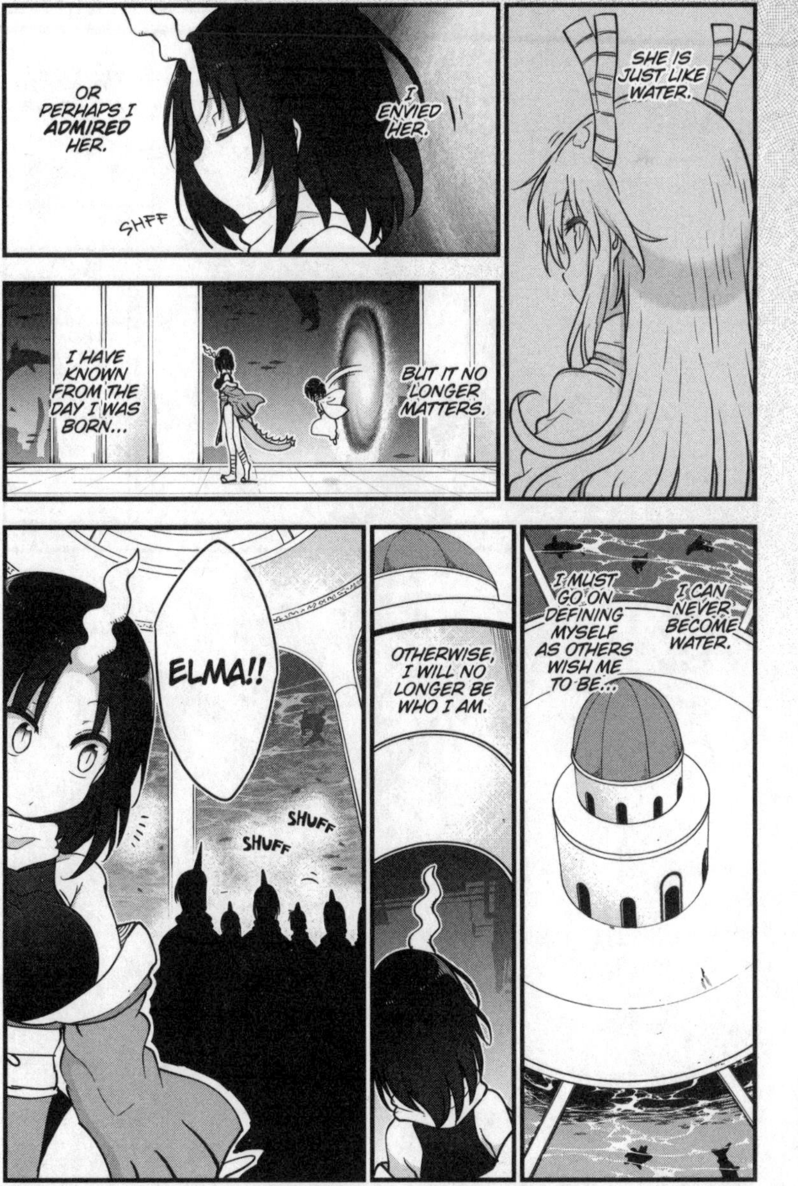
SHE IS JUST LIKE WATER.
I ENVIED HER.
OR PERHAPS I ADMIRED HER.
SHFF
BUT IT NO LONGER MATTERS.
I HAVE KNOWN FROM THE DAY I WAS BORN...
I CAN NEVER BECOME WATER.
I MUST GO ON DEFINING MYSELF AS OTHERS WISH ME TO BE...
OTHERWISE, I WILL NO LONGER BE WHO I AM.
ELMA!!
SHUFF
SHUFF

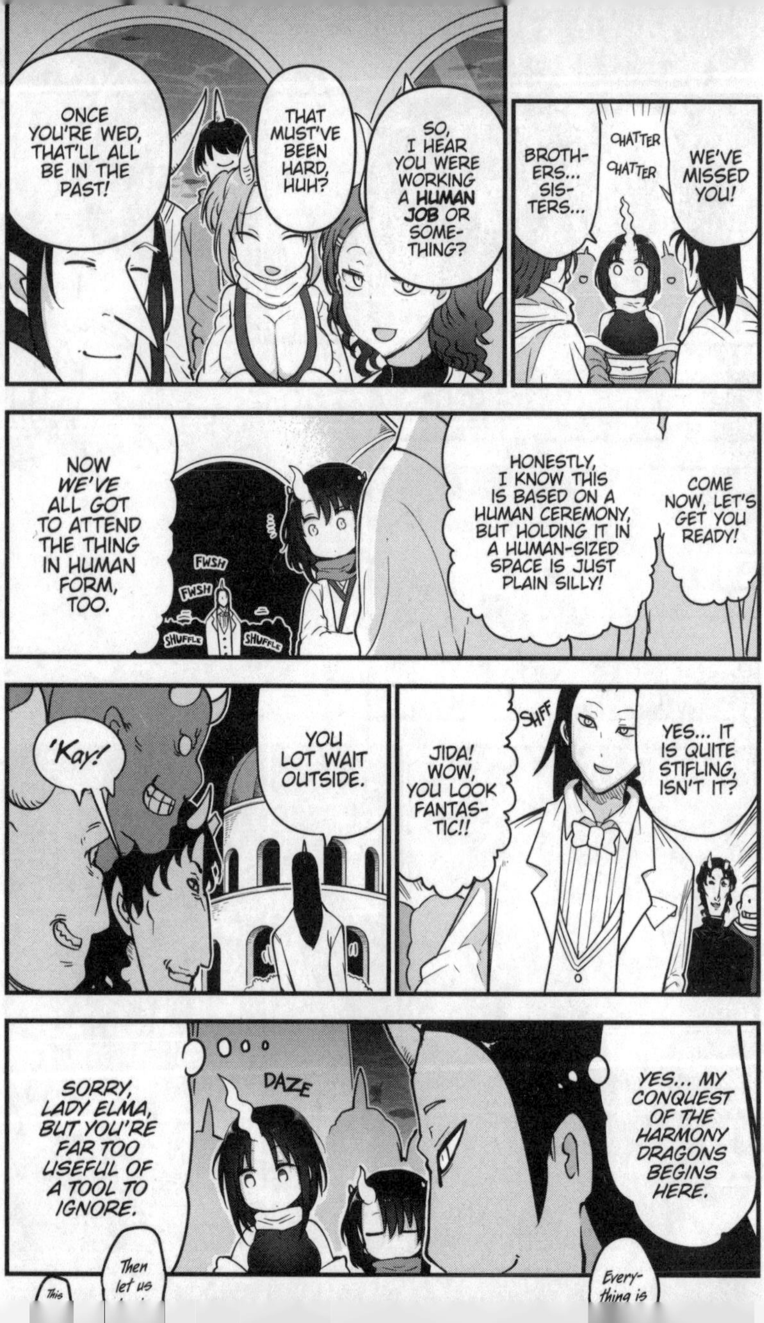
WE'VE MISSED YOU!
CHATTER
CHATTER
BROTHERS... SISTERS...
SO, I HEAR YOU WERE WORKING A **HUMAN JOB** OR SOMETHING?
THAT MUST'VE BEEN HARD, HUH?
ONCE YOU'RE WED, THAT'LL ALL BE IN THE PAST!
COME NOW, LET'S GET YOU READY!
HONESTLY, I KNOW THIS IS BASED ON A HUMAN CEREMONY, BUT HOLDING IT IN A HUMAN-SIZED SPACE IS JUST PLAIN SILLY!
NOW *WE'VE* ALL GOT TO ATTEND THE THING IN HUMAN FORM, TOO.
FWSH
FWSH
SHUFFLE
SHUFFLE
YES... IT IS QUITE STIFLING, ISN'T IT?
SHFF
JIDA! WOW, YOU LOOK FANTASTIC!!
YOU LOT WAIT OUTSIDE.
'Kay!
YES... MY CONQUEST OF THE HARMONY DRAGONS BEGINS HERE.
DAZE
SORRY, LADY ELMA, BUT YOU'RE FAR TOO USEFUL OF A TOOL TO IGNORE.
Every-thing is
Then let us
This

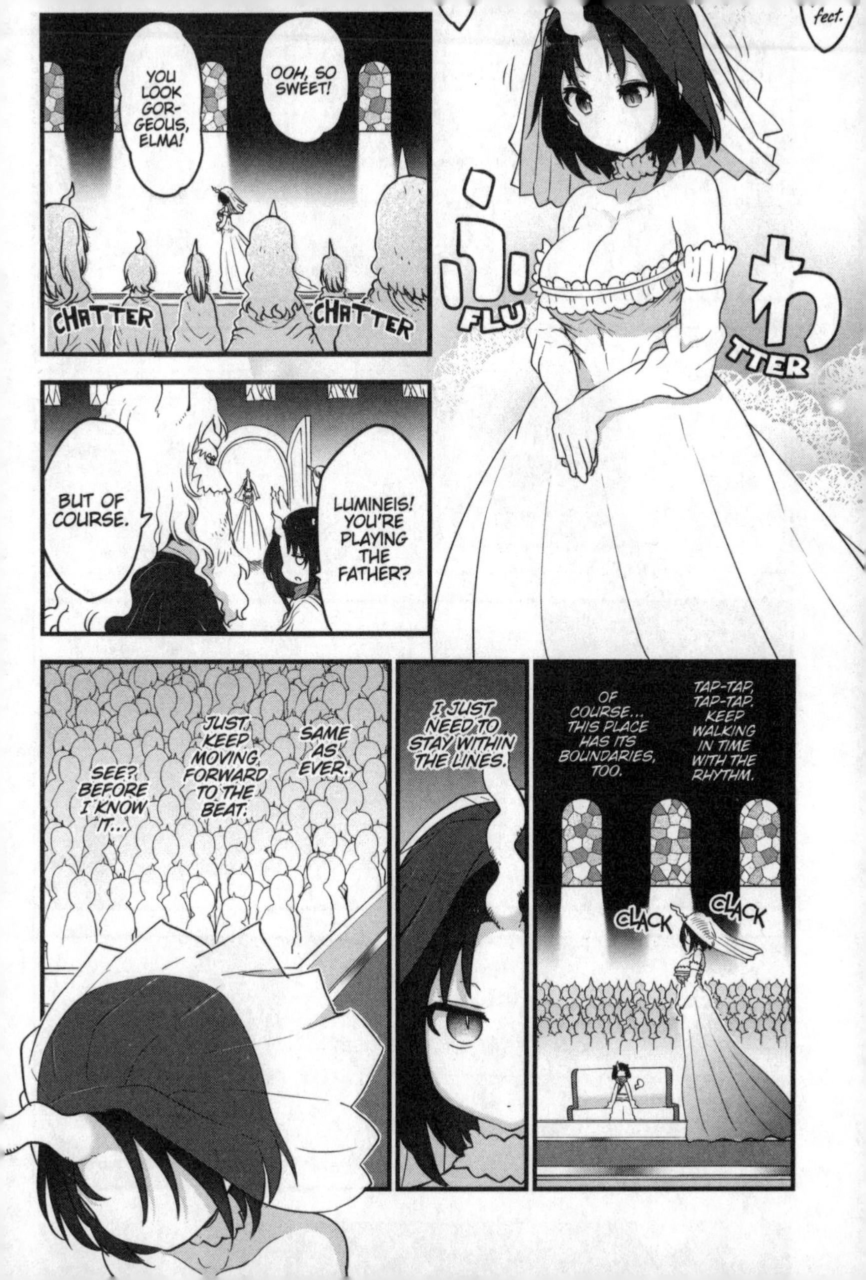
fect.
ふわ
FLUTTER
OOH, SO SWEET!
YOU LOOK GORGEOUS, ELMA!
CHATTER
CHATTER
LUMINEIS! YOU'RE PLAYING THE FATHER?
BUT OF COURSE.
TAP-TAP, TAP-TAP. KEEP WALKING IN TIME WITH THE RHYTHM.
OF COURSE... THIS PLACE HAS ITS BOUNDARIES, TOO.
CLACK
CLACK
I JUST NEED TO STAY WITHIN THE LINES.
SAME AS EVER.
JUST KEEP MOVING FORWARD TO THE BEAT.
SEE? BEFORE I KNOW IT...

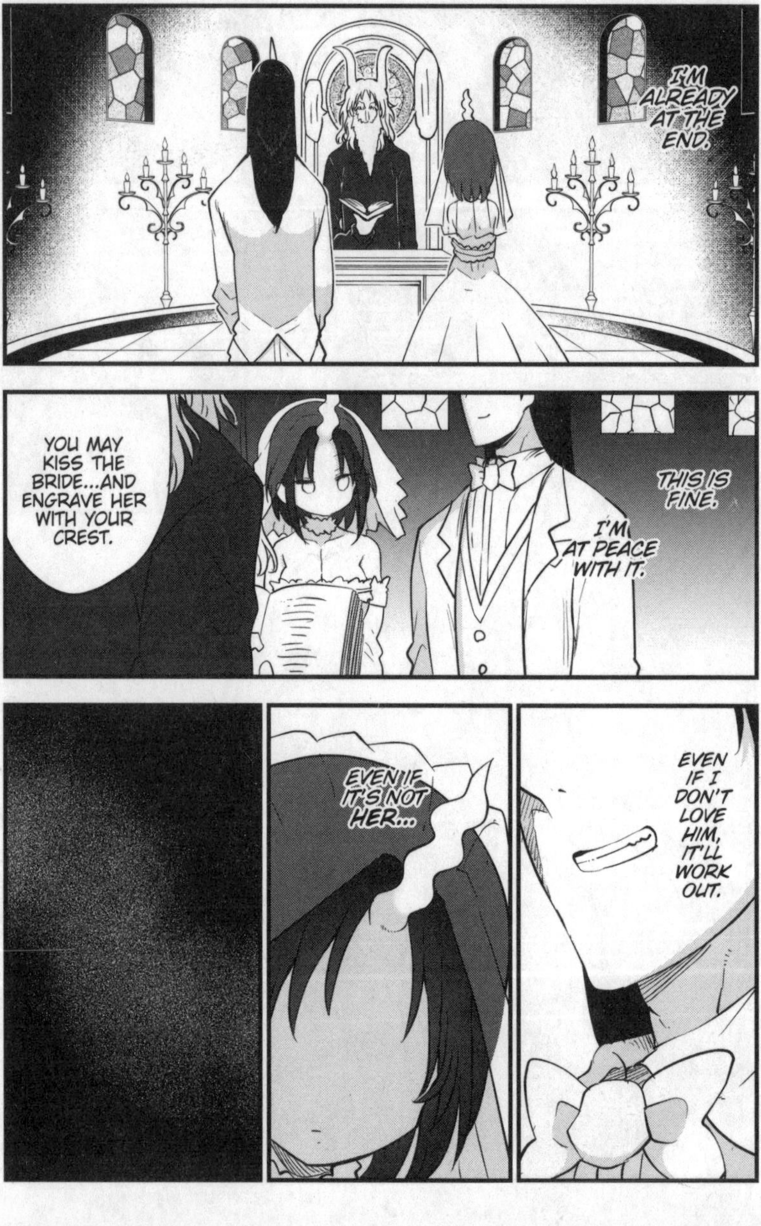
I'M ALREADY AT THE END.
THIS IS FINE.
I'M AT PEACE WITH IT.
YOU MAY KISS THE BRIDE...AND ENGRAVE HER WITH YOUR CREST.
EVEN IF I DON'T LOVE HIM, IT'LL WORK OUT.
EVEN IF IT'S NOT HER...

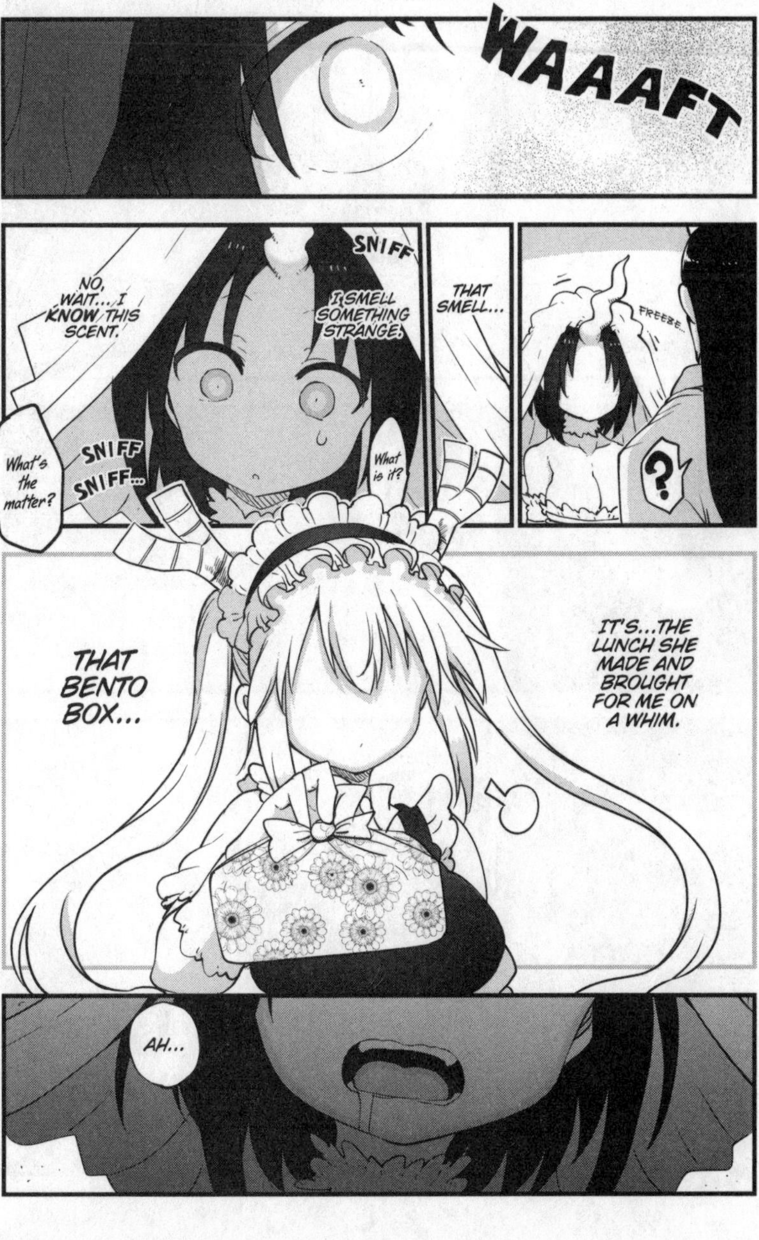
WAAAFT
FREEZE...
?
THAT SMELL...
SNIFF
I SMELL SOMETHING STRANGE.
NO, WAIT... I KNOW THIS SCENT.
What is it?
SNIFF SNIFF...
What's the matter?
IT'S...THE LUNCH SHE MADE AND BROUGHT FOR ME ON A WHIM.
THAT BENTO BOX...
AH...

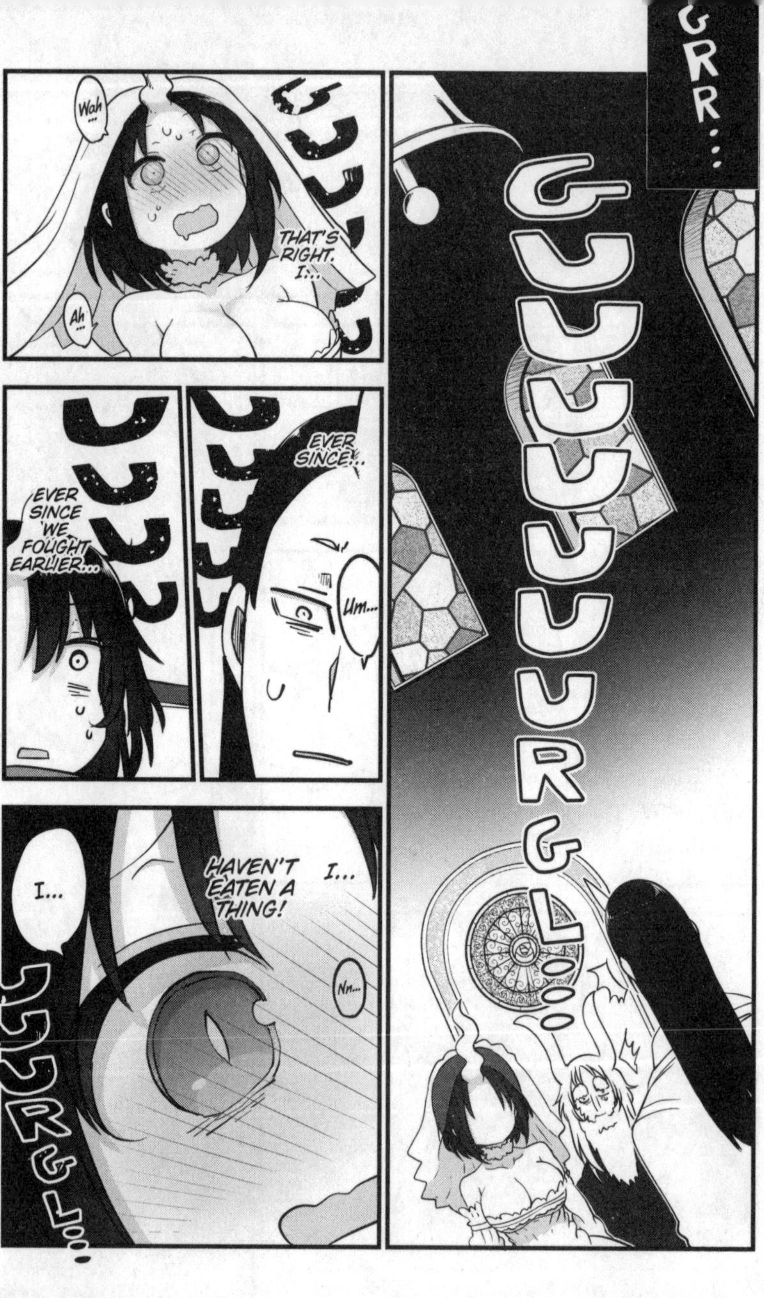
GRR...
GUUUUUUUURGL...
Wah...
THAT'S RIGHT. I...
Ah...
EVER SINCE...
Um...
EVER SINCE WE FOUGHT EARLIER...
I...
HAVEN'T EATEN A THING!
I...
Nn...
UUURGL...

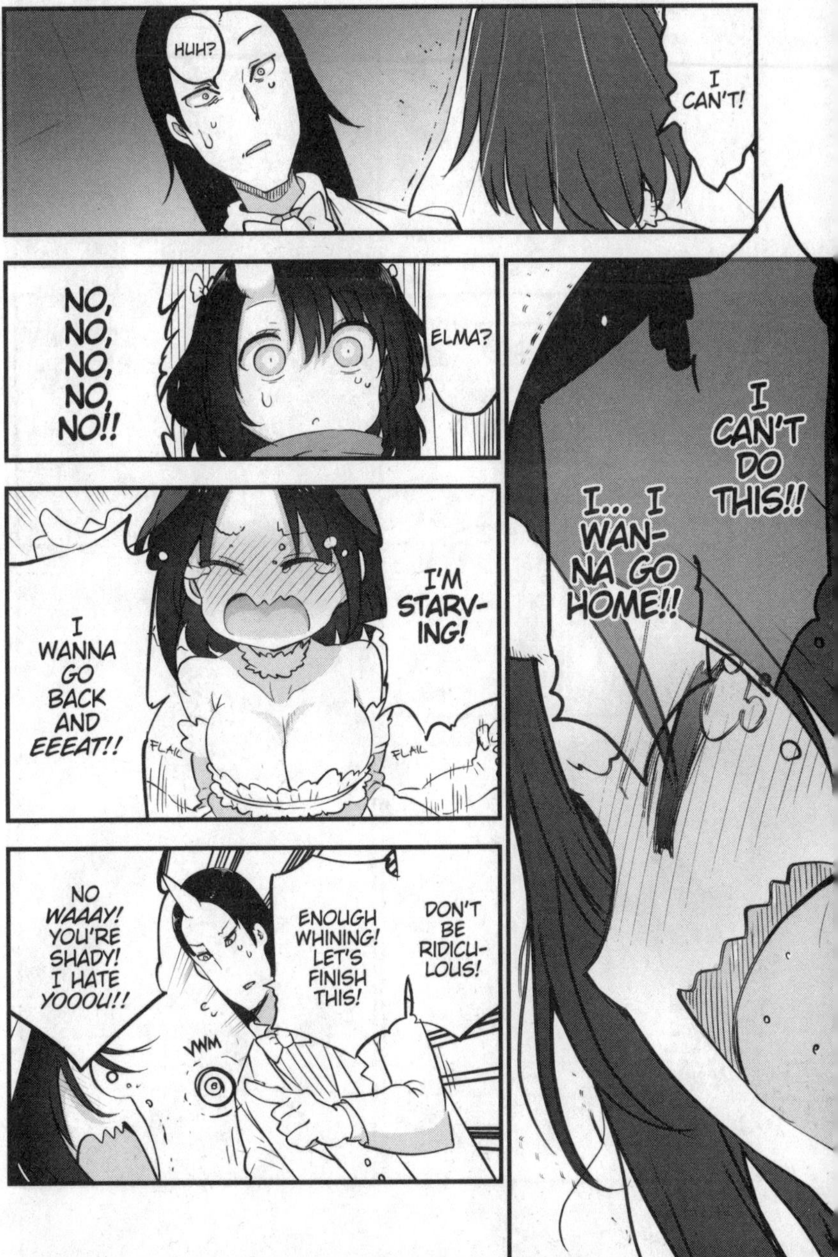
I CAN'T!
HUH?
I CAN'T DO THIS!!
I... I WANNA GO HOME!!
ELMA?
NO, NO, NO, NO, NO!!
I'M STARVING!
I WANNA GO BACK AND EEEAT!!
FLAIL
FLAIL
DON'T BE RIDICULOUS!
ENOUGH WHINING! LET'S FINISH THIS!
NO WAAAY! YOU'RE SHADY! I HATE YOOOU!!
VWM

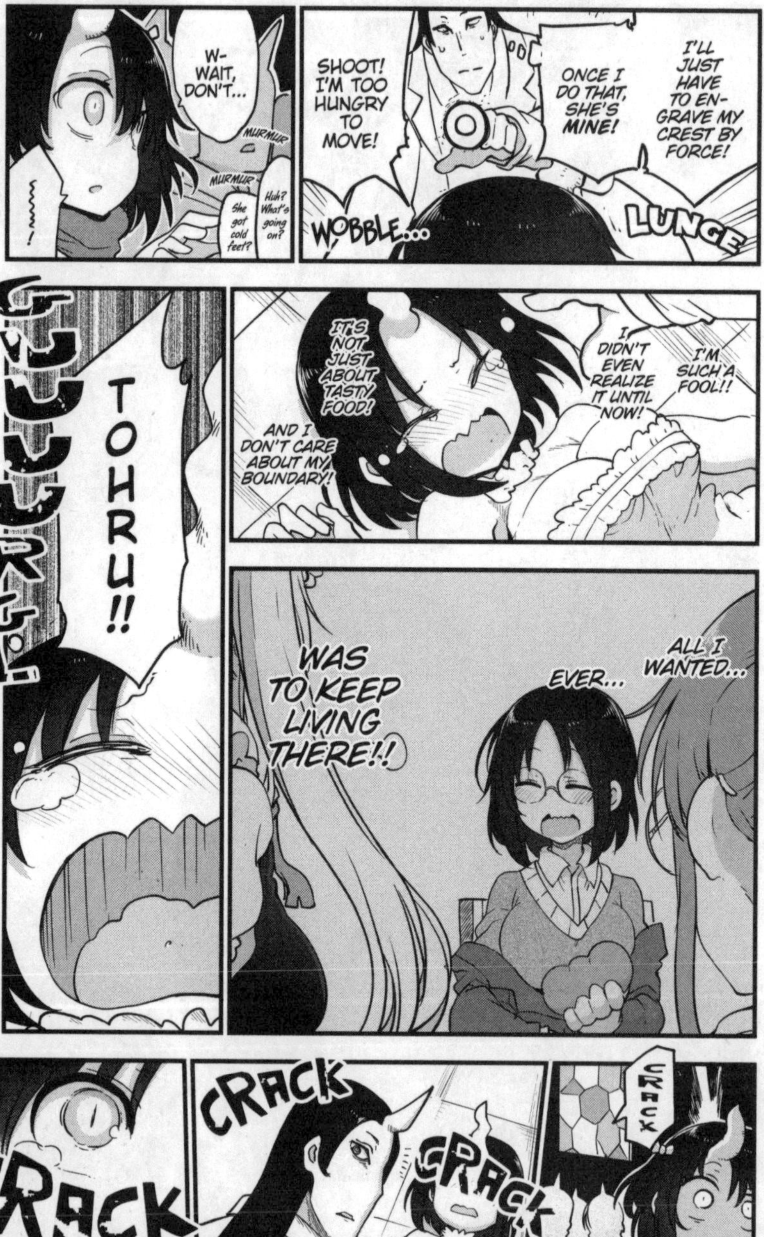
I'LL JUST HAVE TO EN-GRAVE MY CREST BY FORCE!
ONCE I DO THAT, SHE'S MINE!
SHOOT! I'M TOO HUNGRY TO MOVE!
LUNGE
WOBBLE...
W-WAIT, DON'T...
MURMUR
MURMUR
Huh? What's going on?
She got cold feet?
I'M SUCH A FOOL!!
I DIDN'T EVEN REALIZE IT UNTIL NOW!
IT'S NOT JUST ABOUT TASTY FOOD!
AND I DON'T CARE ABOUT MY BOUNDARY!
ALL I WANTED...
EVER...
WAS TO KEEP LIVING THERE!!
TOHRU!!
CRACK
CRACK
CRACK
CRACK
CRACK

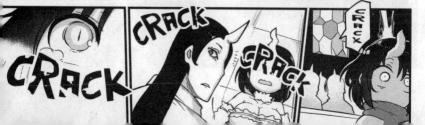

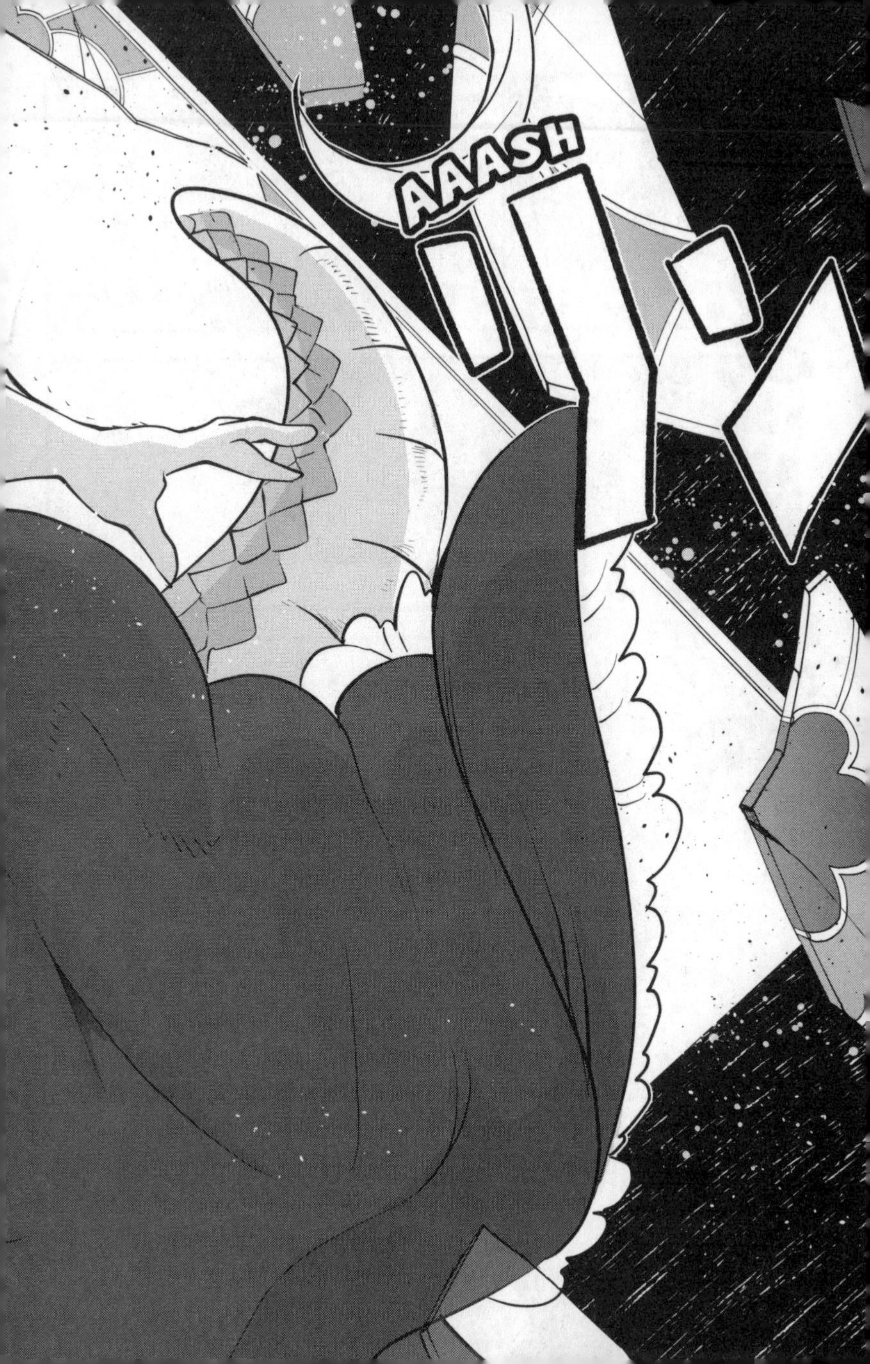
AAASH

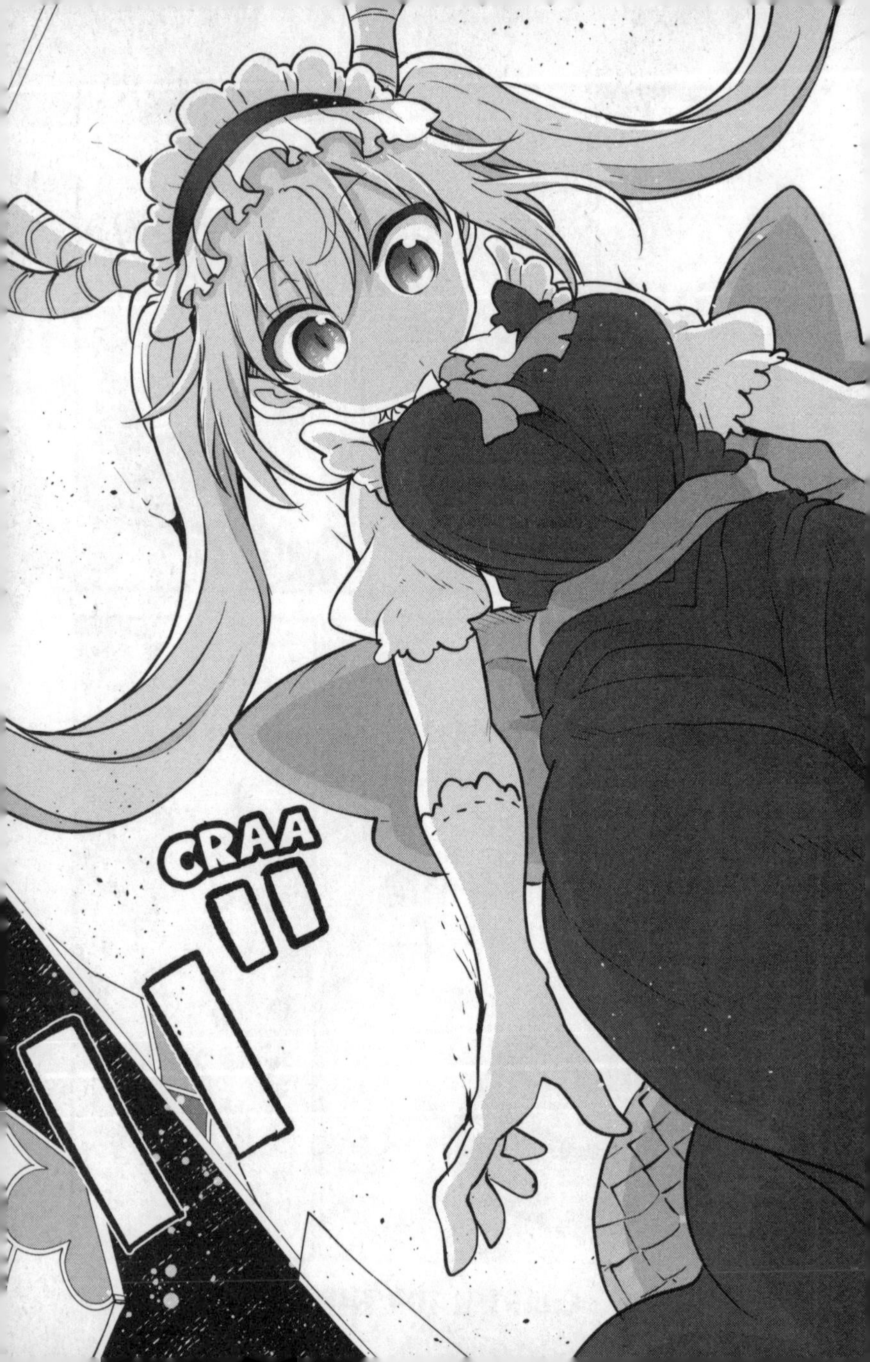
CRAA

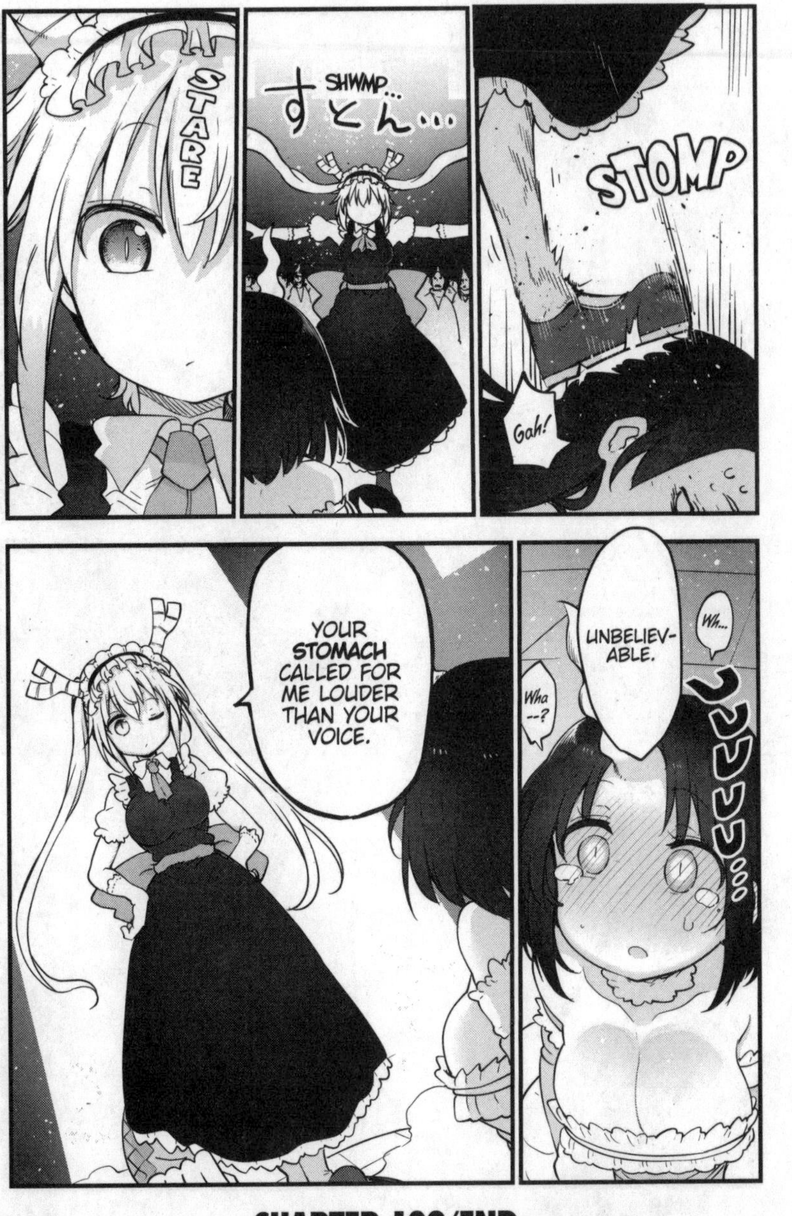
STOMP
Gah!
SHWMP...
すとん...
STARE
Wh...
UNBELIEVABLE.
Wha--?
YOUR STOMACH CALLED FOR ME LOUDER THAN YOUR VOICE.

CHAPTER 109/END

CHAPTER 110

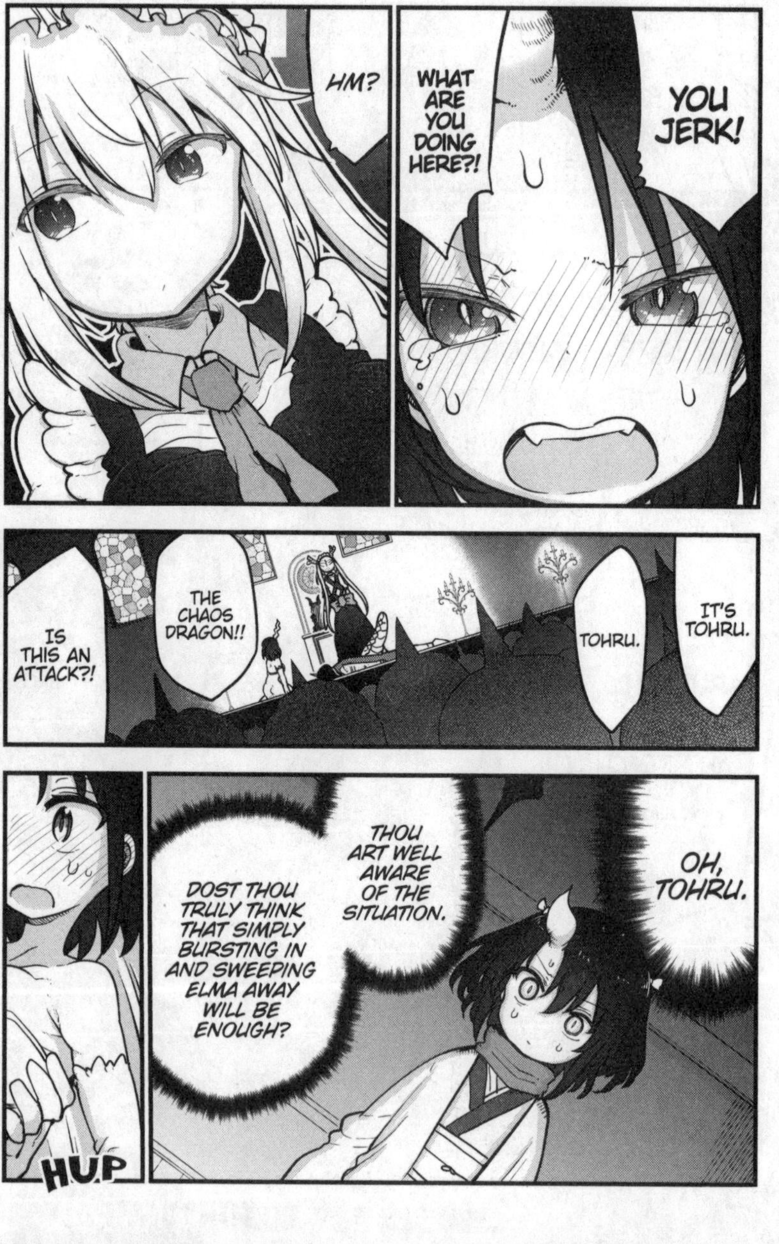
YOU JERK!
WHAT ARE YOU DOING HERE?!
HM?
IT'S TOHRU.
TOHRU.
THE CHAOS DRAGON!!
IS THIS AN ATTACK?!
OH, TOHRU.
THOU ART WELL AWARE OF THE SITUATION.
DOST THOU TRULY THINK THAT SIMPLY BURSTING IN AND SWEEPING ELMA AWAY WILL BE ENOUGH?
HUP

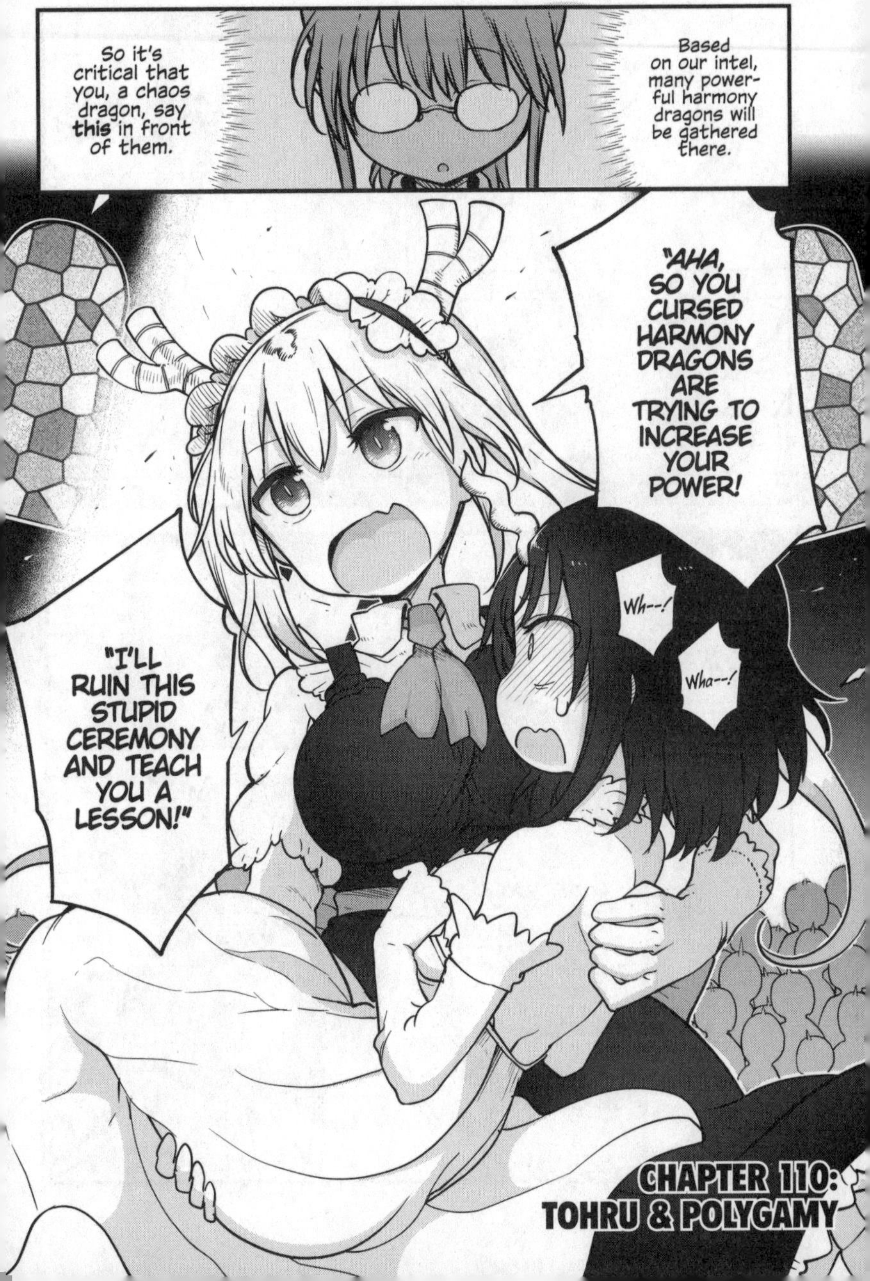
Based on our intel, many powerful harmony dragons will be gathered there.
So it's critical that you, a chaos dragon, say **this** in front of them.
"AHA, SO YOU CURSED HARMONY DRAGONS ARE TRYING TO INCREASE YOUR POWER!
Wh--!
Wha--!
"I'LL RUIN THIS STUPID CEREMONY AND TEACH YOU A LESSON!"
CHAPTER 110: TOHRU & POLYGAMY

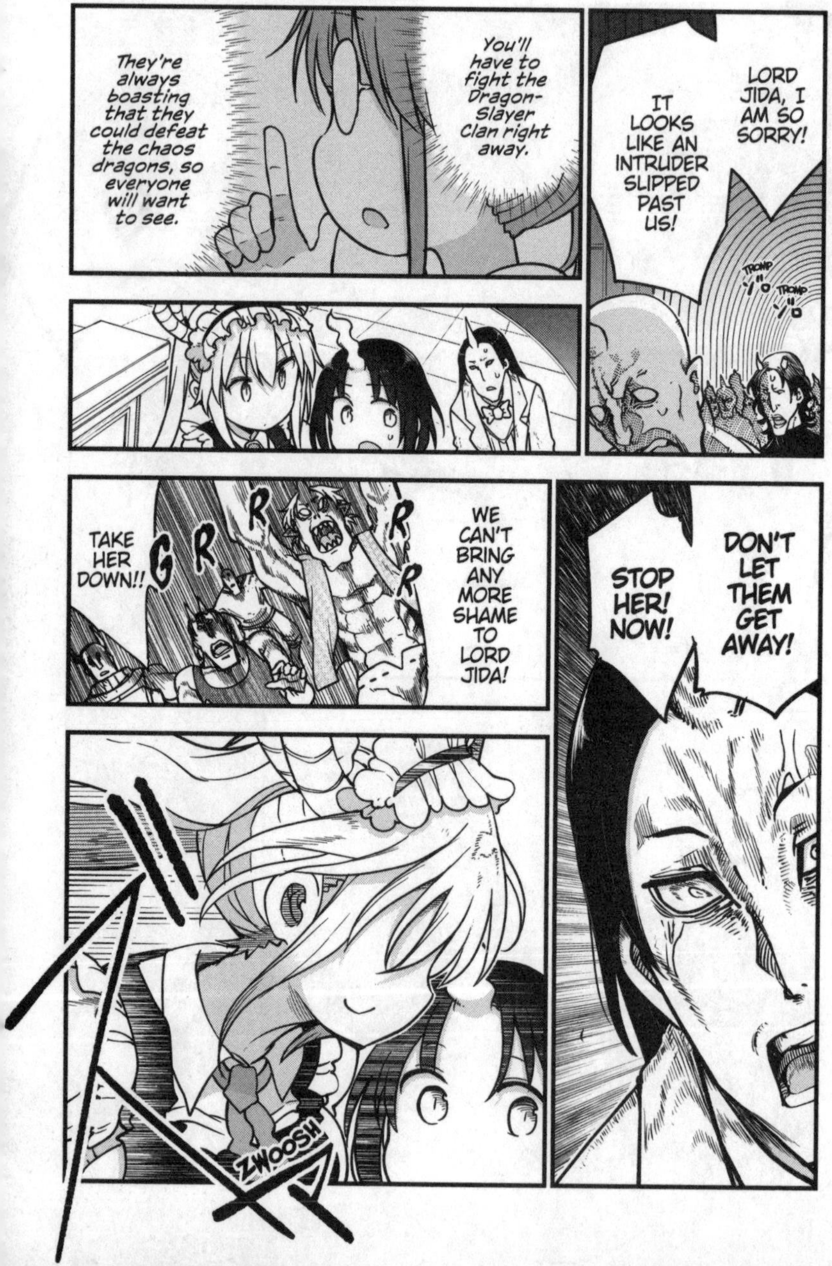
LORD JIDA, I AM SO SORRY!
IT LOOKS LIKE AN INTRUDER SLIPPED PAST US!
You'll have to fight the Dragon-Slayer Clan right away.
They're always boasting that they could defeat the chaos dragons, so everyone will want to see.
TROMP
TROMP
DON'T LET THEM GET AWAY!
STOP HER! NOW!
WE CAN'T BRING ANY MORE SHAME TO LORD JIDA!
GRRRR
TAKE HER DOWN!!
ZWOOSH

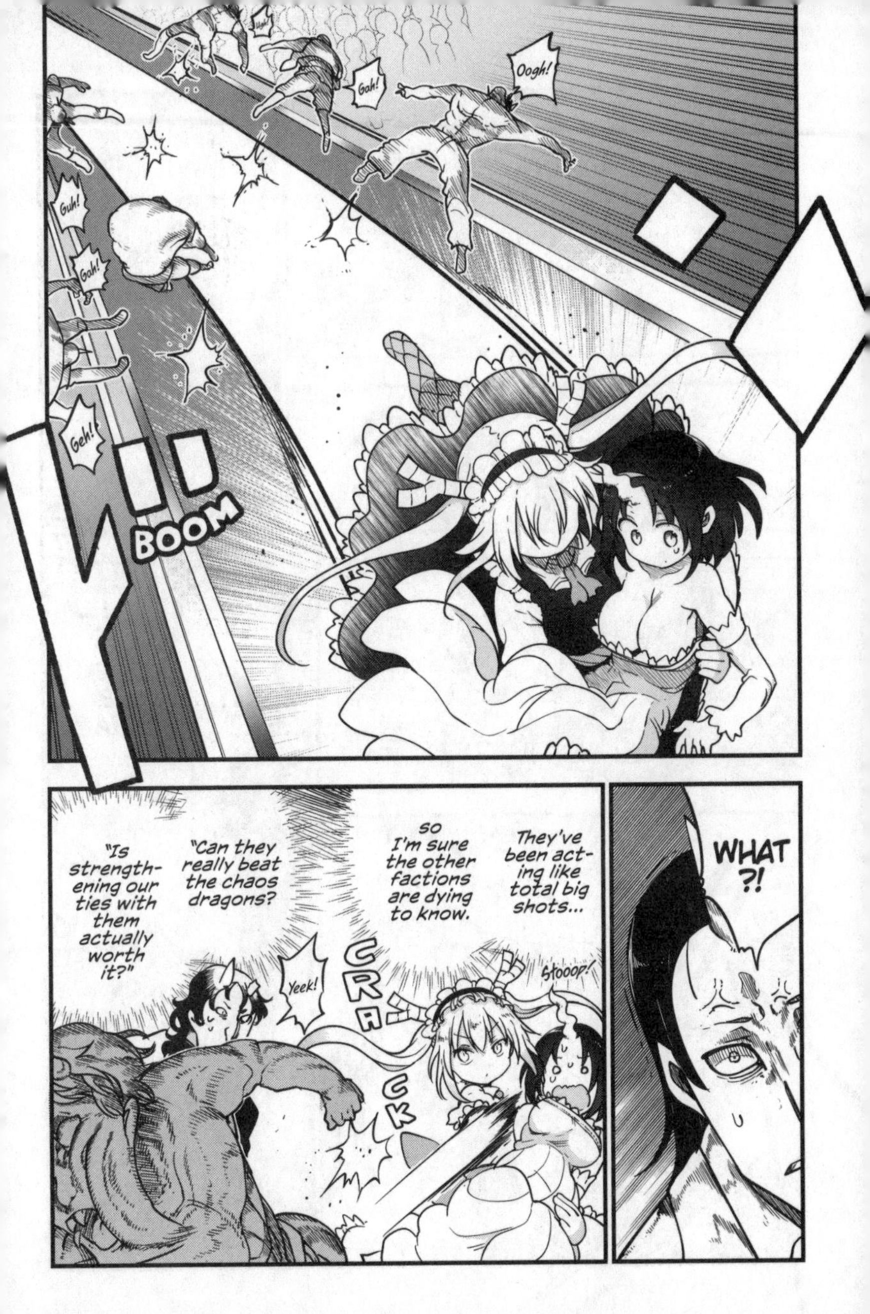
Oogh!
Ugh!
Gah!
Guh!
Gah!
Geh!
BOOM
WHAT ?!
They've been act-ing like total big shots...
so I'm sure the other factions are dying to know.
"Can they really beat the chaos dragons?
"Is strength-ening our ties with them actually worth it?"
Stooop!
CRACK
Yeek!

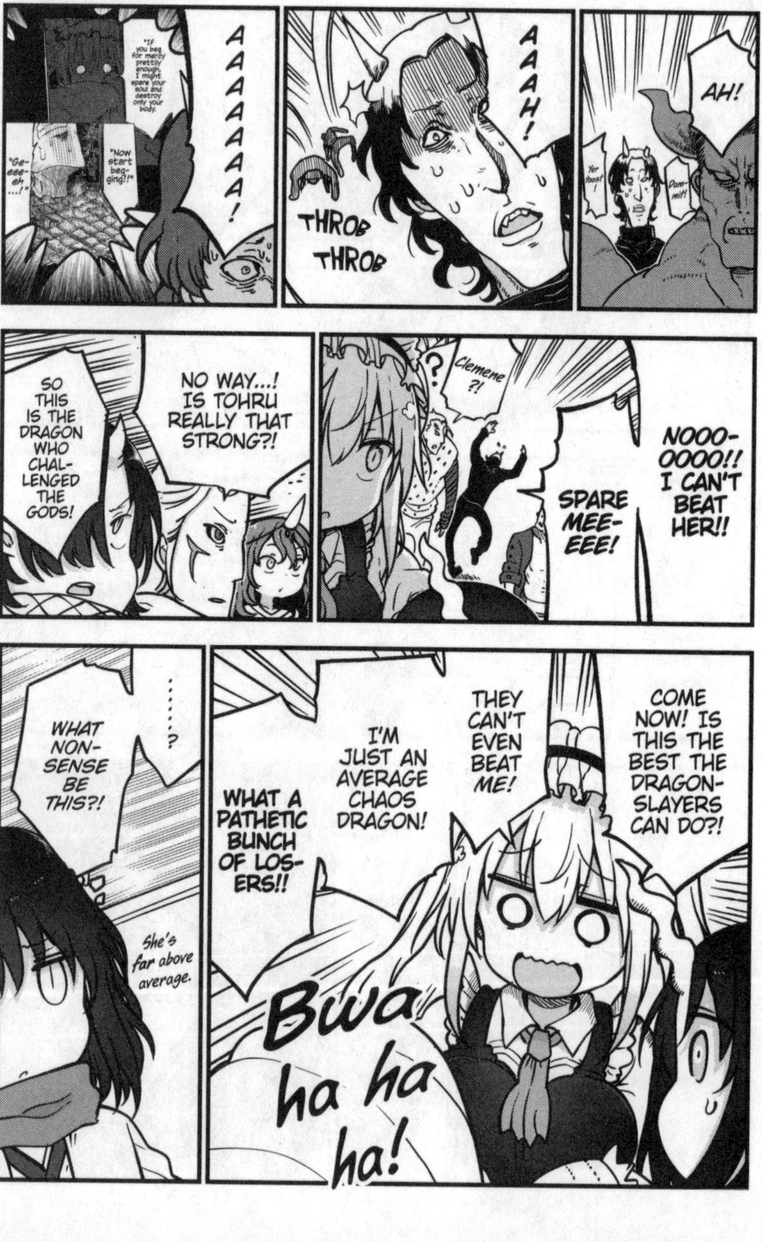
AH!
Dam-mit!
Yer toast!
AAAH!
THROB THROB
AAAAAAAA!
"If you beg for mercy prettily enough, I might spare your soul and destroy only your body.
"Now start beg-ging?!"
"Ge-eee-eh ...!"
NOOO-OOOO!! I CAN'T BEAT HER!!
SPARE MEE-EEE!
Clemene ?!
?
NO WAY...! IS TOHRU REALLY THAT STRONG?!
SO THIS IS THE DRAGON WHO CHAL-LENGED THE GODS!
COME NOW! IS THIS THE BEST THE DRAGON-SLAYERS CAN DO?!
THEY CAN'T EVEN BEAT ME!
I'M JUST AN AVERAGE CHAOS DRAGON!
WHAT A PATHETIC BUNCH OF LOS-ERS!!
Bwa ha ha ha!
......?
WHAT NON-SENSE BE THIS?!
She's far above average.

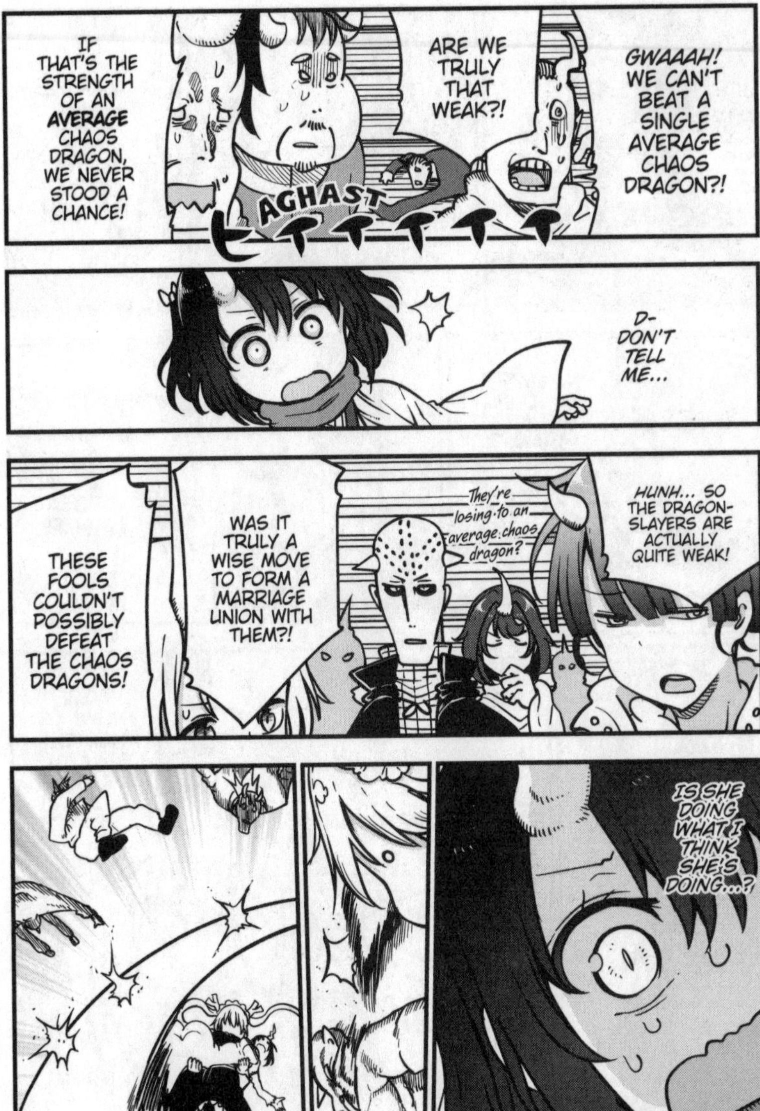
GWAAAH! WE CAN'T BEAT A SINGLE AVERAGE CHAOS DRAGON?!
ARE WE TRULY THAT WEAK?!
IF THAT'S THE STRENGTH OF AN **AVERAGE** CHAOS DRAGON, WE NEVER STOOD A CHANCE!
AGHAST
D-DON'T TELL ME...
HUNH... SO THE DRAGON-SLAYERS ARE ACTUALLY QUITE WEAK!
They're losing to an average chaos dragon?
WAS IT TRULY A WISE MOVE TO FORM A MARRIAGE UNION WITH THEM?!
THESE FOOLS COULDN'T POSSIBLY DEFEAT THE CHAOS DRAGONS!
IS SHE DOING WHAT I THINK SHE'S DOING...?

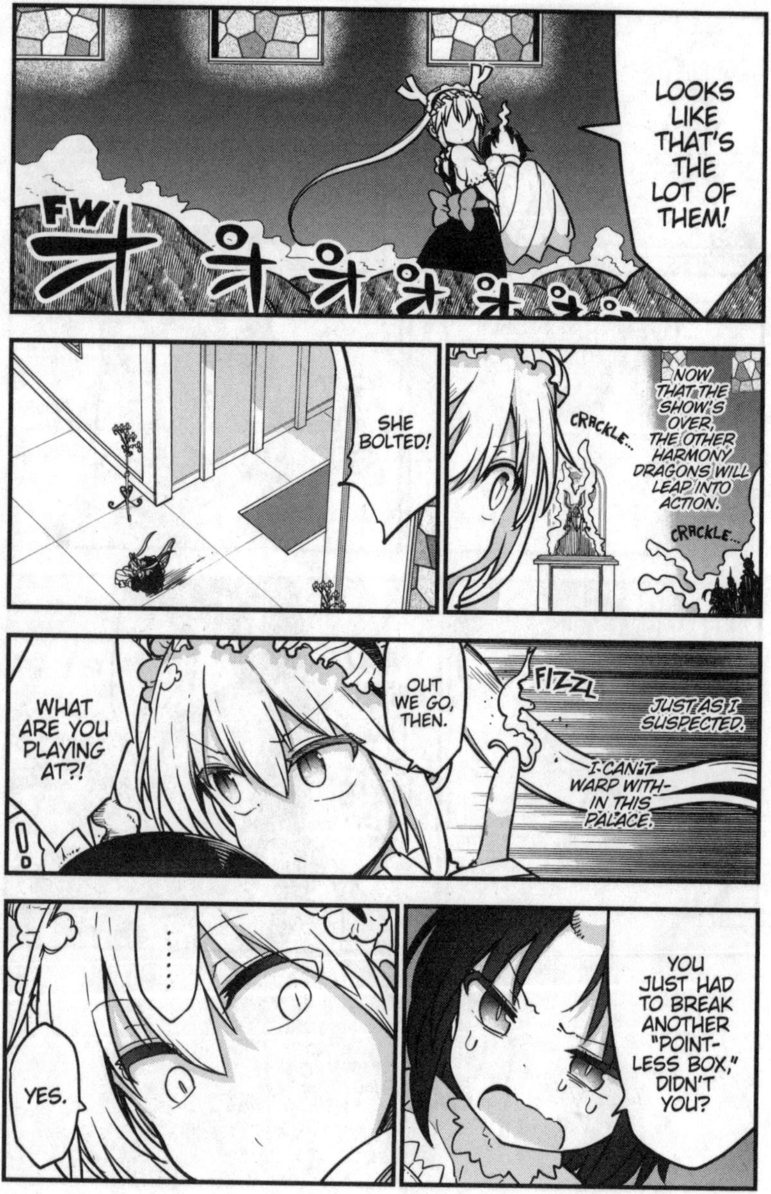
LOOKS LIKE THAT'S THE LOT OF THEM!
FW
CRACKLE...
NOW THAT THE SHOW'S OVER, THE OTHER HARMONY DRAGONS WILL LEAP INTO ACTION.
CRACKLE...
SHE BOLTED!
FIZZL
JUST AS I SUSPECTED.
I CAN'T WARP WITH-IN THIS PALACE.
OUT WE GO, THEN.
WHAT ARE YOU PLAYING AT?!
YOU JUST HAD TO BREAK ANOTHER "POINT-LESS BOX," DIDN'T YOU?
......
YES.

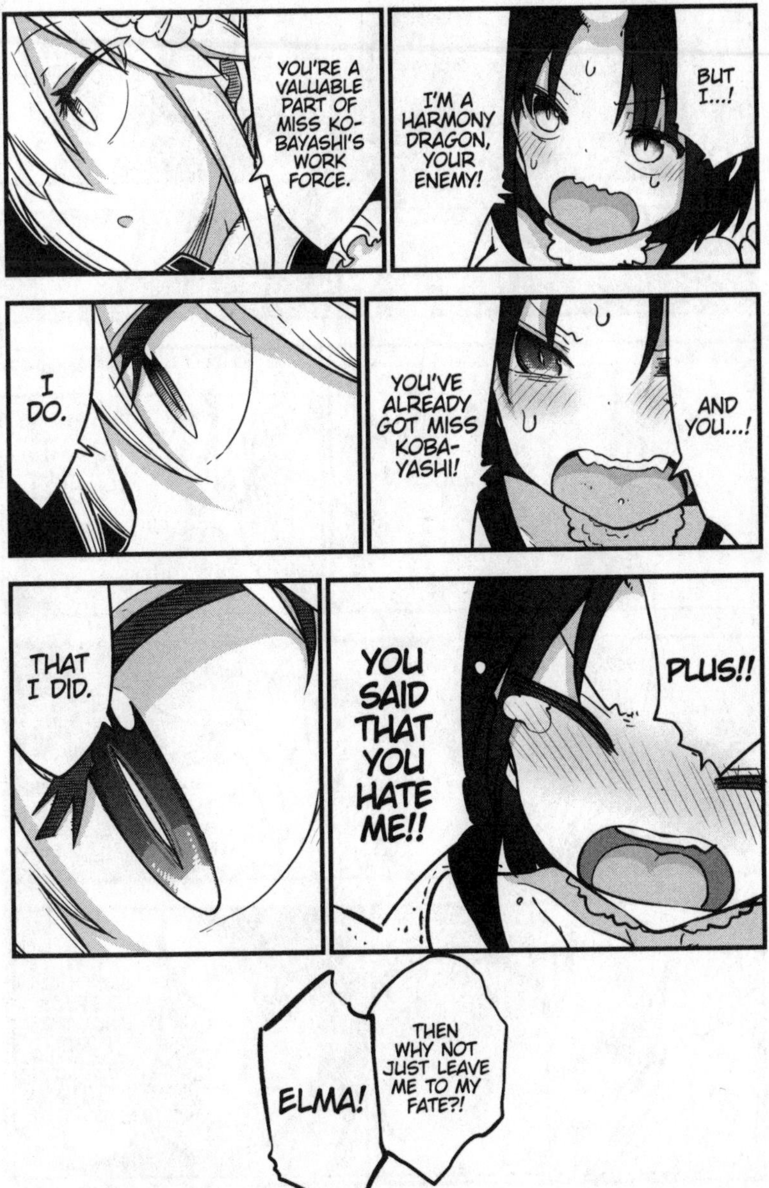
BUT I...!
I'M A HARMONY DRAGON, YOUR ENEMY!
YOU'RE A VALUABLE PART OF MISS KOBAYASHI'S WORK FORCE.
AND YOU...!
YOU'VE ALREADY GOT MISS KOBAYASHI!
I DO.
PLUS!!
YOU SAID THAT YOU HATE ME!!
THAT I DID.
THEN WHY NOT JUST LEAVE ME TO MY FATE?!
ELMA!

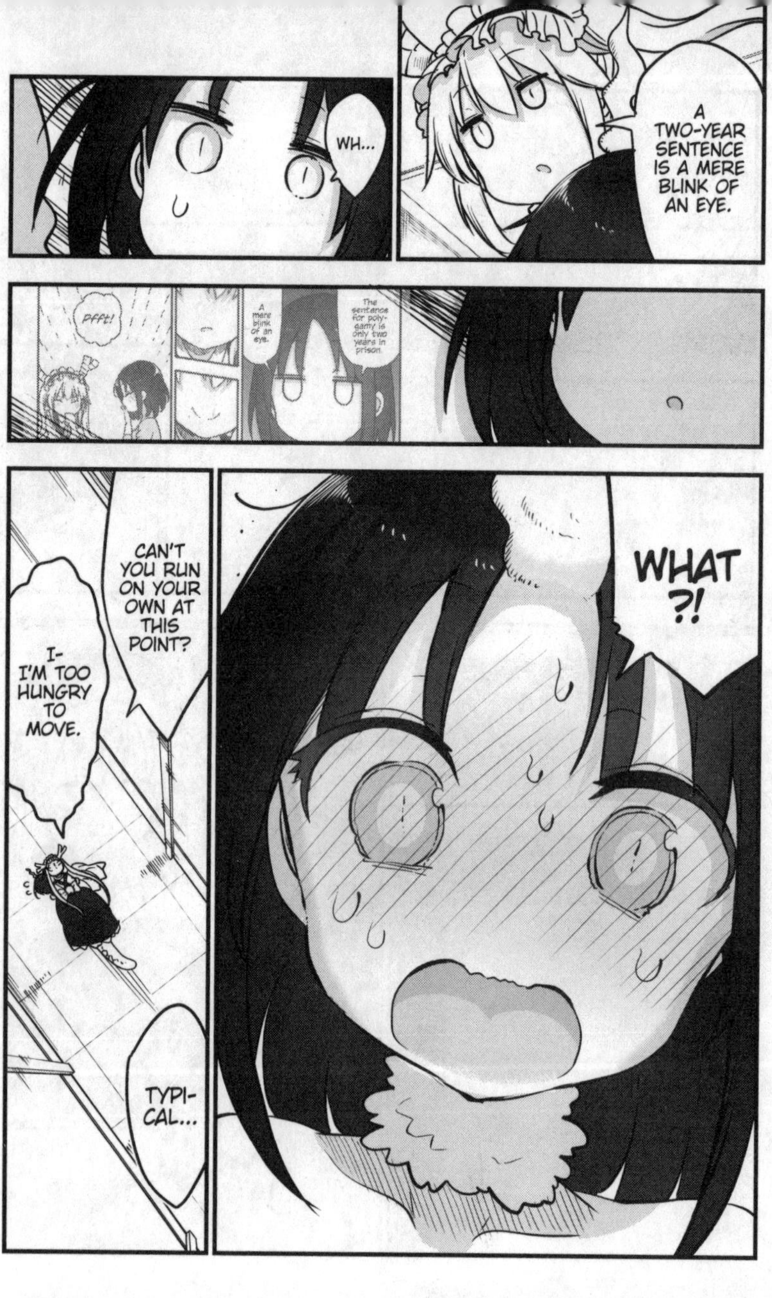
A TWO-YEAR SENTENCE IS A MERE BLINK OF AN EYE.
WH...
The sentence for polygamy is only two years in prison.
A mere blink of an eye.
Pfft!
WHAT?!
CAN'T YOU RUN ON YOUR OWN AT THIS POINT?
I- I'M TOO HUNGRY TO MOVE.
TYPICAL...

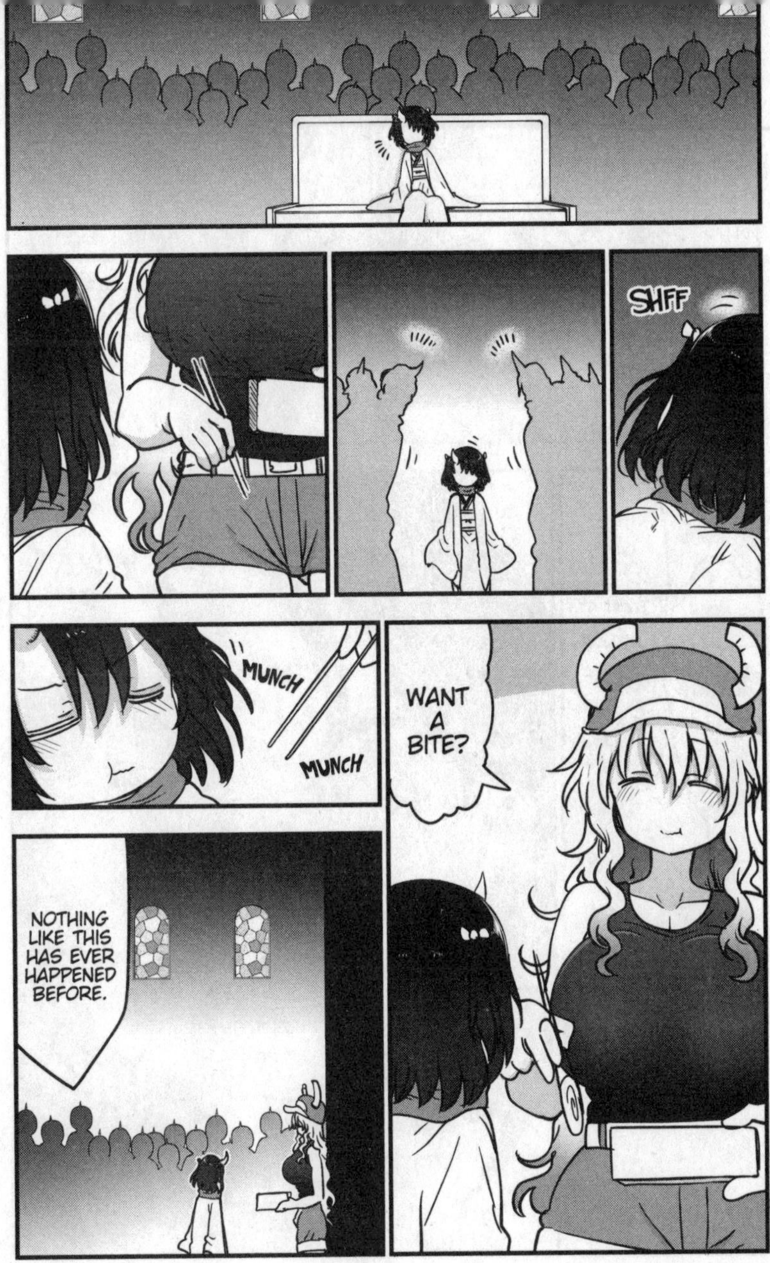
SHFF
WANT A BITE?
MUNCH
MUNCH
NOTHING LIKE THIS HAS EVER HAPPENED BEFORE.

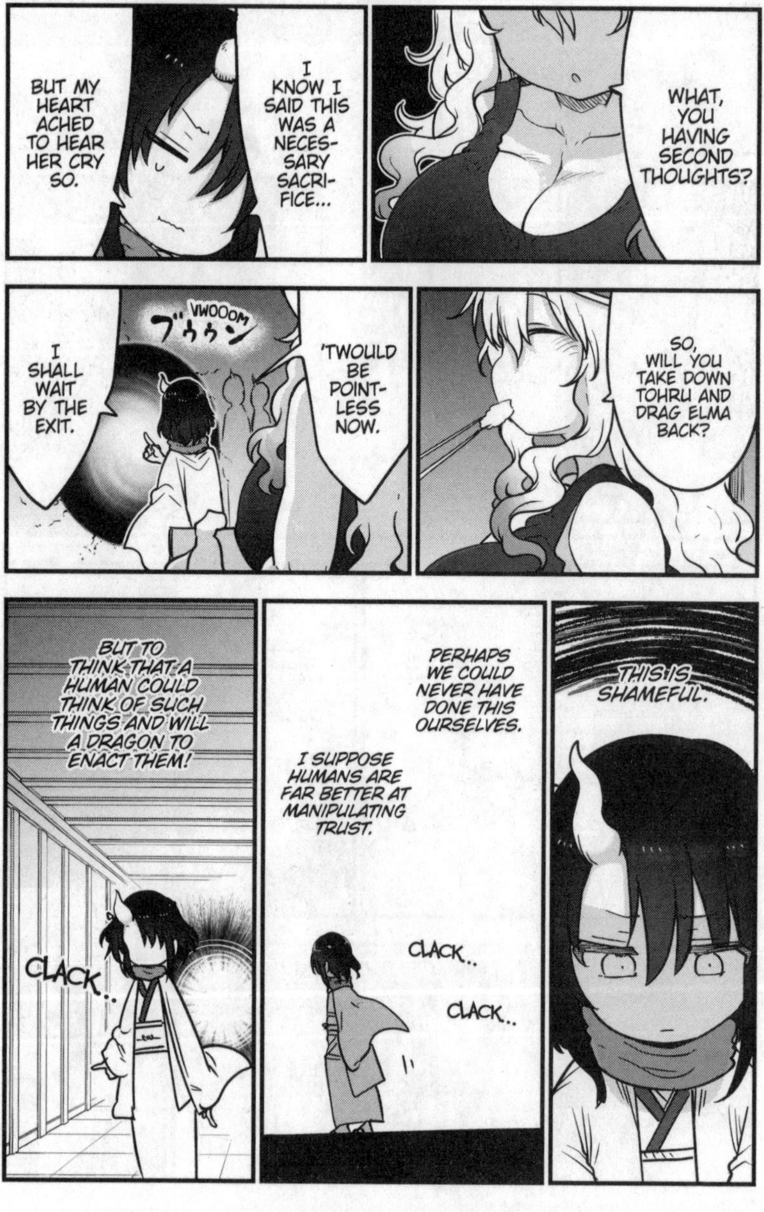
WHAT, YOU HAVING SECOND THOUGHTS?
I KNOW I SAID THIS WAS A NECESSARY SACRIFICE...
BUT MY HEART ACHED TO HEAR HER CRY SO.
SO, WILL YOU TAKE DOWN TOHRU AND DRAG ELMA BACK?
'TWOULD BE POINTLESS NOW.
VWOOOM
ブウウン
I SHALL WAIT BY THE EXIT.
THIS IS SHAMEFUL.
PERHAPS WE COULD NEVER HAVE DONE THIS OURSELVES.
I SUPPOSE HUMANS ARE FAR BETTER AT MANIPULATING TRUST.
CLACK...
CLACK...
BUT TO THINK THAT A HUMAN COULD THINK OF SUCH THINGS AND WILL A DRAGON TO ENACT THEM!
CLACK...

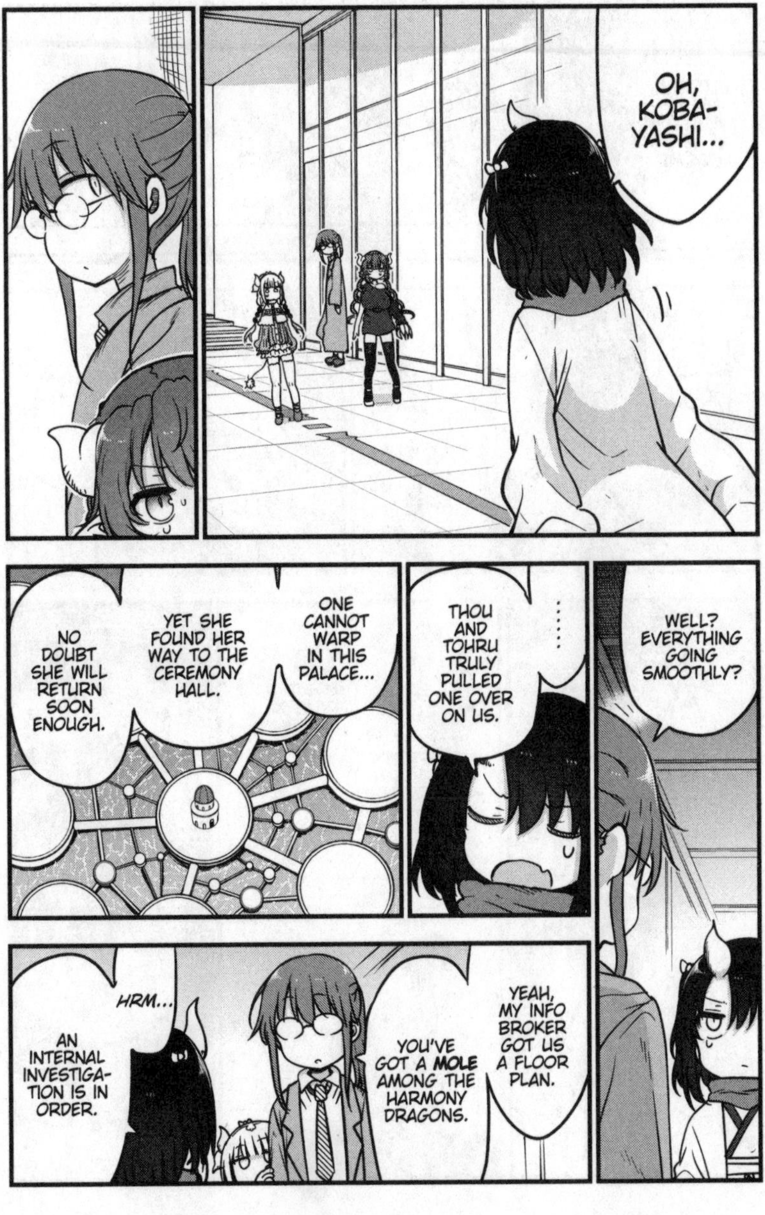
OH, KOBA-YASHI...
WELL? EVERYTHING GOING SMOOTHLY?
......
THOU AND TOHRU TRULY PULLED ONE OVER ON US.
ONE CANNOT WARP IN THIS PALACE...
YET SHE FOUND HER WAY TO THE CEREMONY HALL.
NO DOUBT SHE WILL RETURN SOON ENOUGH.
YEAH, MY INFO BROKER GOT US A FLOOR PLAN.
YOU'VE GOT A **MOLE** AMONG THE HARMONY DRAGONS.
HRM...
AN INTERNAL INVESTIGA-TION IS IN ORDER.

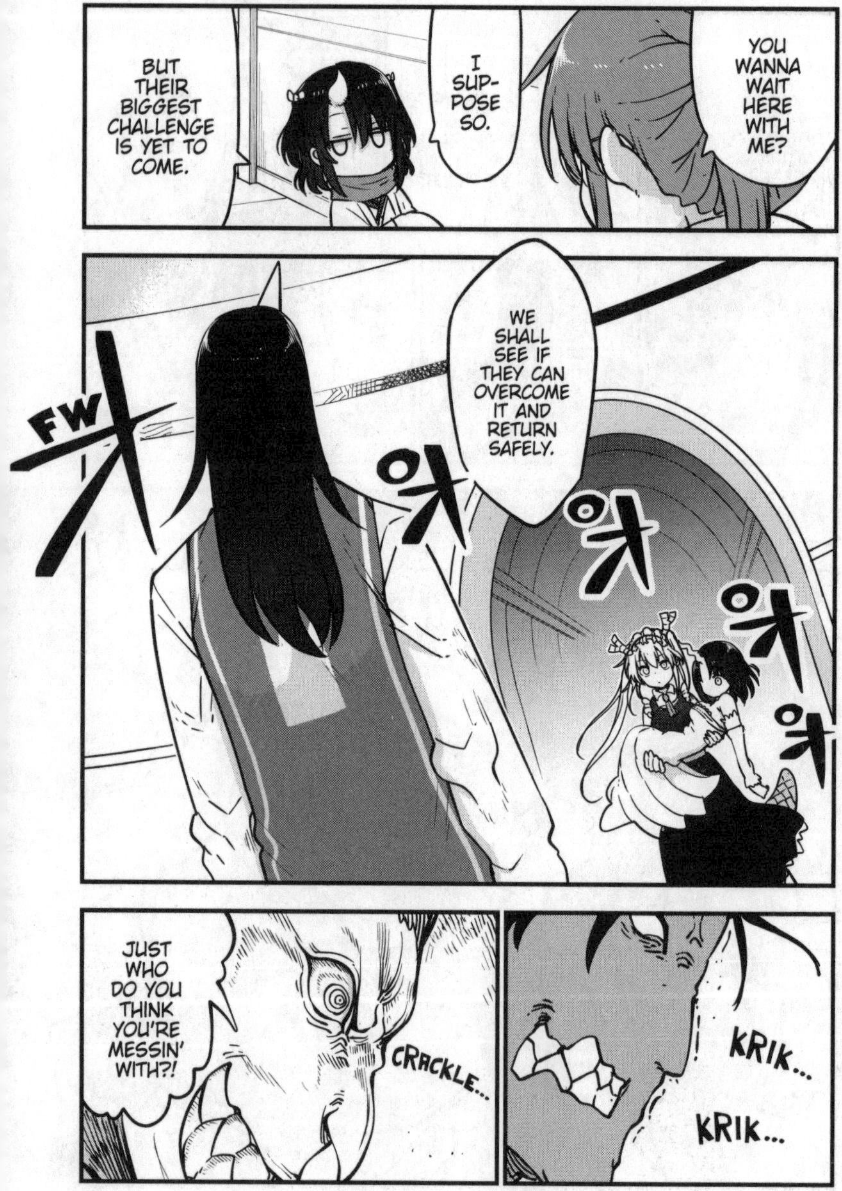
YOU WANNA WAIT HERE WITH ME?
I SUP-POSE SO.
BUT THEIR BIGGEST CHALLENGE IS YET TO COME.
WE SHALL SEE IF THEY CAN OVERCOME IT AND RETURN SAFELY.
FW
KRIK...
KRIK...
JUST WHO DO YOU THINK YOU'RE MESSIN' WITH?!
CRACKLE...

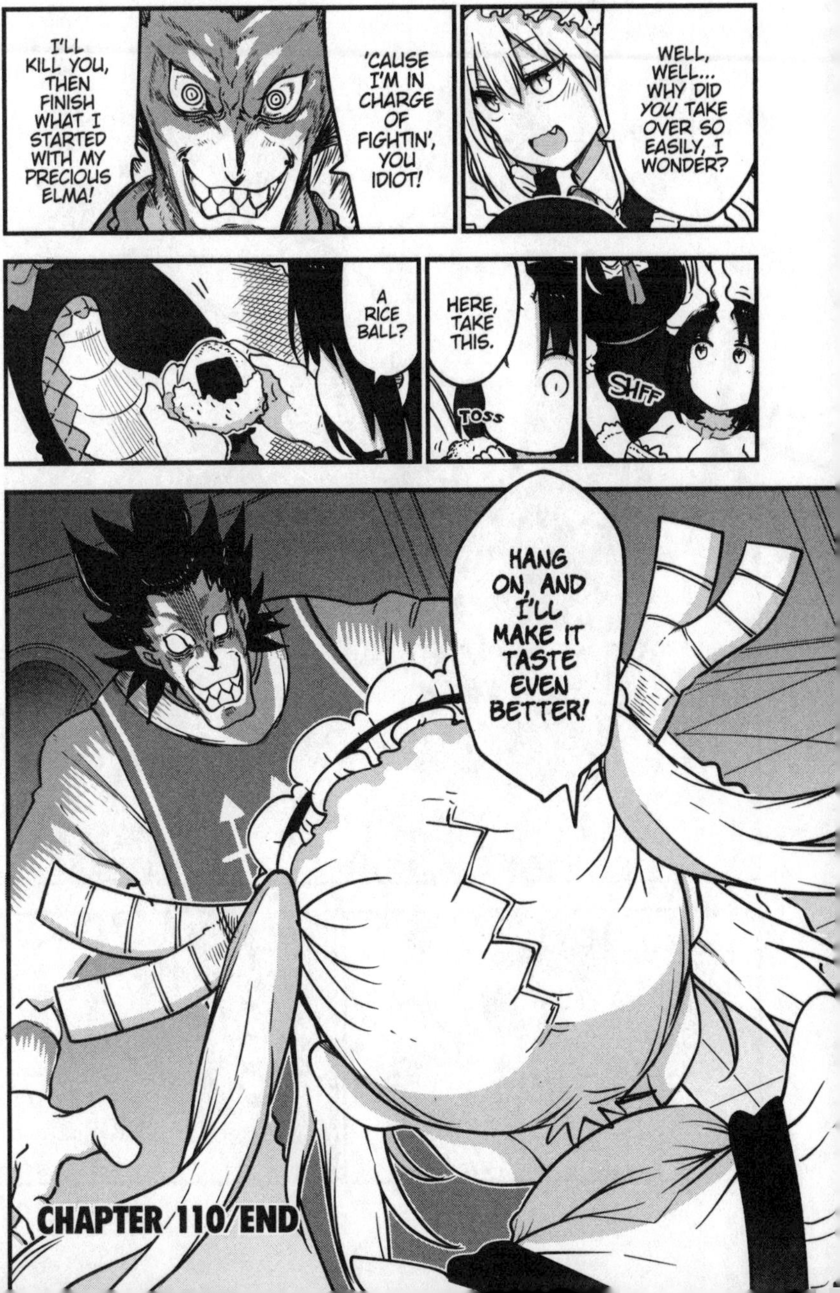
WELL, WELL... WHY DID YOU TAKE OVER SO EASILY, I WONDER?
'CAUSE I'M IN CHARGE OF FIGHTIN', YOU IDIOT!
I'LL KILL YOU, THEN FINISH WHAT I STARTED WITH MY PRECIOUS ELMA!
SHFF
HERE, TAKE THIS.
TOSS
A RICE BALL?
HANG ON, AND I'LL MAKE IT TASTE EVEN BETTER!
CHAPTER 110/END

It already tastes just fine, though.

Miss Kobayashi's
DRAGON MAID

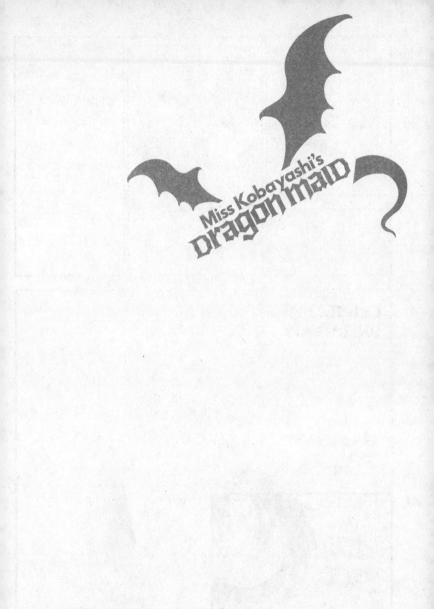

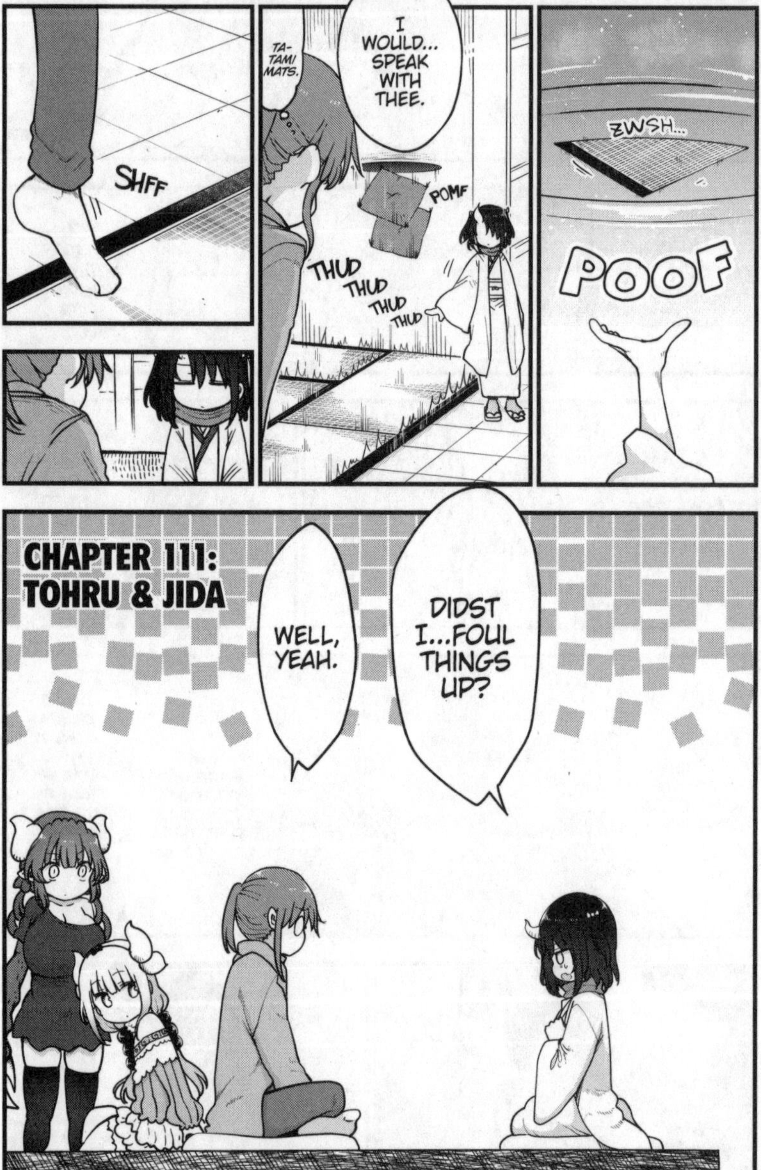
ZWSH...
POOF
I WOULD... SPEAK WITH THEE.
TA-TAMI MATS.
POMF
THUD THUD THUD THUD
SHFF
CHAPTER 111: TOHRU & JIDA
DIDST I...FOUL THINGS UP?
WELL, YEAH.

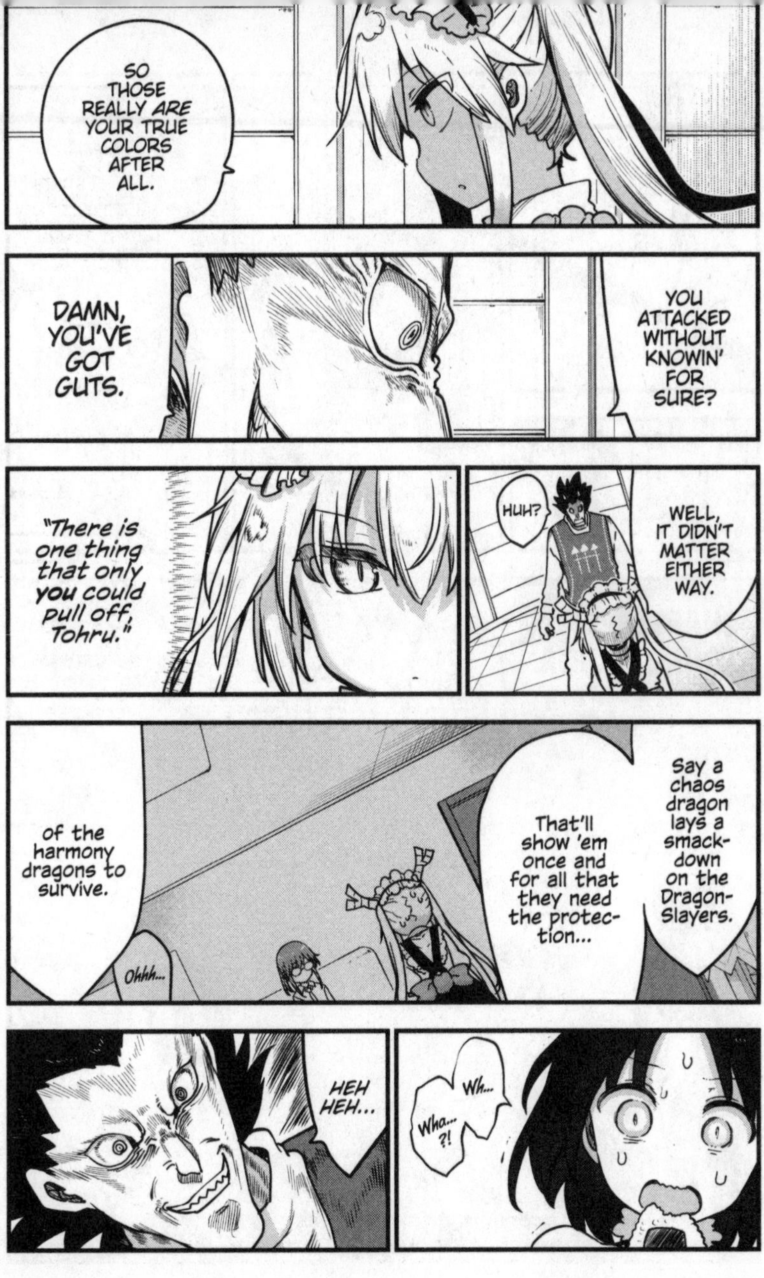
SO THOSE REALLY *ARE* YOUR TRUE COLORS AFTER ALL.
YOU ATTACKED WITHOUT KNOWIN' FOR SURE?
DAMN, YOU'VE GOT GUTS.
WELL, IT DIDN'T MATTER EITHER WAY.
HUH?
"There is one thing that only **you** could pull off, Tohru."
Say a chaos dragon lays a smack-down on the Dragon-Slayers.
That'll show 'em once and for all that they need the protec-tion...
of the harmony dragons to survive.
Ohhh...
Wh...
Wha... ?!
HEH HEH...

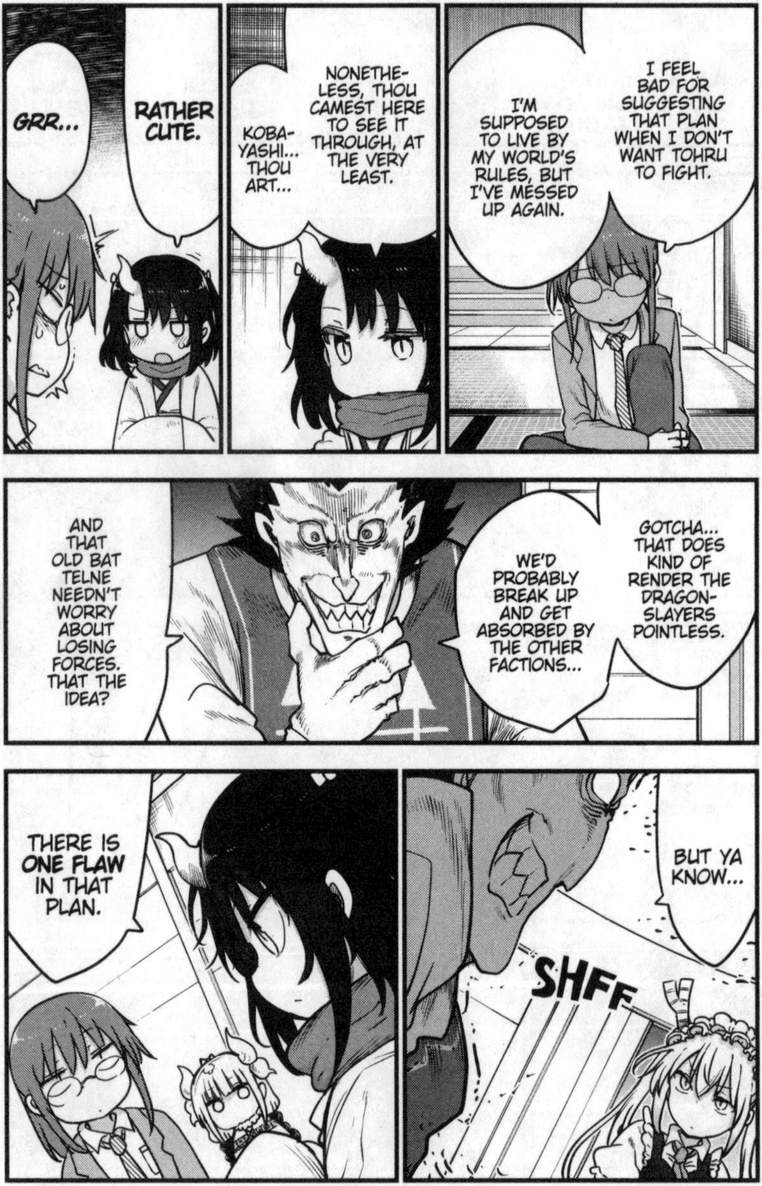
I FEEL BAD FOR SUGGESTING THAT PLAN WHEN I DON'T WANT TOHRU TO FIGHT.
I'M SUPPOSED TO LIVE BY MY WORLD'S RULES, BUT I'VE MESSED UP AGAIN.
NONETHELESS, THOU CAMEST HERE TO SEE IT THROUGH, AT THE VERY LEAST.
KOBAYASHI... THOU ART...
RATHER CUTE.
GRR...
GOTCHA... THAT DOES KIND OF RENDER THE DRAGON-SLAYERS POINTLESS.
WE'D PROBABLY BREAK UP AND GET ABSORBED BY THE OTHER FACTIONS...
AND THAT OLD BAT TELNE NEEDN'T WORRY ABOUT LOSING FORCES. THAT THE IDEA?
BUT YA KNOW...
SHFF
THERE IS ONE FLAW IN THAT PLAN.

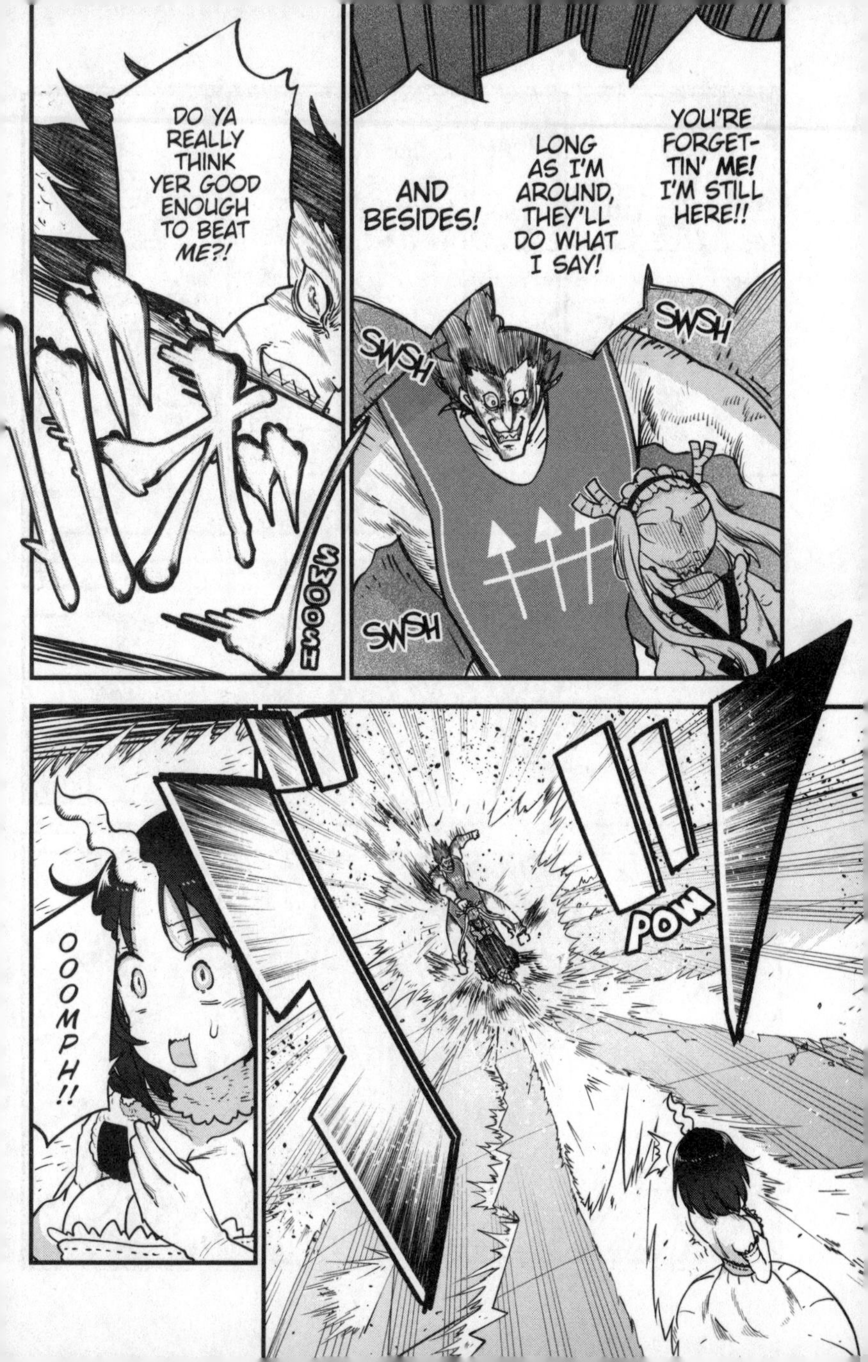
YOU'RE FORGETTIN' ME! I'M STILL HERE!!
LONG AS I'M AROUND, THEY'LL DO WHAT I SAY!
AND BESIDES!
SWSH
SWSH
SWSH
DO YA REALLY THINK YER GOOD ENOUGH TO BEAT ME?!
SWOOOSH
POW
OOOOMPH!!

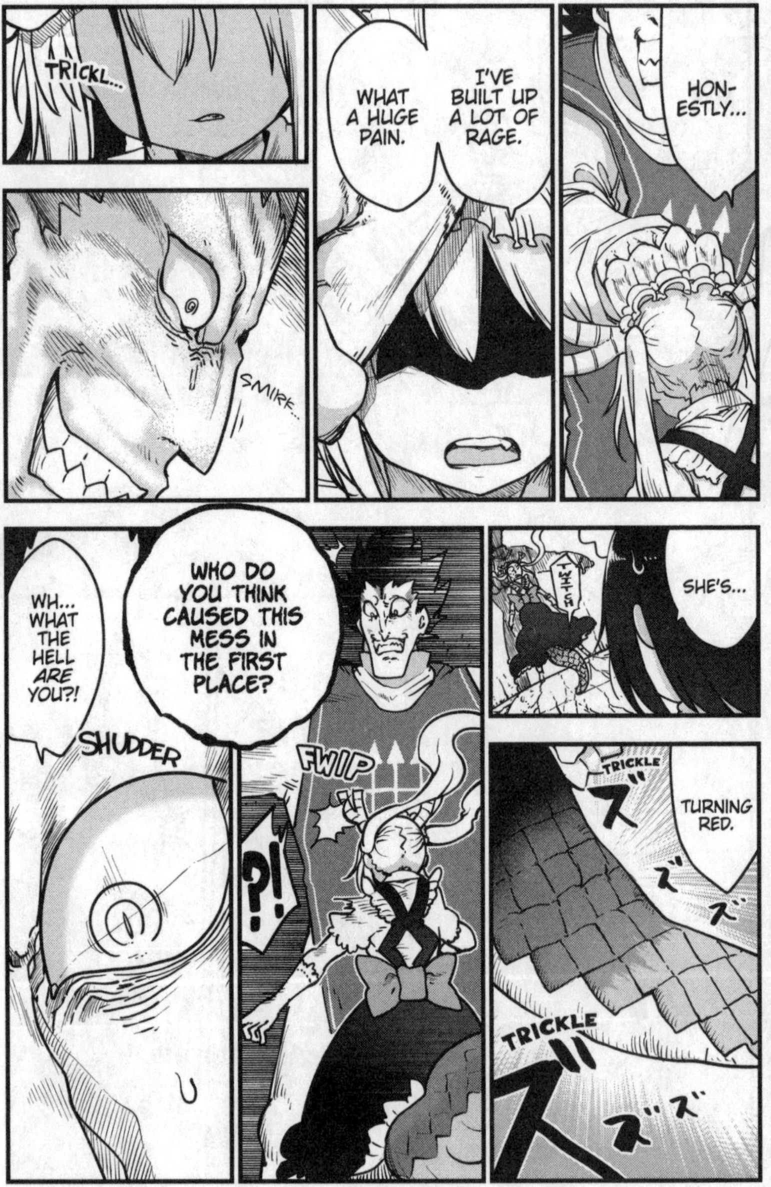
HON-ESTLY...
I'VE BUILT UP A LOT OF RAGE.
WHAT A HUGE PAIN.
TRICKL...
SMIRK...
SHE'S...
TWITCH
TRICKLE
TURNING RED.
TRICKLE
WHO DO YOU THINK CAUSED THIS MESS IN THE FIRST PLACE?
FWIP
?!
WH... WHAT THE HELL ARE YOU?!
SHUDDER

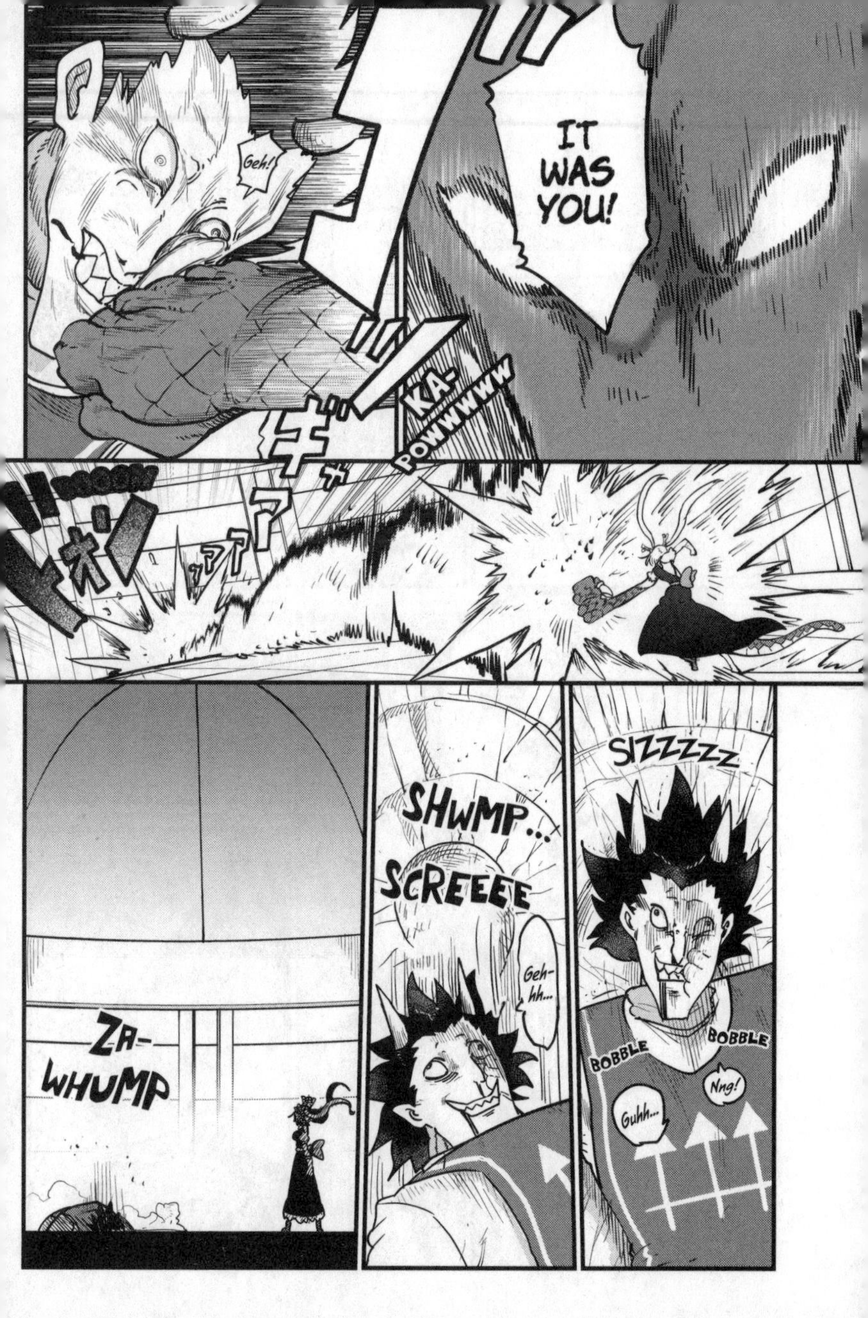
IT WAS YOU!
Geh!
KA-POWWWWW
SIZZZZZ
BOBBLE
BOBBLE
Nng!
Guhh...
SHWMP...
SCREEEE
Geh-hh...
ZA-WHUMP

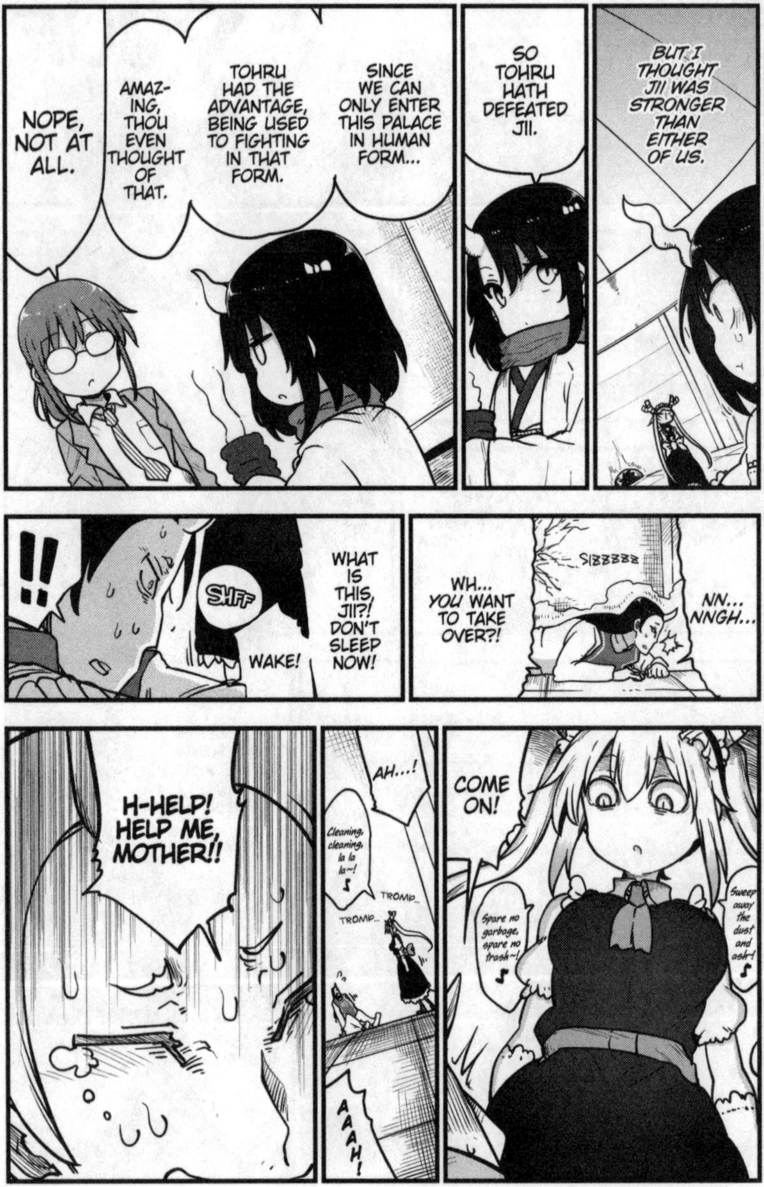
BUT I THOUGHT JII WAS STRONGER THAN EITHER OF US.
SO TOHRU HATH DEFEATED JII.
SINCE WE CAN ONLY ENTER THIS PALACE IN HUMAN FORM...
TOHRU HAD THE ADVANTAGE, BEING USED TO FIGHTING IN THAT FORM.
AMAZING, THOU EVEN THOUGHT OF THAT.
NOPE, NOT AT ALL.
NN... NNGH...
SIZZZZZ
WH... YOU WANT TO TAKE OVER?!
WHAT IS THIS, JII?! DON'T SLEEP NOW!
SHFF
WAKE!
!!
Sweep away the dust and ash! ♪
COME ON!
Spare no garbage, spare no trash~! ♪
AH...!
Cleaning, cleaning, la la la~! ♪
TROMP...
TROMP...
AAAAH!
H-HELP! HELP ME, MOTHER!!

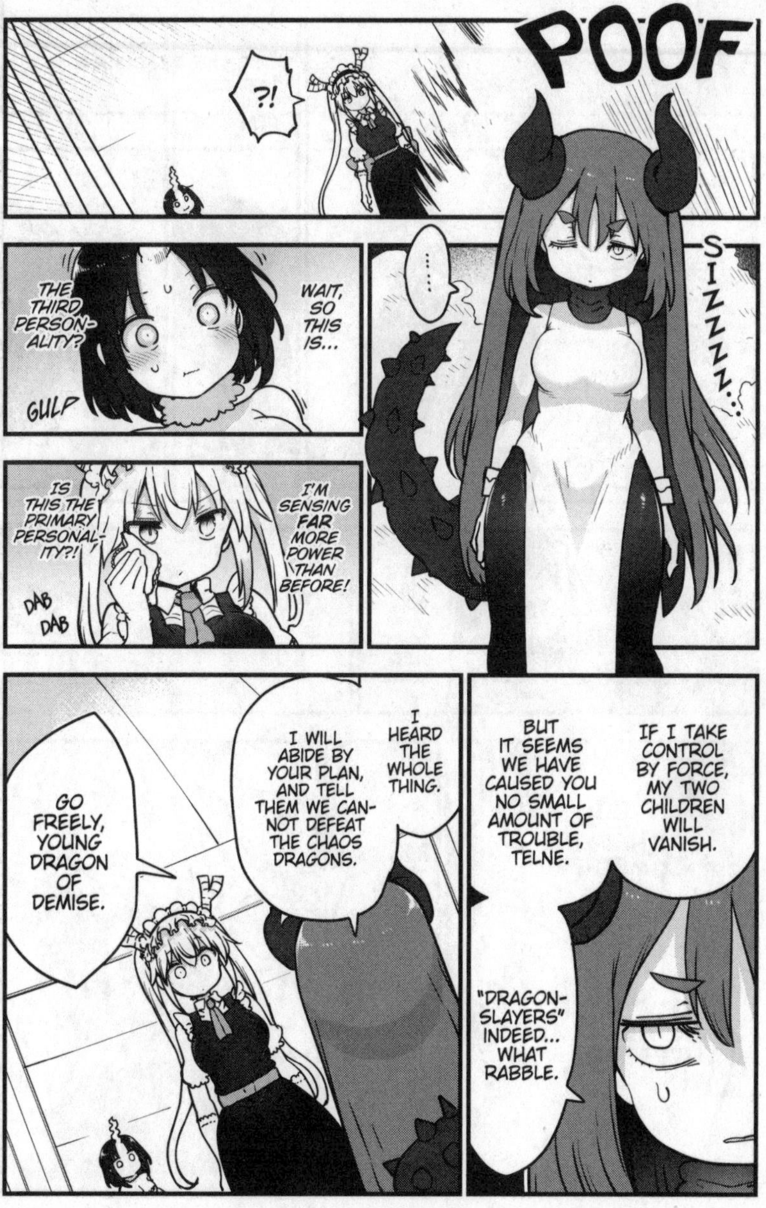
POOF
?!
SIZZZZ...
......
WAIT, SO THIS IS...
THE THIRD PERSON-ALITY?
GULP
I'M SENSING FAR MORE POWER THAN BEFORE!
IS THIS THE PRIMARY PERSONAL-ITY?!
DAB DAB
IF I TAKE CONTROL BY FORCE, MY TWO CHILDREN WILL VANISH.
BUT IT SEEMS WE HAVE CAUSED YOU NO SMALL AMOUNT OF TROUBLE, TELNE.
"DRAGON-SLAYERS" INDEED... WHAT RABBLE.
I HEARD THE WHOLE THING.
I WILL ABIDE BY YOUR PLAN, AND TELL THEM WE CAN-NOT DEFEAT THE CHAOS DRAGONS.
GO FREELY, YOUNG DRAGON OF DEMISE.

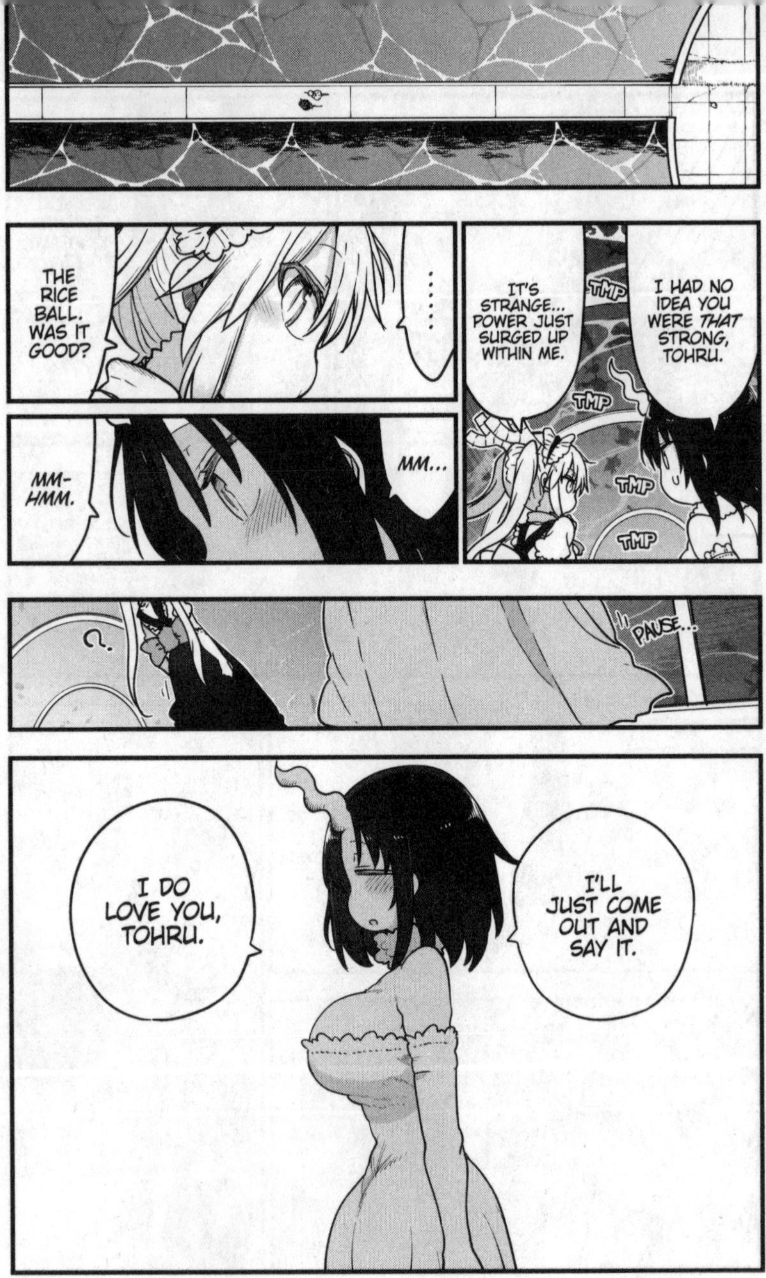
I HAD NO IDEA YOU WERE *THAT* STRONG, TOHRU.
IT'S STRANGE... POWER JUST SURGED UP WITHIN ME.
TMP
TMP
TMP
TMP
......
THE RICE BALL. WAS IT GOOD?
MM...
MM-HMM.
PAUSE...
?
I'LL JUST COME OUT AND SAY IT.
I DO LOVE YOU, TOHRU.

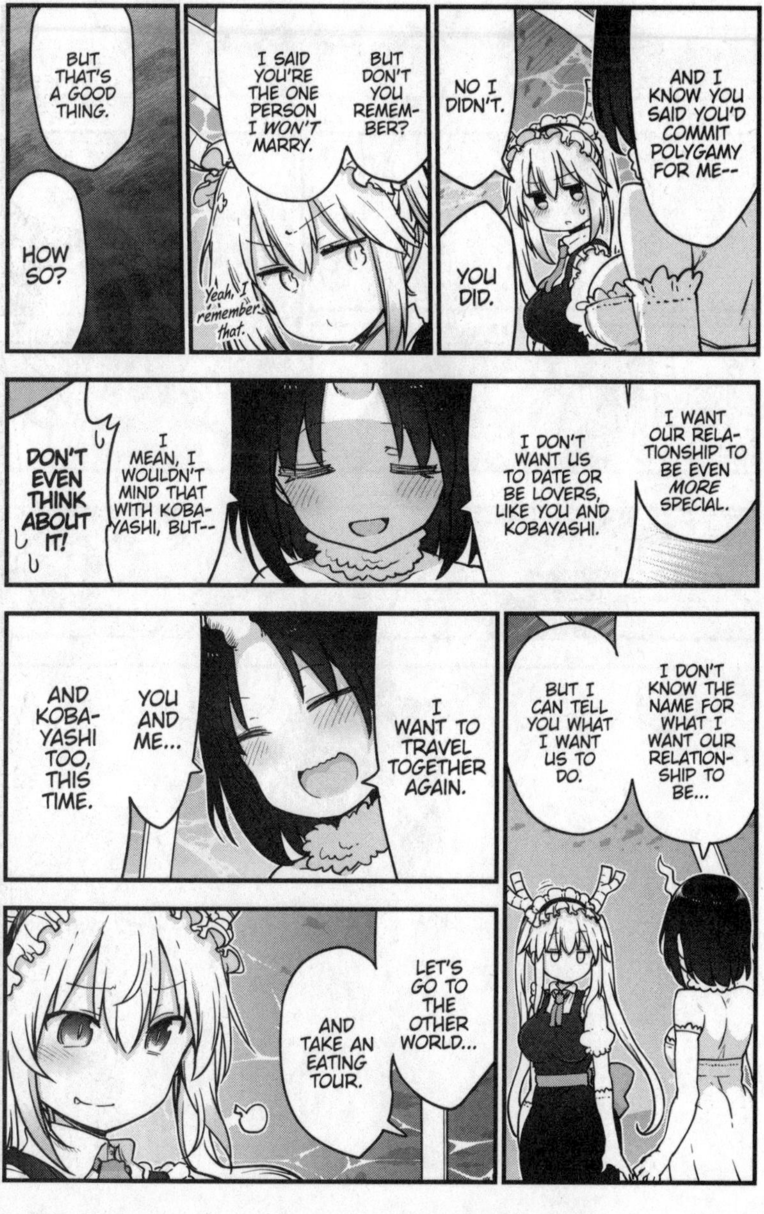
AND I KNOW YOU SAID YOU'D COMMIT POLYGAMY FOR ME--
NO I DIDN'T.
YOU DID.
BUT DON'T YOU REMEMBER?
I SAID YOU'RE THE ONE PERSON I *WON'T* MARRY.
Yeah, I remember that.
BUT THAT'S A GOOD THING.
HOW SO?
I WANT OUR RELATIONSHIP TO BE EVEN *MORE* SPECIAL.
I DON'T WANT US TO DATE OR BE LOVERS, LIKE YOU AND KOBAYASHI.
I MEAN, I WOULDN'T MIND THAT WITH KOBAYASHI, BUT--
DON'T EVEN THINK ABOUT IT!
I DON'T KNOW THE NAME FOR WHAT I WANT OUR RELATIONSHIP TO BE...
BUT I CAN TELL YOU WHAT I WANT US TO DO.
I WANT TO TRAVEL TOGETHER AGAIN.
YOU AND ME...
AND KOBAYASHI TOO, THIS TIME.
LET'S GO TO THE OTHER WORLD...
AND TAKE AN EATING TOUR.

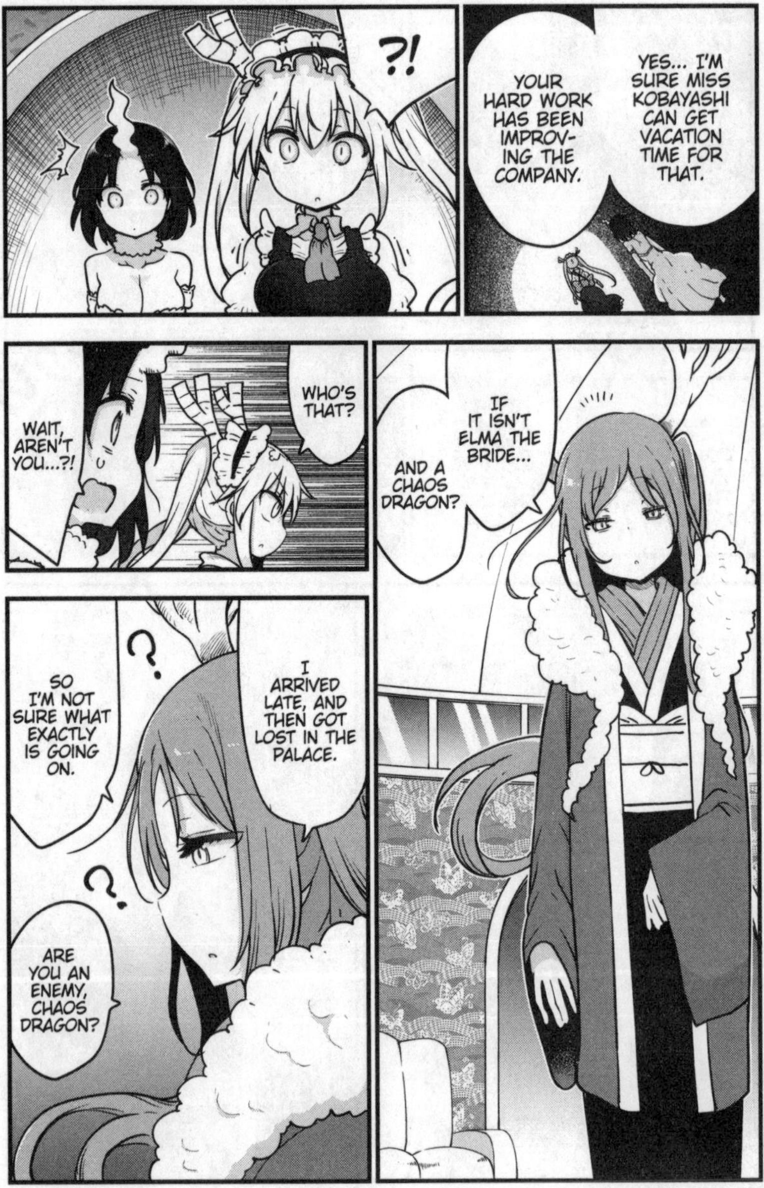
YES... I'M SURE MISS KOBAYASHI CAN GET VACATION TIME FOR THAT.
YOUR HARD WORK HAS BEEN IMPROVING THE COMPANY.
?!
IF IT ISN'T ELMA THE BRIDE...
AND A CHAOS DRAGON?
WHO'S THAT?
WAIT, AREN'T YOU...?!
?
I ARRIVED LATE, AND THEN GOT LOST IN THE PALACE.
SO I'M NOT SURE WHAT EXACTLY IS GOING ON.
?
ARE YOU AN ENEMY, CHAOS DRAGON?

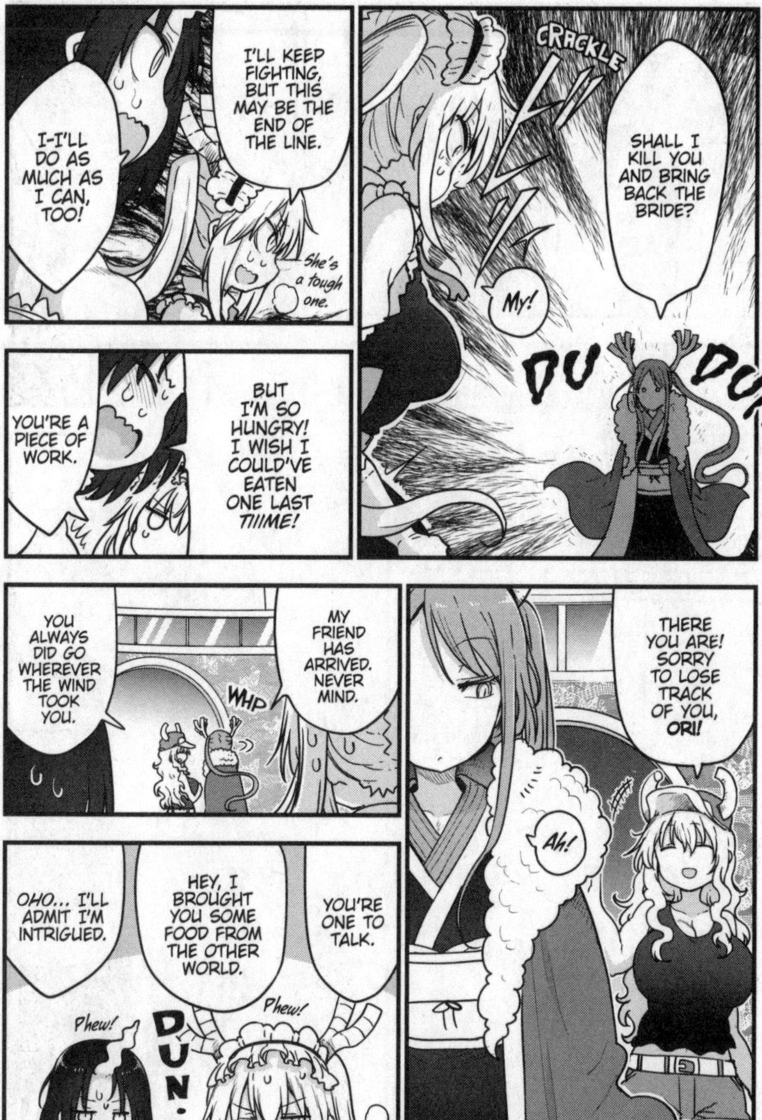
CRACKLE
SHALL I KILL YOU AND BRING BACK THE BRIDE?
My!
DU DUN
I'LL KEEP FIGHTING, BUT THIS MAY BE THE END OF THE LINE.
I-I'LL DO AS MUCH AS I CAN, TOO!
She's a tough one.
BUT I'M SO HUNGRY! I WISH I COULD'VE EATEN ONE LAST TIIIME!
YOU'RE A PIECE OF WORK.
THERE YOU ARE! SORRY TO LOSE TRACK OF YOU, ORI!
Ah!
MY FRIEND HAS ARRIVED. NEVER MIND.
WHP
YOU ALWAYS DID GO WHEREVER THE WIND TOOK YOU.
YOU'RE ONE TO TALK.
HEY, I BROUGHT YOU SOME FOOD FROM THE OTHER WORLD.
OHO... I'LL ADMIT I'M INTRIGUED.
Phew!
Phew!
DUN...

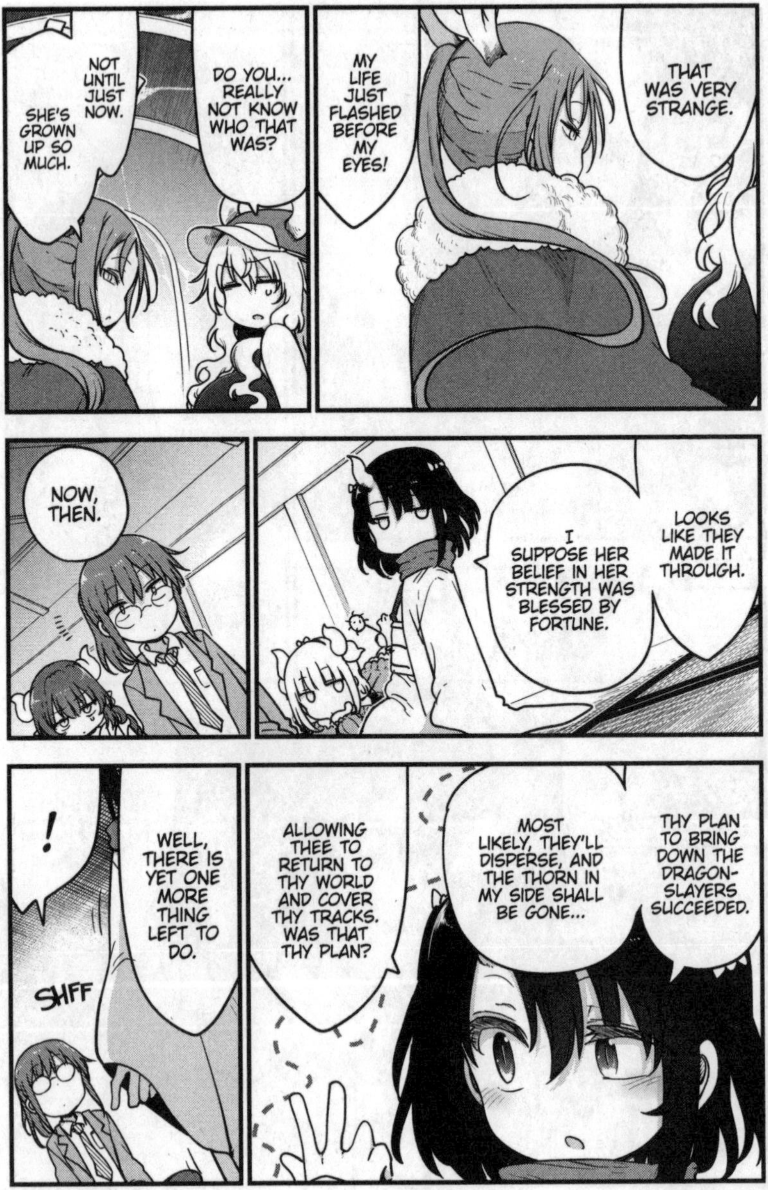
THAT WAS VERY STRANGE.
MY LIFE JUST FLASHED BEFORE MY EYES!
DO YOU... REALLY NOT KNOW WHO THAT WAS?
NOT UNTIL JUST NOW.
SHE'S GROWN UP SO MUCH.
LOOKS LIKE THEY MADE IT THROUGH.
I SUPPOSE HER BELIEF IN HER STRENGTH WAS BLESSED BY FORTUNE.
NOW, THEN.
THY PLAN TO BRING DOWN THE DRAGON-SLAYERS SUCCEEDED.
MOST LIKELY, THEY'LL DISPERSE, AND THE THORN IN MY SIDE SHALL BE GONE...
ALLOWING THEE TO RETURN TO THY WORLD AND COVER THY TRACKS. WAS THAT THY PLAN?
!
WELL, THERE IS YET ONE MORE THING LEFT TO DO.
SHFF

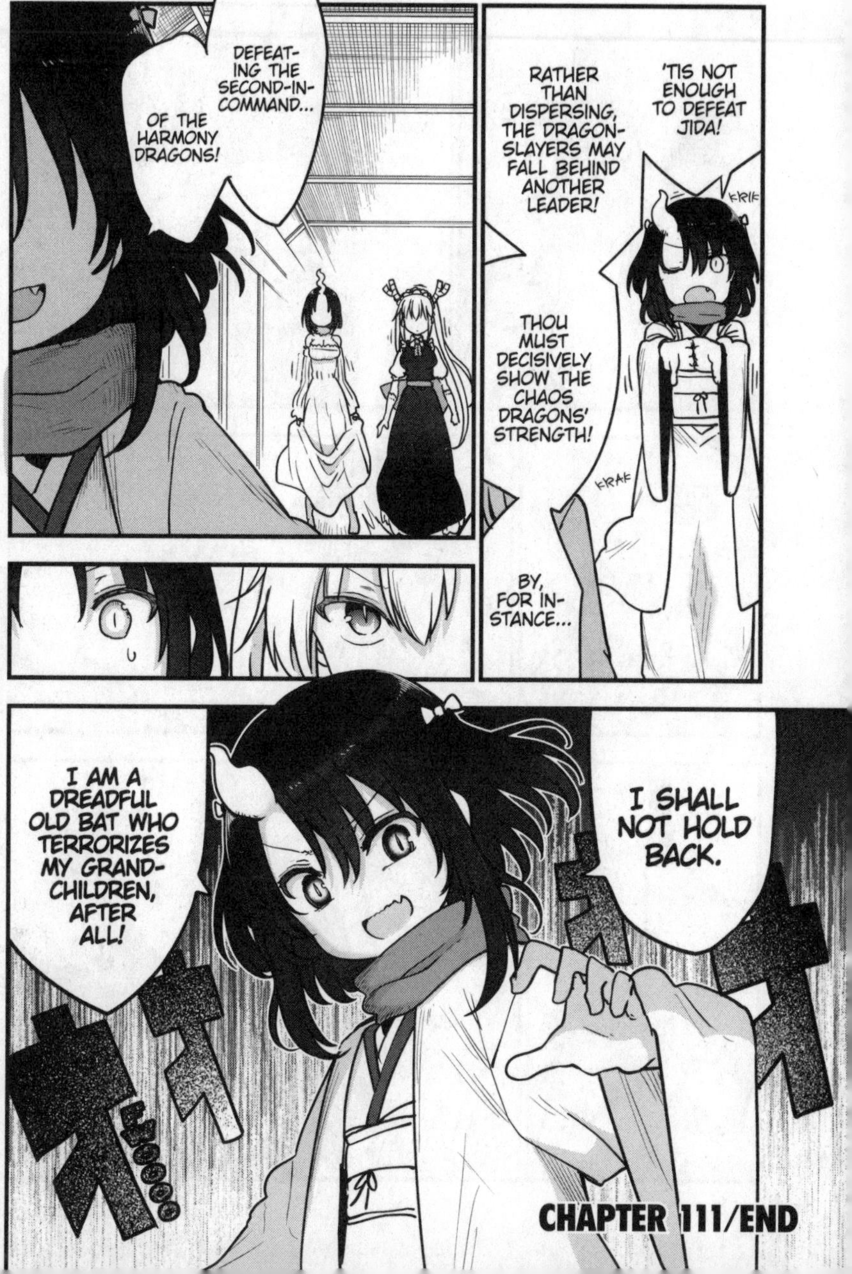
'TIS NOT ENOUGH TO DEFEAT JIDA!
KRIK
RATHER THAN DISPERSING, THE DRAGON-SLAYERS MAY FALL BEHIND ANOTHER LEADER!
THOU MUST DECISIVELY SHOW THE CHAOS DRAGONS' STRENGTH!
KRAK
BY, FOR IN-STANCE...
DEFEAT-ING THE SECOND-IN-COMMAND...
OF THE HARMONY DRAGONS!
I SHALL NOT HOLD BACK.
I AM A DREADFUL OLD BAT WHO TERRORIZES MY GRAND-CHILDREN, AFTER ALL!

CHAPTER 111/END

CHAPTER 112: TELNE & ELMA & TOHRU

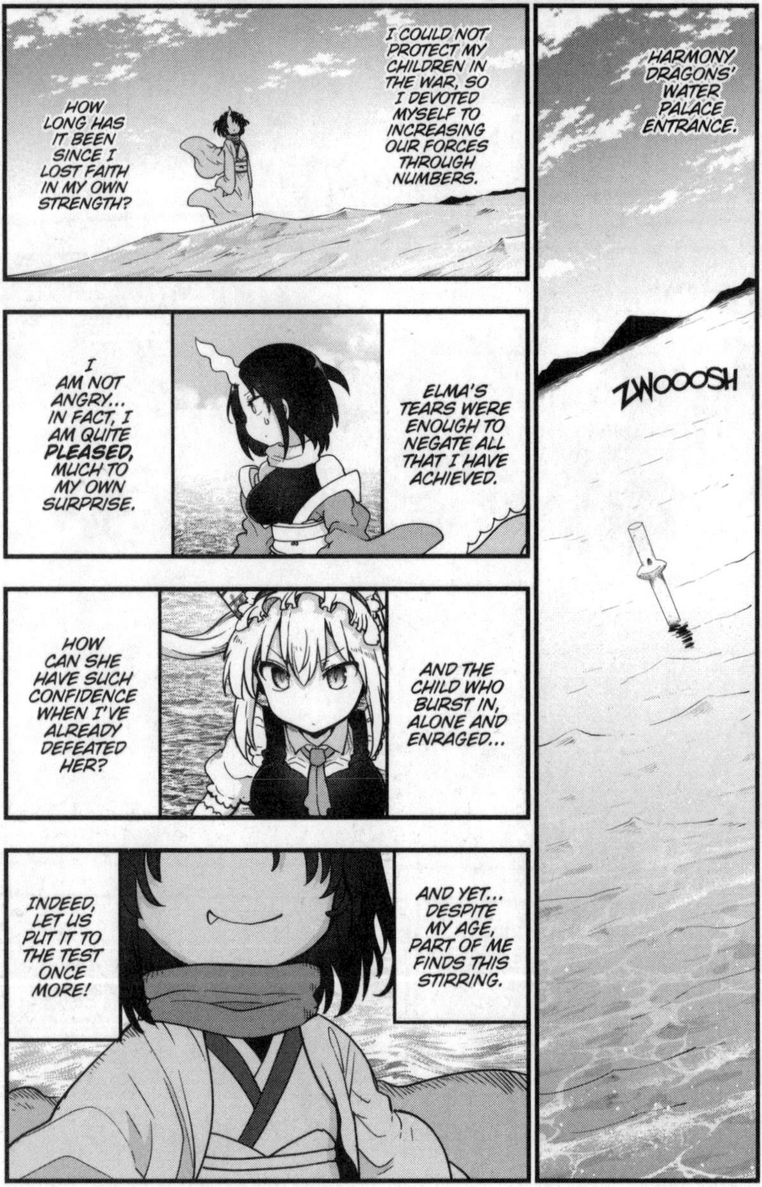

HARMONY DRAGONS' WATER PALACE ENTRANCE.
ZWOOOSH
I COULD NOT PROTECT MY CHILDREN IN THE WAR, SO I DEVOTED MYSELF TO INCREASING OUR FORCES THROUGH NUMBERS.
HOW LONG HAS IT BEEN SINCE I LOST FAITH IN MY OWN STRENGTH?
ELMA'S TEARS WERE ENOUGH TO NEGATE ALL THAT I HAVE ACHIEVED.
I AM NOT ANGRY... IN FACT, I AM QUITE **PLEASED**, MUCH TO MY OWN SURPRISE.
AND THE CHILD WHO BURST IN, ALONE AND ENRAGED...
HOW CAN SHE HAVE SUCH CONFIDENCE WHEN I'VE ALREADY DEFEATED HER?
AND YET... DESPITE MY AGE, PART OF ME FINDS THIS STIRRING.
INDEED, LET US PUT IT TO THE TEST ONCE MORE!

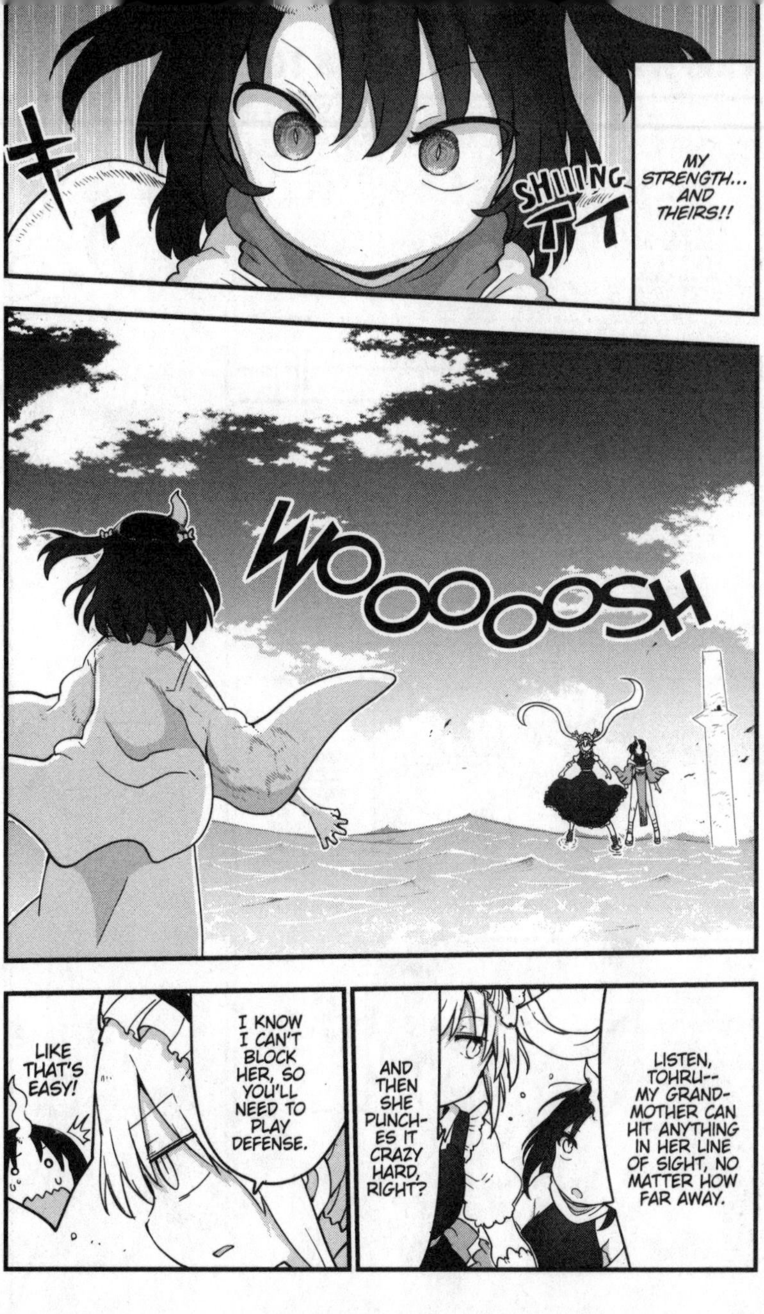
MY STRENGTH... AND THEIRS!!
SHIIING
WOOOOOOSH
LISTEN, TOHRU-- MY GRAND-MOTHER CAN HIT ANYTHING IN HER LINE OF SIGHT, NO MATTER HOW FAR AWAY.
AND THEN SHE PUNCH-ES IT CRAZY HARD, RIGHT?
I KNOW I CAN'T BLOCK HER, SO YOU'LL NEED TO PLAY DEFENSE.
LIKE THAT'S EASY!

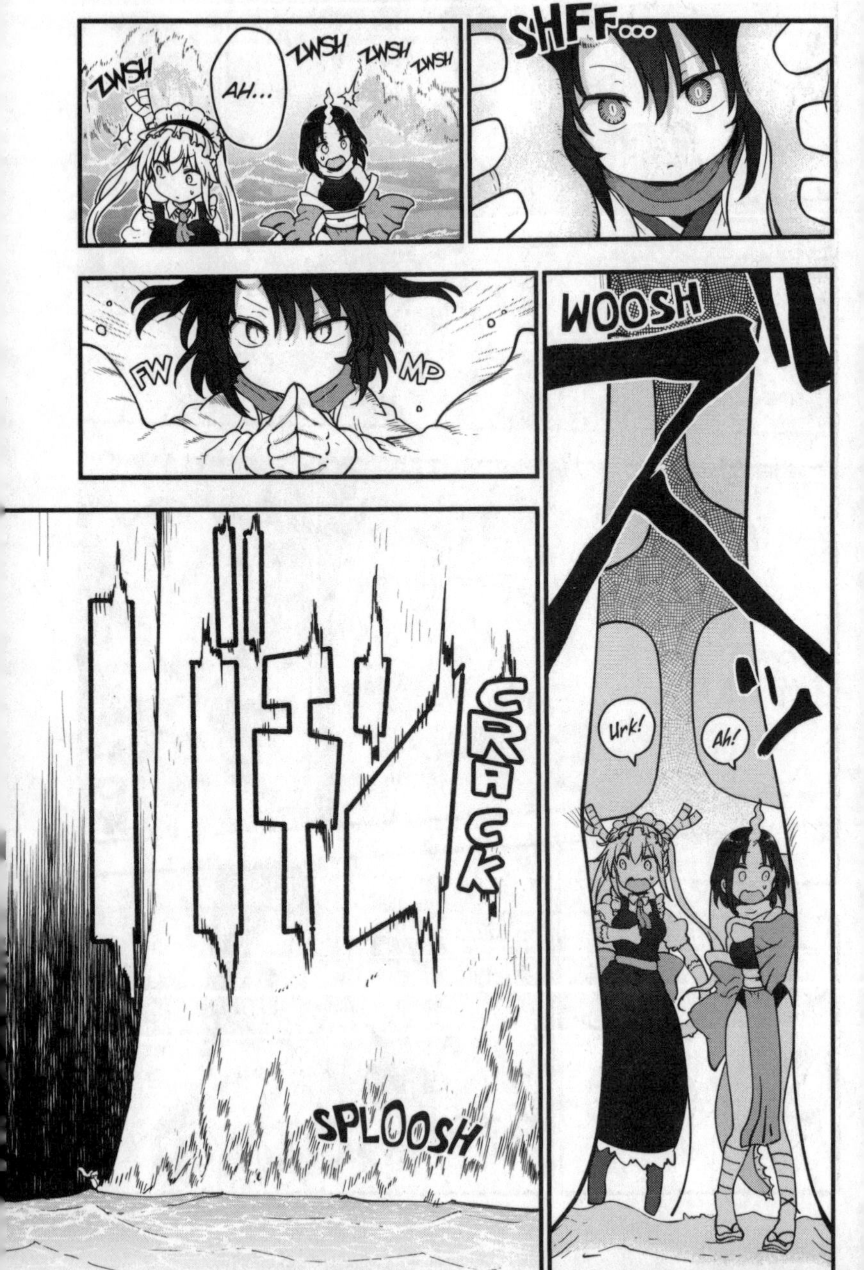
SHFF...
ZWSH
ZWSH
ZWSH
AH...
ZWSH
WOOSH
Ah!
Urk!
FW
MP
CRACK
SPLOOSH

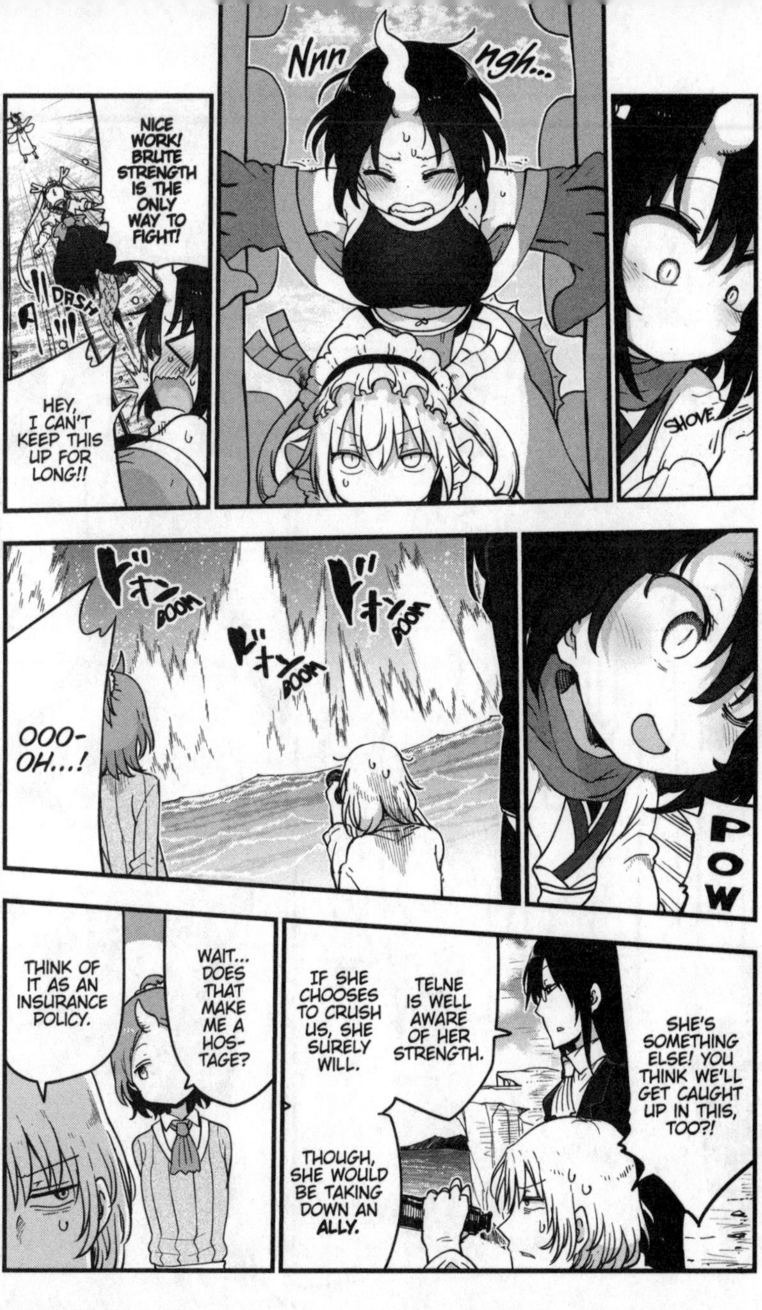
SHOVE
Nnn ngh...
NICE WORK! BRUTE STRENGTH IS THE ONLY WAY TO FIGHT!
DRSH
HEY, I CAN'T KEEP THIS UP FOR LONG!!
POW
ドオン BOOM
ドオン BOOM
ドオン BOOM
OOO-OH...!
SHE'S SOMETHING ELSE! YOU THINK WE'LL GET CAUGHT UP IN THIS, TOO?!
TELNE IS WELL AWARE OF HER STRENGTH.
IF SHE CHOOSES TO CRUSH US, SHE SURELY WILL.
THOUGH, SHE WOULD BE TAKING DOWN AN ALLY.
WAIT... DOES THAT MAKE ME A HOS-TAGE?
THINK OF IT AS AN INSURANCE POLICY.

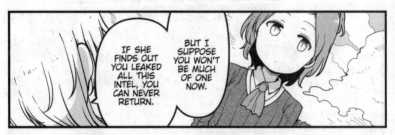

BUT I SUPPOSE YOU WON'T BE MUCH OF ONE NOW.
IF SHE FINDS OUT YOU LEAKED ALL THIS INTEL, YOU CAN NEVER RETURN.
IT'S FINE. I LIKE WORKING WITH LADY ELMA.
I'LL NEVER UNDERSTAND YOU DRAGONS.
......
THAT ASIDE, AZAD, SURELY YOU HAVE NOT FORGOTTEN?
Urk...
I AGREED TO GIVE YOU A FEW OF MY TREASURES, YES?
THAT'S HIGHWAY ROBBERY...
BUT I SUPPOSE A CURSE DRAGON'S HELP IS WELL WORTH IT.
AND YOU SWEAR YOU WON'T ASK FOR ANYTHING MORE?
INDEED.
?
FOR THE COMMUNITY... I SUPPOSE.
SO, YOU'RE NOT JOINING IN THE FIGHT?
NO, IT IS BUT A FARCE.
POW POW POW POW POW

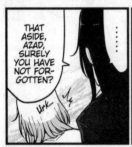

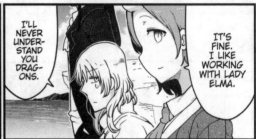

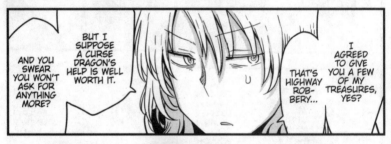

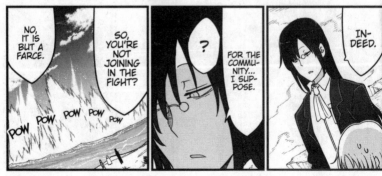

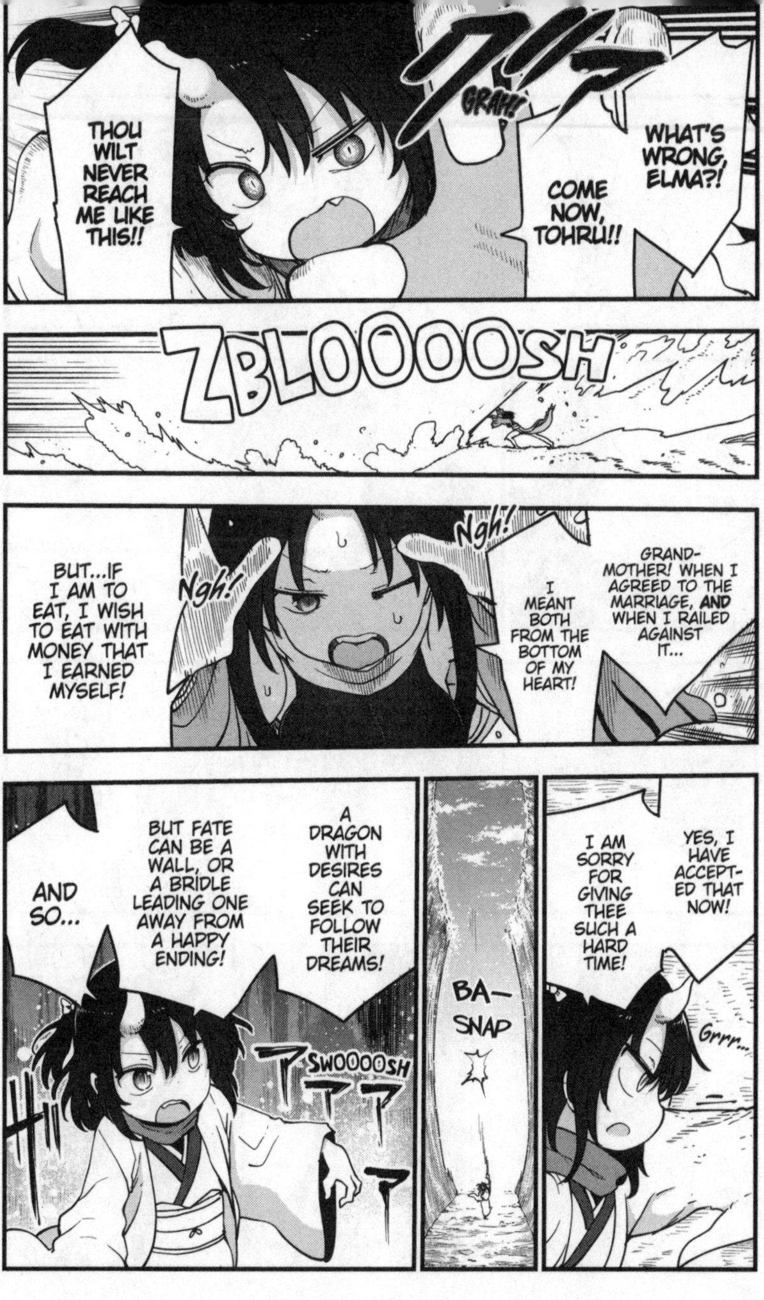
WHAT'S WRONG, ELMA?!
GRAH!!
COME NOW, TOHRU!!
THOU WILT NEVER REACH ME LIKE THIS!!
ZBLOOOOSH
GRAND-MOTHER! WHEN I AGREED TO THE MARRIAGE, AND WHEN I RAILED AGAINST IT...
Ngh!
I MEANT BOTH FROM THE BOTTOM OF MY HEART!
Ngh!
BUT...IF I AM TO EAT, I WISH TO EAT WITH MONEY THAT I EARNED MYSELF!
YES, I HAVE ACCEPT-ED THAT NOW!
I AM SORRY FOR GIVING THEE SUCH A HARD TIME!
Grrr...
BA-SNAP
A DRAGON WITH DESIRES CAN SEEK TO FOLLOW THEIR DREAMS!
BUT FATE CAN BE A WALL, OR A BRIDLE LEADING ONE AWAY FROM A HAPPY ENDING!
AND SO...
SWOOOOSH

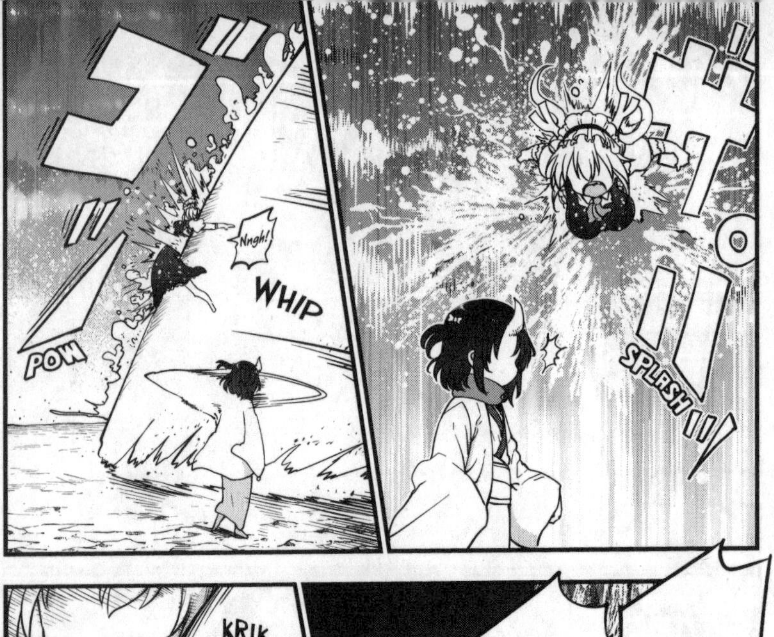
SPLASH!!
Nngh!
WHIP
POW
THOU MUST DIG IN WITH THY TEETH!
UNTIL THOU CANST BREAK FREE...
EVEN IF IT SHATTERS THY JAW!
KRIK...
KRIK...
Grr...!
Ah!
Aaaaaa!
Nnngh...
CHARGE

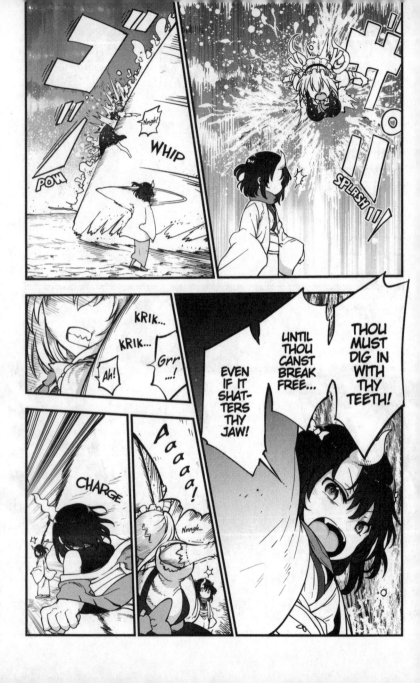

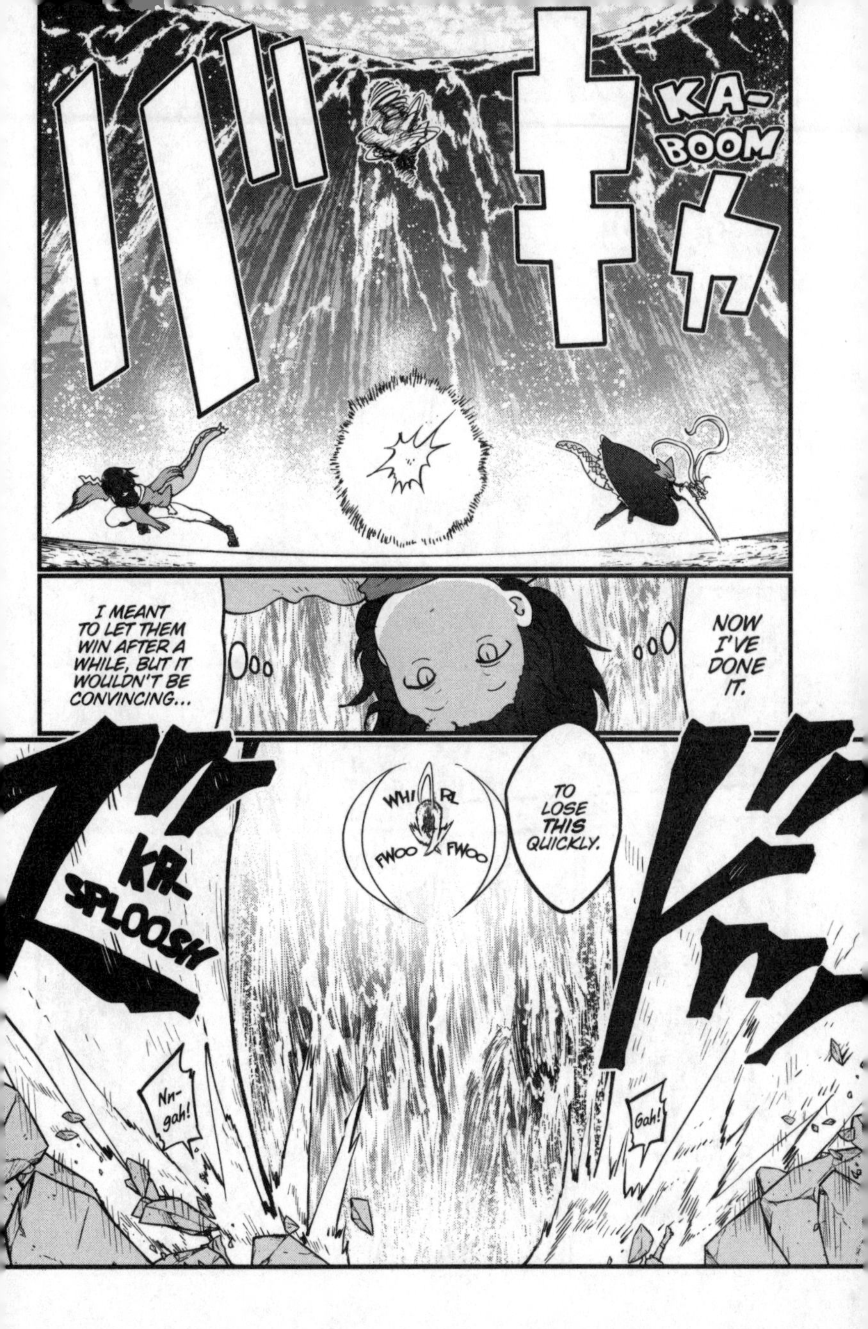
KA-BOOM
NOW I'VE DONE IT.
I MEANT TO LET THEM WIN AFTER A WHILE, BUT IT WOULDN'T BE CONVINCING...
TO LOSE THIS QUICKLY.
WHIRL
FWOO FWOO
KR-SPLOOSH
Gah!
Nn-gah!

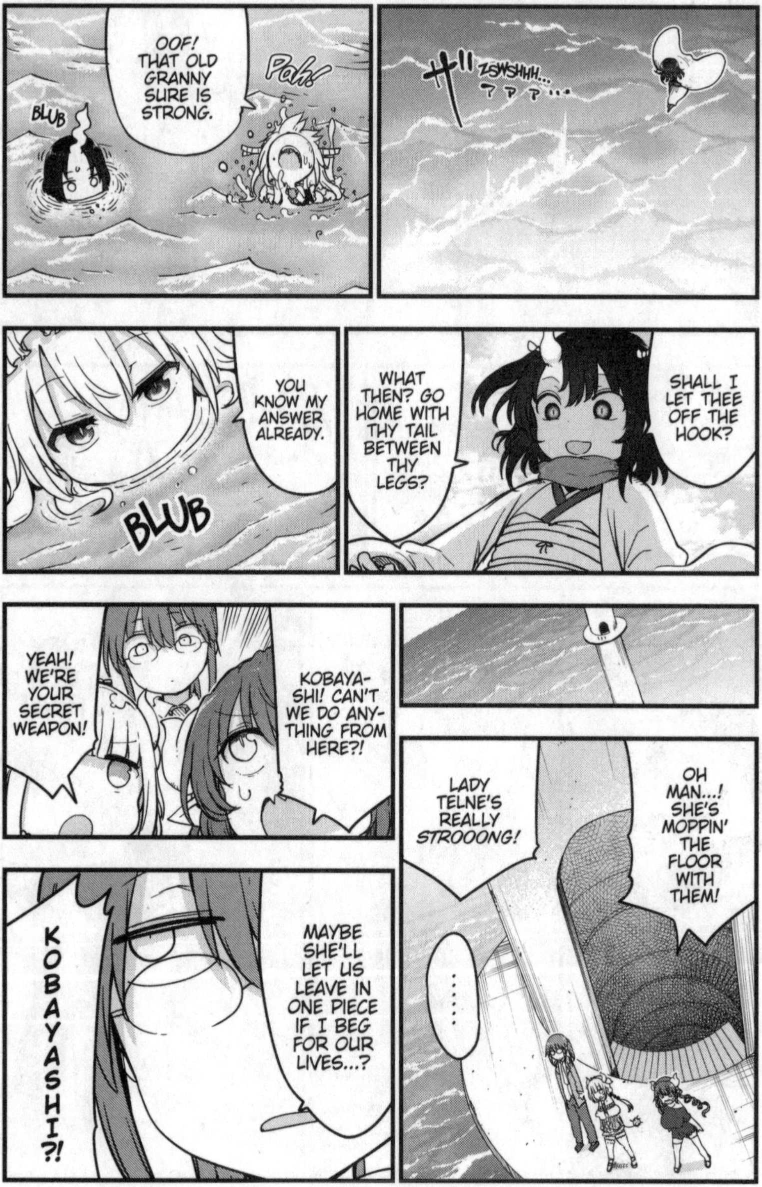
ZSWSHHH...
Pah!
OOF! THAT OLD GRANNY SURE IS STRONG.
BLUB
SHALL I LET THEE OFF THE HOOK?
WHAT THEN? GO HOME WITH THY TAIL BETWEEN THY LEGS?
YOU KNOW MY ANSWER ALREADY.
BLUB
OH MAN...! SHE'S MOPPIN' THE FLOOR WITH THEM!
LADY TELNE'S REALLY STROOONG!
......
KOBAYASHI! CAN'T WE DO ANYTHING FROM HERE?!
YEAH! WE'RE YOUR SECRET WEAPON!
MAYBE SHE'LL LET US LEAVE IN ONE PIECE IF I BEG FOR OUR LIVES...?
KOBAYASHI?!

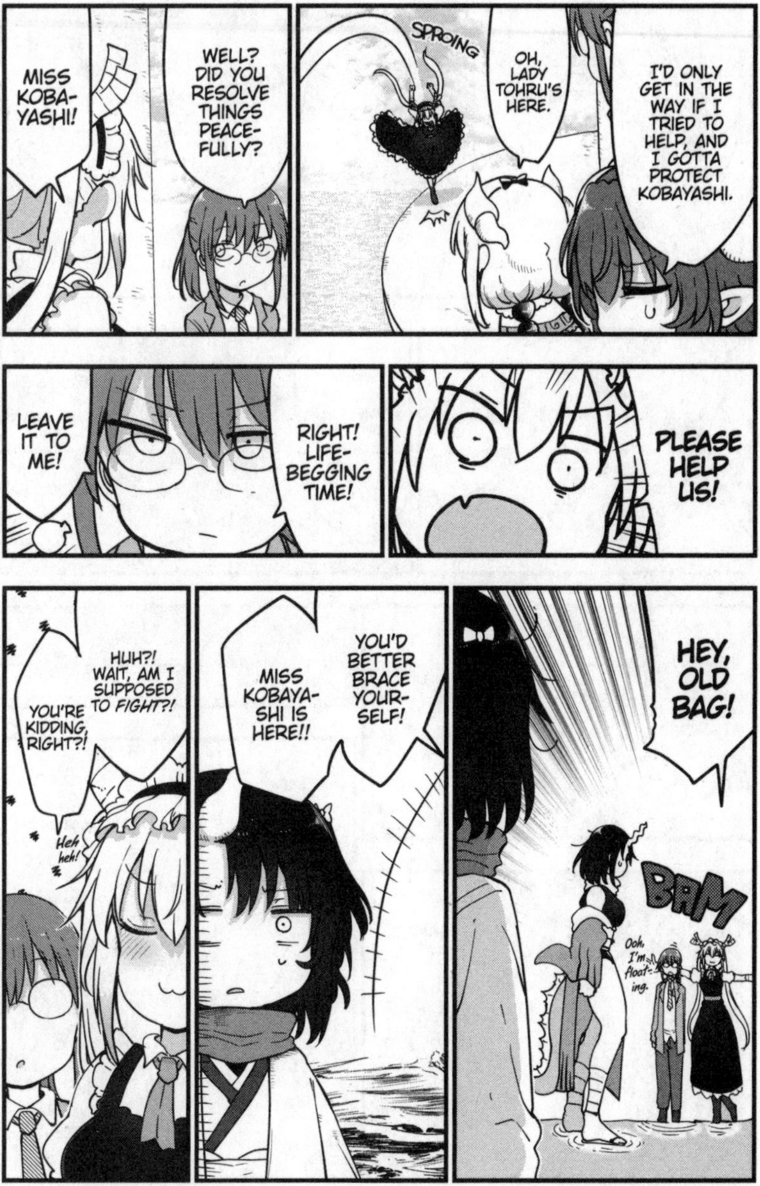
I'D ONLY GET IN THE WAY IF I TRIED TO HELP, AND I GOTTA PROTECT KOBAYASHI.
OH, LADY TOHRU'S HERE.
SPROING
WELL? DID YOU RESOLVE THINGS PEACEFULLY?
MISS KOBAYASHI!
PLEASE HELP US!
RIGHT! LIFE-BEGGING TIME!
LEAVE IT TO ME!
HEY, OLD BAG!
BAM
Ooh, I'm floating.
YOU'D BETTER BRACE YOURSELF!
MISS KOBAYASHI IS HERE!!
HUH?! WAIT, AM I SUPPOSED TO *FIGHT*?!
YOU'RE KIDDING, RIGHT?!
Heh heh!

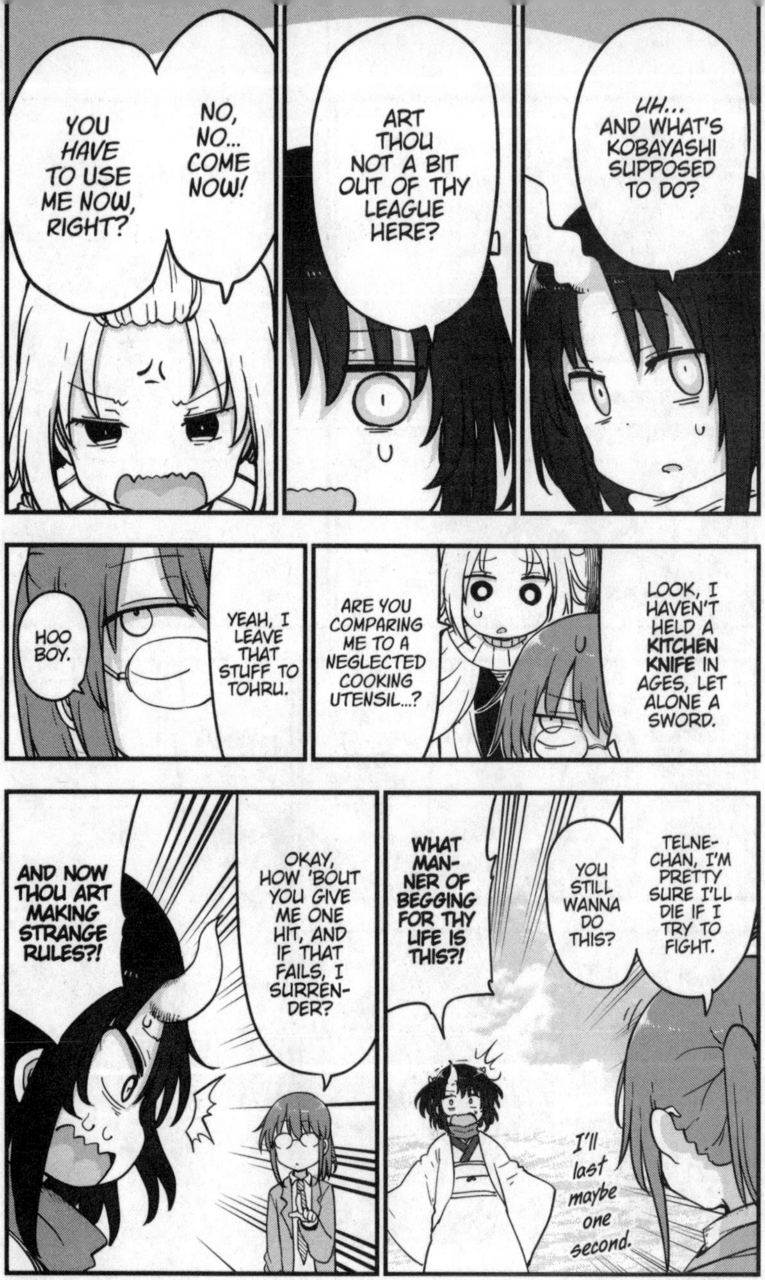
UH... AND WHAT'S KOBAYASHI SUPPOSED TO DO?
ART THOU NOT A BIT OUT OF THY LEAGUE HERE?
NO, NO... COME NOW!
YOU HAVE TO USE ME NOW, RIGHT?
LOOK, I HAVEN'T HELD A **KITCHEN KNIFE** IN AGES, LET ALONE A SWORD.
ARE YOU COMPARING ME TO A NEGLECTED COOKING UTENSIL...?
YEAH, I LEAVE THAT STUFF TO TOHRU.
HOO BOY.
TELNE-CHAN, I'M PRETTY SURE I'LL DIE IF I TRY TO FIGHT.
YOU STILL WANNA DO THIS?
WHAT MANNER OF BEGGING FOR THY LIFE IS THIS?!
I'll last maybe one second.
OKAY, HOW 'BOUT YOU GIVE ME ONE HIT, AND IF THAT FAILS, I SURRENDER?
AND NOW THOU ART MAKING STRANGE RULES?!

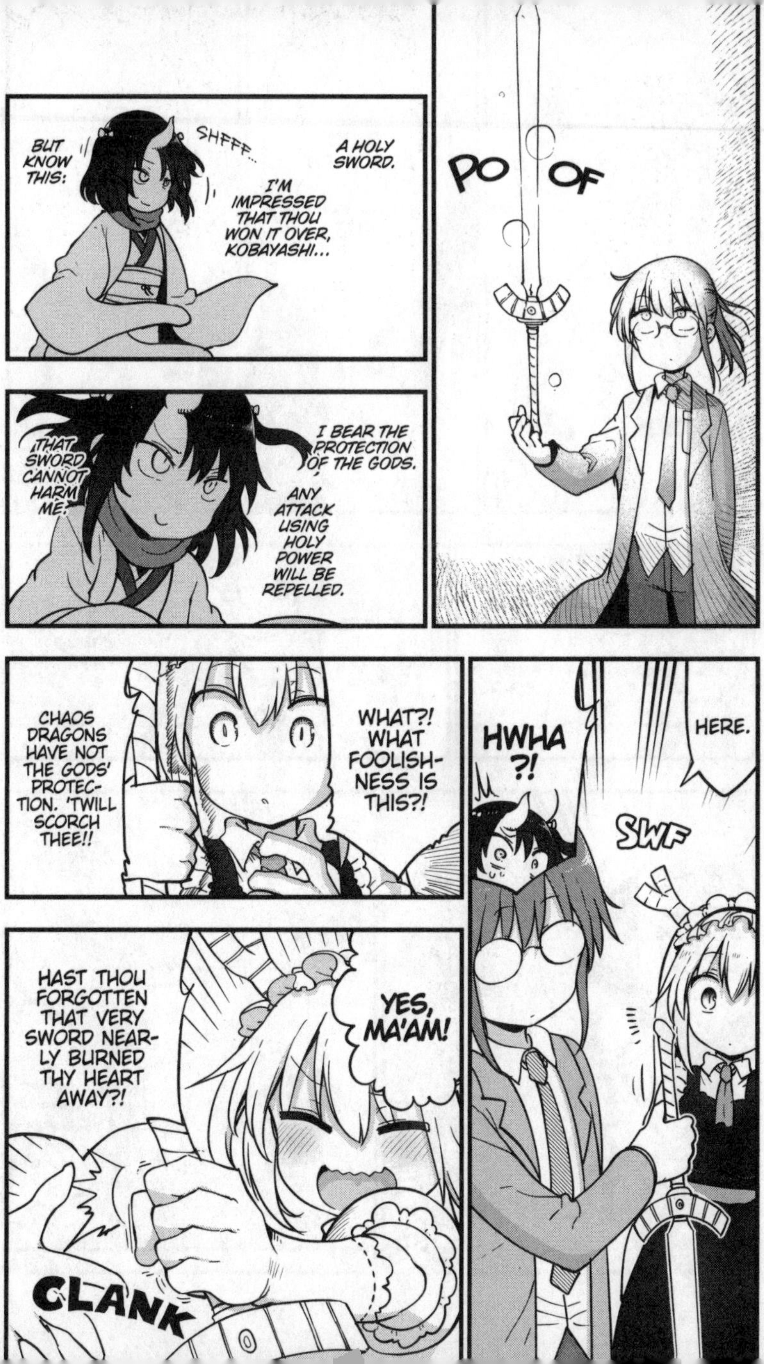
POOF
A HOLY SWORD.
I'M IMPRESSED THAT THOU WON IT OVER, KOBAYASHI...
SHFFF...
BUT KNOW THIS:
I BEAR THE PROTECTION OF THE GODS.
ANY ATTACK USING HOLY POWER WILL BE REPELLED.
THAT SWORD CANNOT HARM ME.
HERE.
SWF
HWHA?!
WHAT?! WHAT FOOLISHNESS IS THIS?!
CHAOS DRAGONS HAVE NOT THE GODS' PROTECTION. 'TWILL SCORCH THEE!!
YES, MA'AM!
HAST THOU FORGOTTEN THAT VERY SWORD NEARLY BURNED THY HEART AWAY?!
CLANK

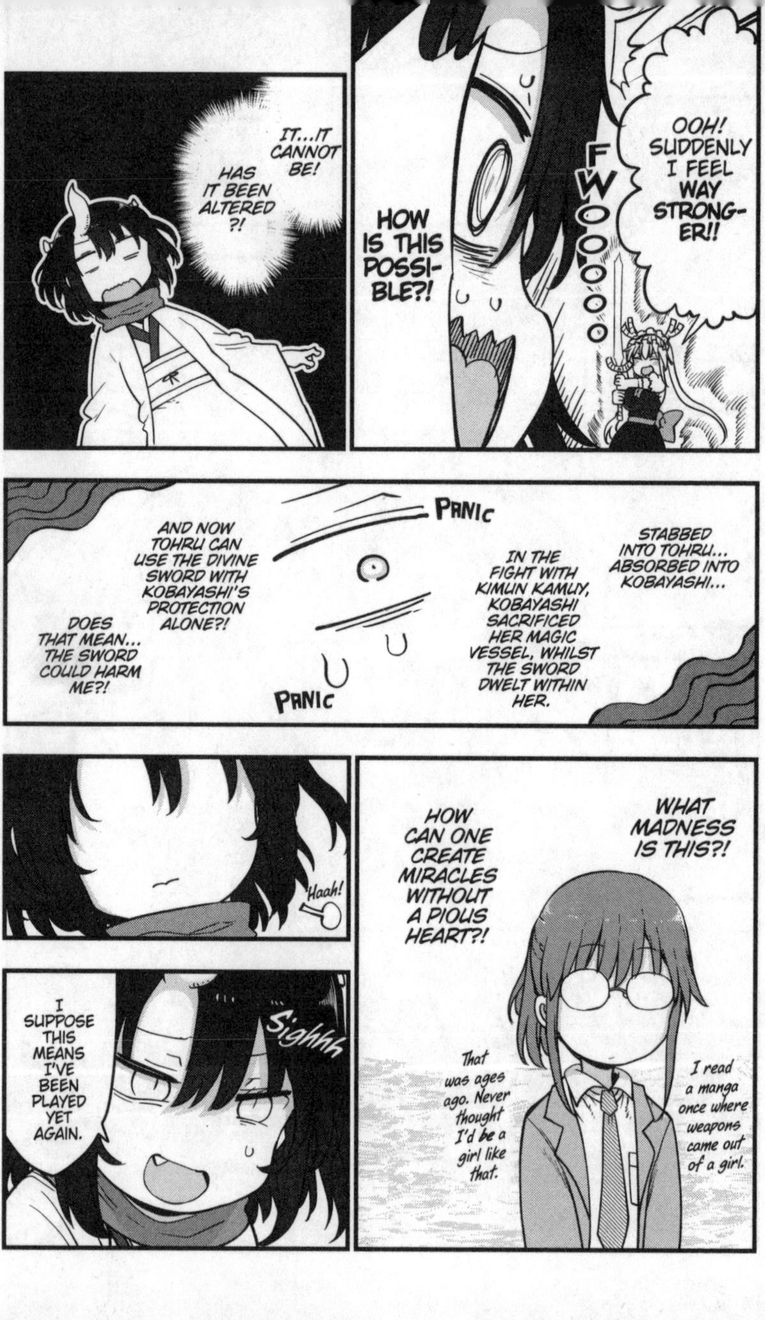
OOH! SUDDENLY I FEEL WAY STRONG-ER!!
FWOOOOOOO
HOW IS THIS POSSI-BLE?!
IT...IT CANNOT BE!
HAS IT BEEN ALTERED ?!
STABBED INTO TOHRU... ABSORBED INTO KOBAYASHI...
IN THE FIGHT WITH KIMUN KAMUY, KOBAYASHI SACRIFICED HER MAGIC VESSEL, WHILST THE SWORD DWELT WITHIN HER.
PANIC
AND NOW TOHRU CAN USE THE DIVINE SWORD WITH KOBAYASHI'S PROTECTION ALONE?!
DOES THAT MEAN... THE SWORD COULD HARM ME?!
PANIC
WHAT MADNESS IS THIS?!
HOW CAN ONE CREATE MIRACLES WITHOUT A PIOUS HEART?!
I read a manga once where weapons came out of a girl.
That was ages ago. Never thought I'd be a girl like that.
Haah!
Sighhh
I SUPPOSE THIS MEANS I'VE BEEN PLAYED YET AGAIN.

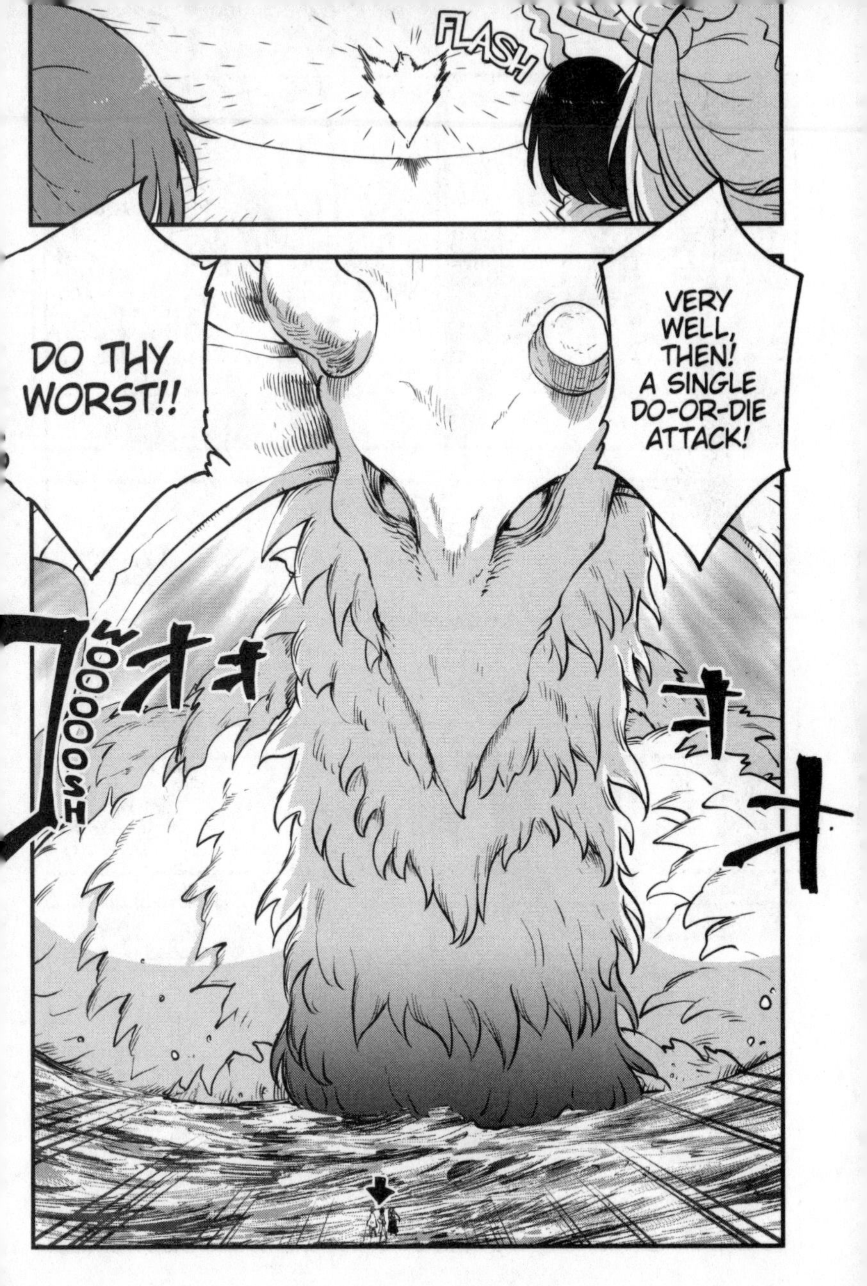
FLASH
VERY WELL, THEN! A SINGLE DO-OR-DIE ATTACK!
DO THY WORST!!
WOOOOOOOSH

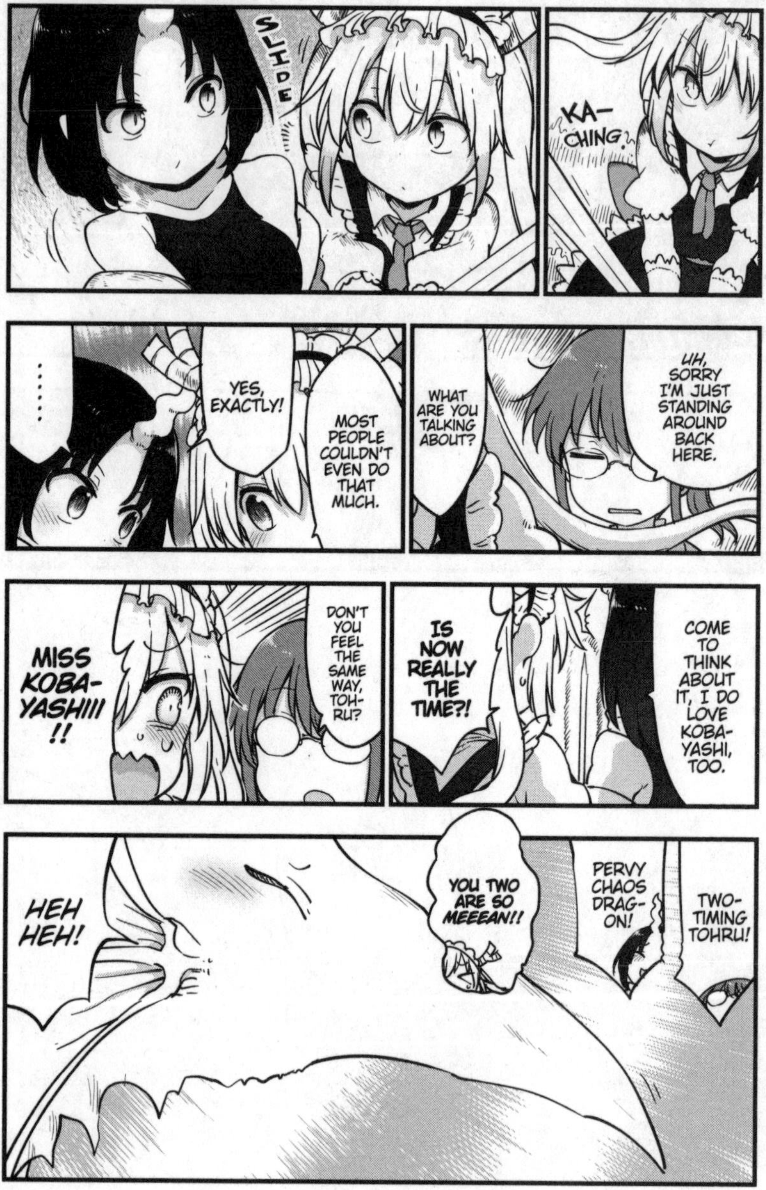
KA-CHING
SLIDE
UH, SORRY I'M JUST STANDING AROUND BACK HERE.
WHAT ARE YOU TALKING ABOUT?
MOST PEOPLE COULDN'T EVEN DO THAT MUCH.
YES, EXACTLY!
......
COME TO THINK ABOUT IT, I DO LOVE KOBA-YASHI, TOO.
IS NOW REALLY THE TIME?!
DON'T YOU FEEL THE SAME WAY, TOH-RU?
MISS KOBA-YASHIII !!
TWO-TIMING TOHRU!
PERVY CHAOS DRAG-ON!
YOU TWO ARE SO MEEEAN!!
HEH HEH!

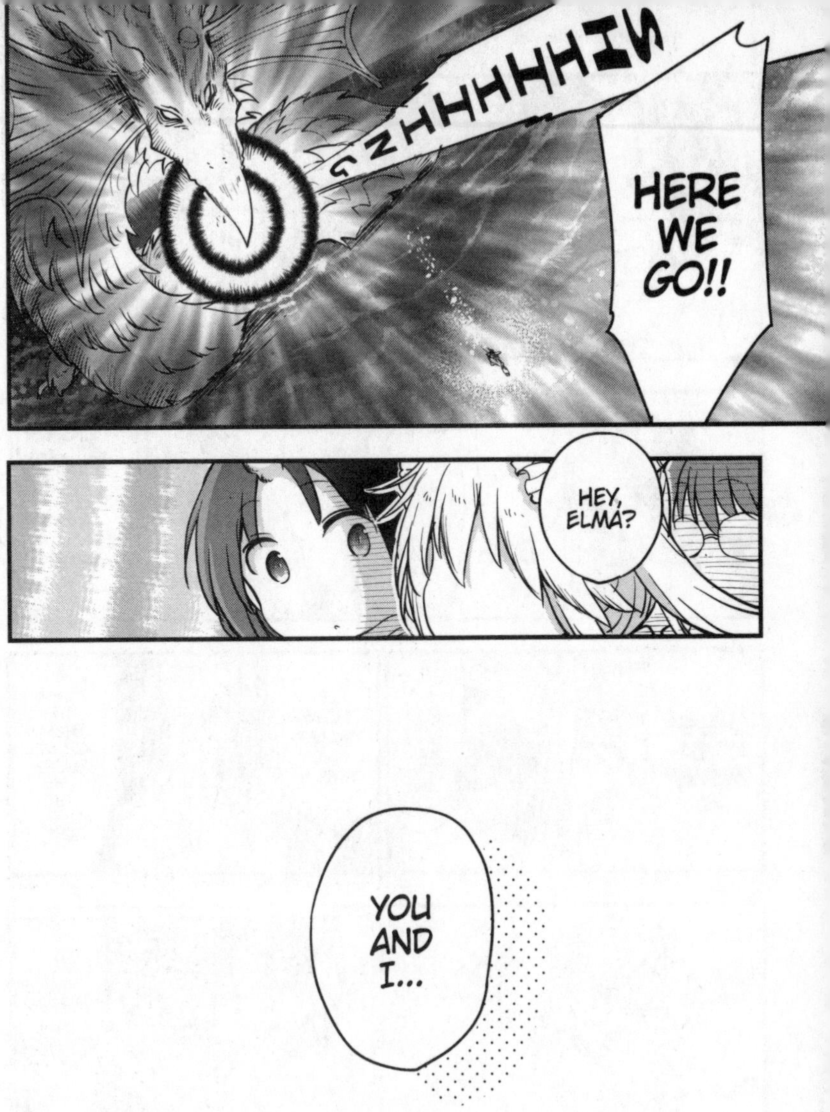
SIHHHHHHNG
HERE WE GO!!
HEY, ELMA?
YOU AND I...

CHAPTER 112/END

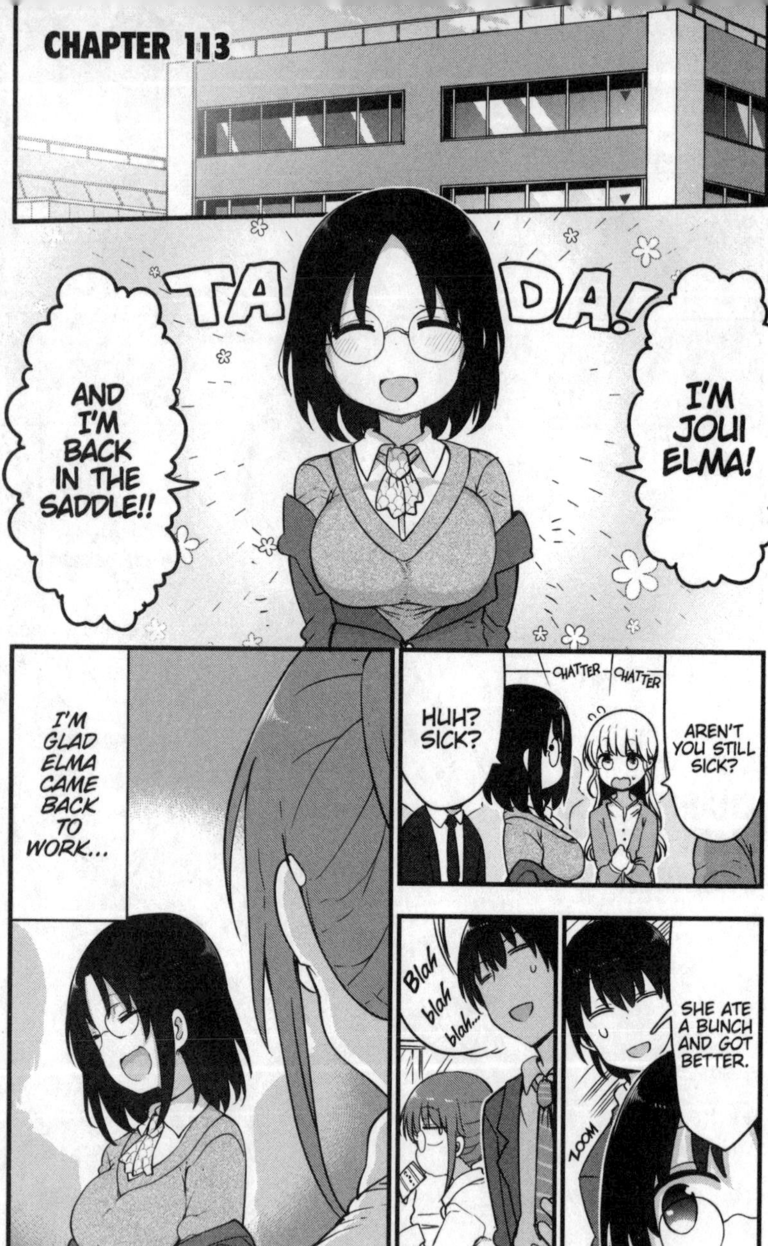
CHAPTER 113
TA DA!
I'M JOUI ELMA!
AND I'M BACK IN THE SADDLE!!
CHATTER CHATTER
AREN'T YOU STILL SICK?
HUH? SICK?
SHE ATE A BUNCH AND GOT BETTER.
ZOOM
Blah blah blah...
I'M GLAD ELMA CAME BACK TO WORK...

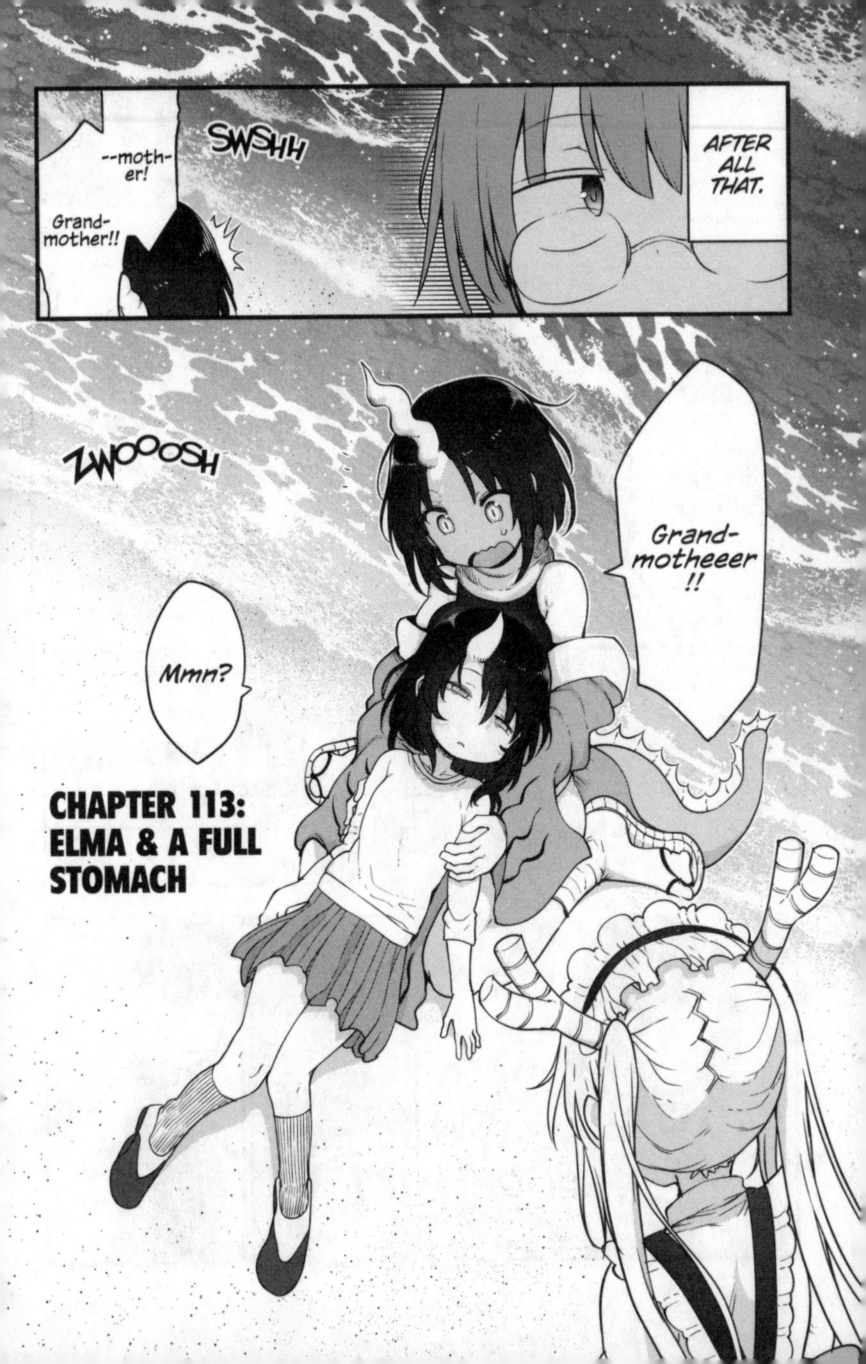
AFTER ALL THAT.
SWSHH
--moth-er!
Grand-mother!!
Grand-motheeer!!
ZWOOOSH
Mmn?
CHAPTER 113: ELMA & A FULL STOMACH

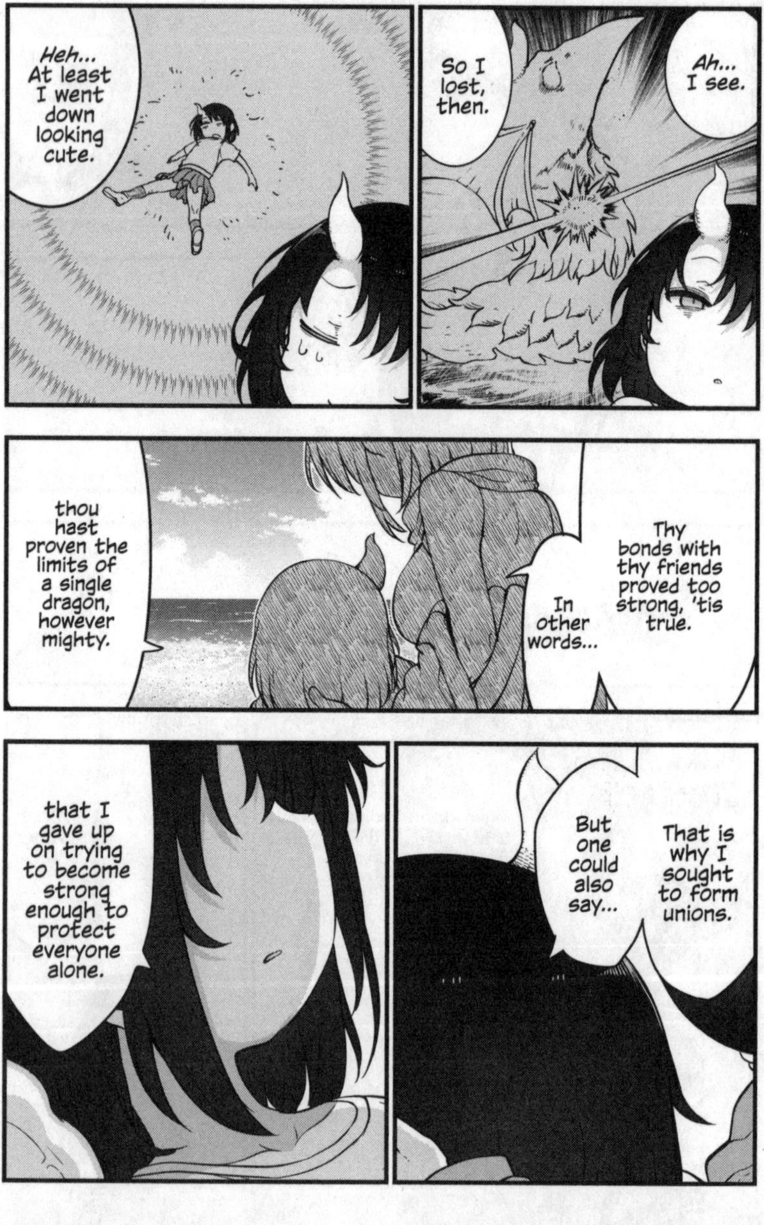
Ah... I see.
So I lost, then.
Heh... At least I went down looking cute.
Thy bonds with thy friends proved too strong, 'tis true.
In other words...
thou hast proven the limits of a single dragon, however mighty.
That is why I sought to form unions.
But one could also say...
that I gave up on trying to become strong enough to protect everyone alone.

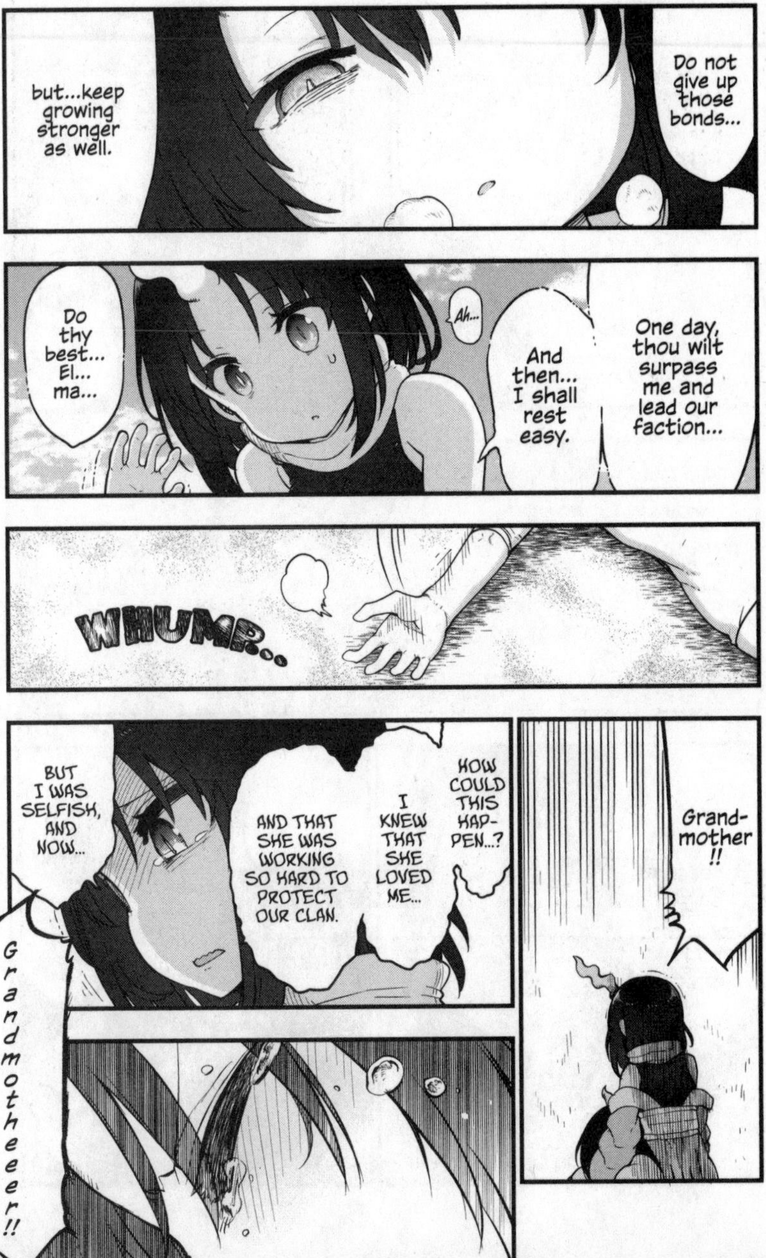
Do not give up those bonds...
but...keep growing stronger as well.
One day, thou wilt surpass me and lead our faction...
And then... I shall rest easy.
Ah...
Do thy best... El... ma...
WHUMP...
Grand-mother!!
HOW COULD THIS HAP-PEN...?
I KNEW THAT SHE LOVED ME...
AND THAT SHE WAS WORKING SO HARD TO PROTECT OUR CLAN.
BUT I WAS SELFISH, AND NOW...
Grandmotheeeer!!

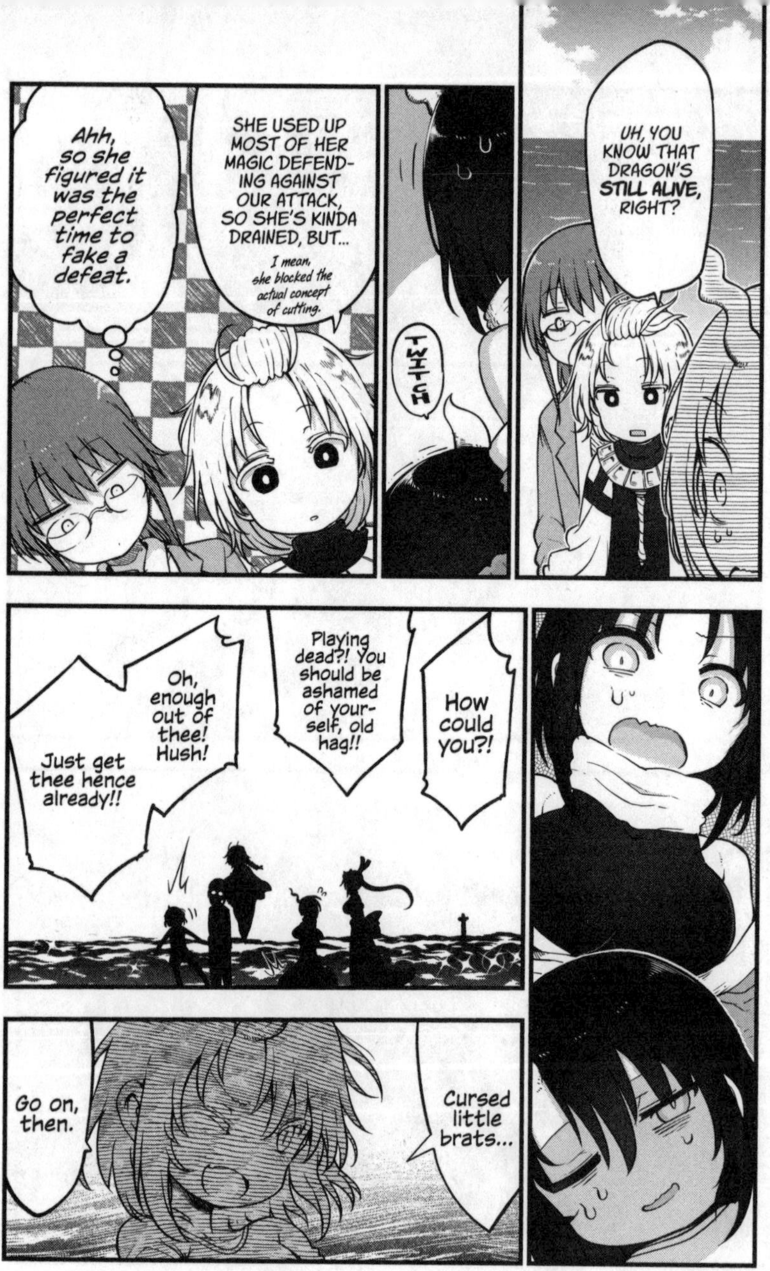
UH, YOU KNOW THAT DRAGON'S **STILL ALIVE,** RIGHT?
TWITCH
SHE USED UP MOST OF HER MAGIC DEFEND-ING AGAINST OUR ATTACK, SO SHE'S KINDA DRAINED, BUT...
I mean, she blocked the actual concept of cutting.
Ahh, so she figured it was the perfect time to fake a defeat.
How could you?!
Playing dead?! You should be ashamed of your-self, old hag!!
Oh, enough out of thee! Hush!
Just get thee hence already!!
Cursed little brats...
Go on, then.

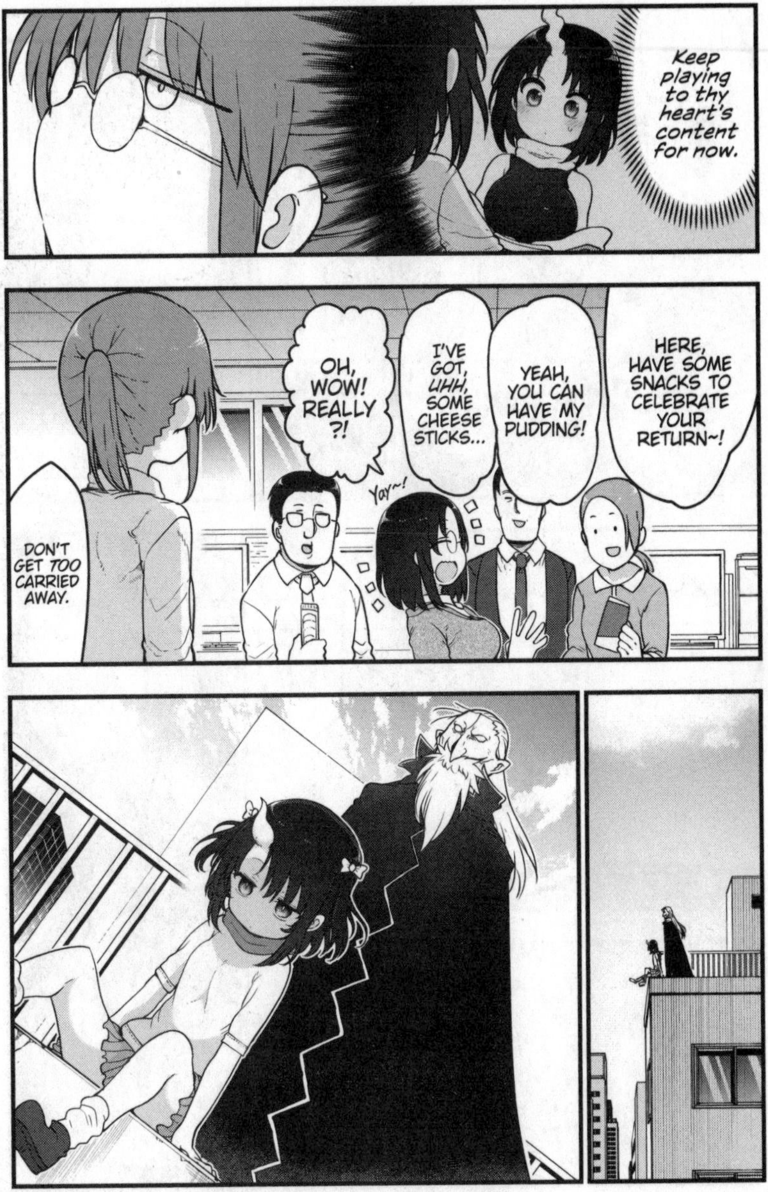
Keep playing to thy heart's content for now.
HERE, HAVE SOME SNACKS TO CELEBRATE YOUR RETURN~!
YEAH, YOU CAN HAVE MY PUDDING!
I'VE GOT, *UHH*, SOME CHEESE STICKS...
OH, WOW! REALLY?!
Yay~!
DON'T GET *TOO* CARRIED AWAY.

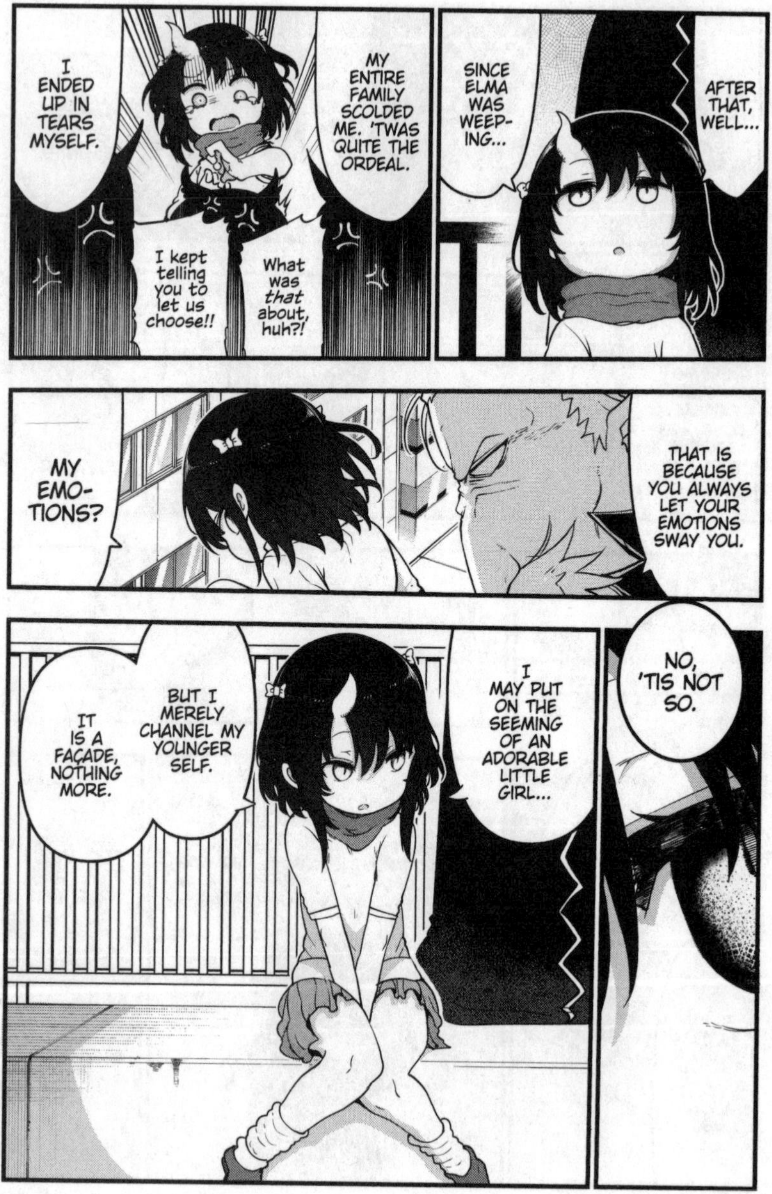
AFTER THAT, WELL...
SINCE ELMA WAS WEEPING...
MY ENTIRE FAMILY SCOLDED ME. 'TWAS QUITE THE ORDEAL.
I ENDED UP IN TEARS MYSELF.
What was *that* about, huh?!
I kept telling you to let us choose!!
THAT IS BECAUSE YOU ALWAYS LET YOUR EMOTIONS SWAY YOU.
MY EMOTIONS?
NO, 'TIS NOT SO.
I MAY PUT ON THE SEEMING OF AN ADORABLE LITTLE GIRL...
BUT I MERELY CHANNEL MY YOUNGER SELF.
IT IS A FAÇADE, NOTHING MORE.

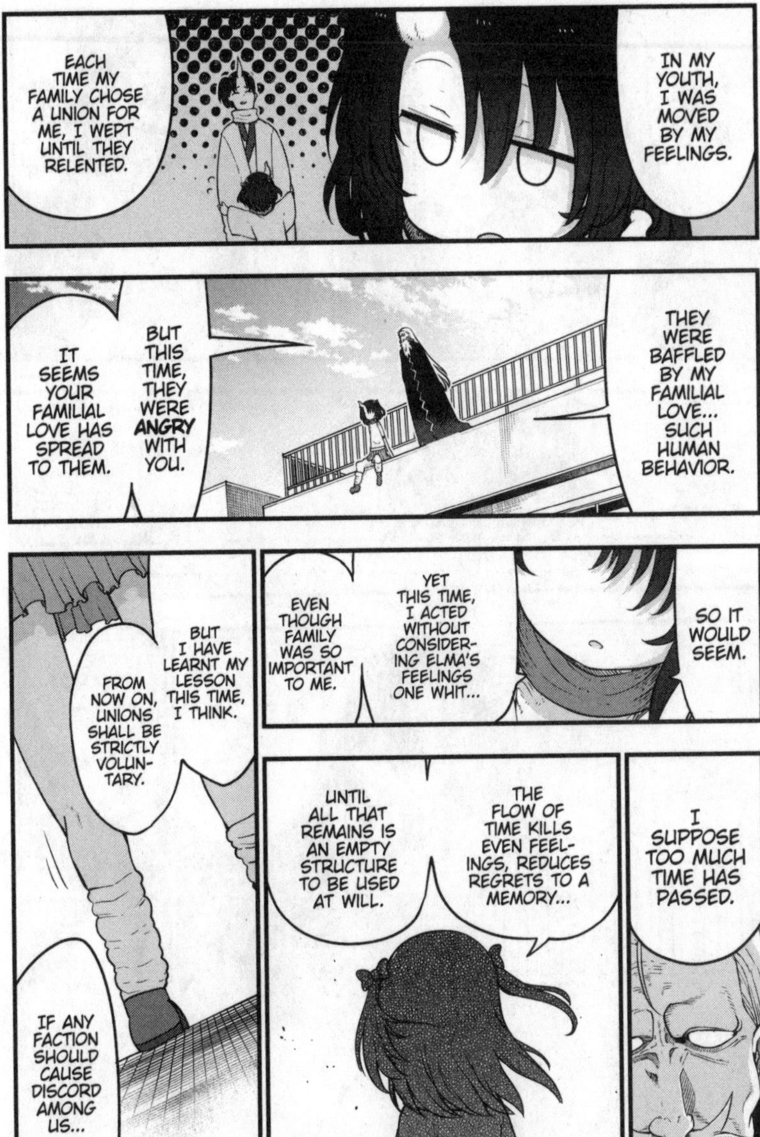
IN MY YOUTH, I WAS MOVED BY MY FEELINGS.
EACH TIME MY FAMILY CHOSE A UNION FOR ME, I WEPT UNTIL THEY RELENTED.
THEY WERE BAFFLED BY MY FAMILIAL LOVE... SUCH HUMAN BEHAVIOR.
BUT THIS TIME, THEY WERE **ANGRY** WITH YOU.
IT SEEMS YOUR FAMILIAL LOVE HAS SPREAD TO THEM.
SO IT WOULD SEEM.
YET THIS TIME, I ACTED WITHOUT CONSIDERING ELMA'S FEELINGS ONE WHIT...
EVEN THOUGH FAMILY WAS SO IMPORTANT TO ME.
I SUPPOSE TOO MUCH TIME HAS PASSED.
THE FLOW OF TIME KILLS EVEN FEELINGS, REDUCES REGRETS TO A MEMORY...
UNTIL ALL THAT REMAINS IS AN EMPTY STRUCTURE TO BE USED AT WILL.
BUT I HAVE LEARNT MY LESSON THIS TIME, I THINK.
FROM NOW ON, UNIONS SHALL BE STRICTLY VOLUNTARY.
IF ANY FACTION SHOULD CAUSE DISCORD AMONG US...

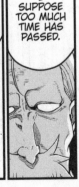

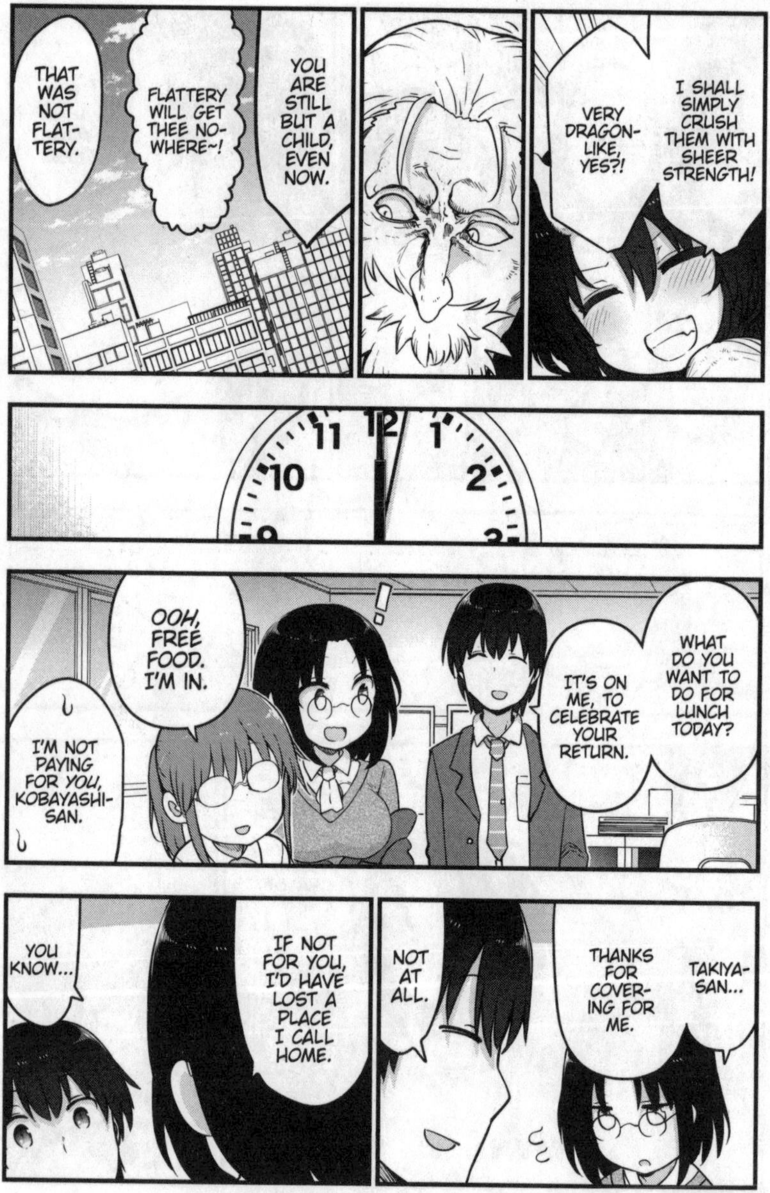
I SHALL SIMPLY CRUSH THEM WITH SHEER STRENGTH!
VERY DRAGON-LIKE, YES?!
YOU ARE STILL BUT A CHILD, EVEN NOW.
FLATTERY WILL GET THEE NO-WHERE~!
THAT WAS NOT FLAT-TERY.
WHAT DO YOU WANT TO DO FOR LUNCH TODAY?
IT'S ON ME, TO CELEBRATE YOUR RETURN.
!
OOH, FREE FOOD. I'M IN.
I'M NOT PAYING FOR YOU, KOBAYASHI-SAN.
TAKIYA-SAN...
THANKS FOR COVER-ING FOR ME.
NOT AT ALL.
IF NOT FOR YOU, I'D HAVE LOST A PLACE I CALL HOME.
YOU KNOW...

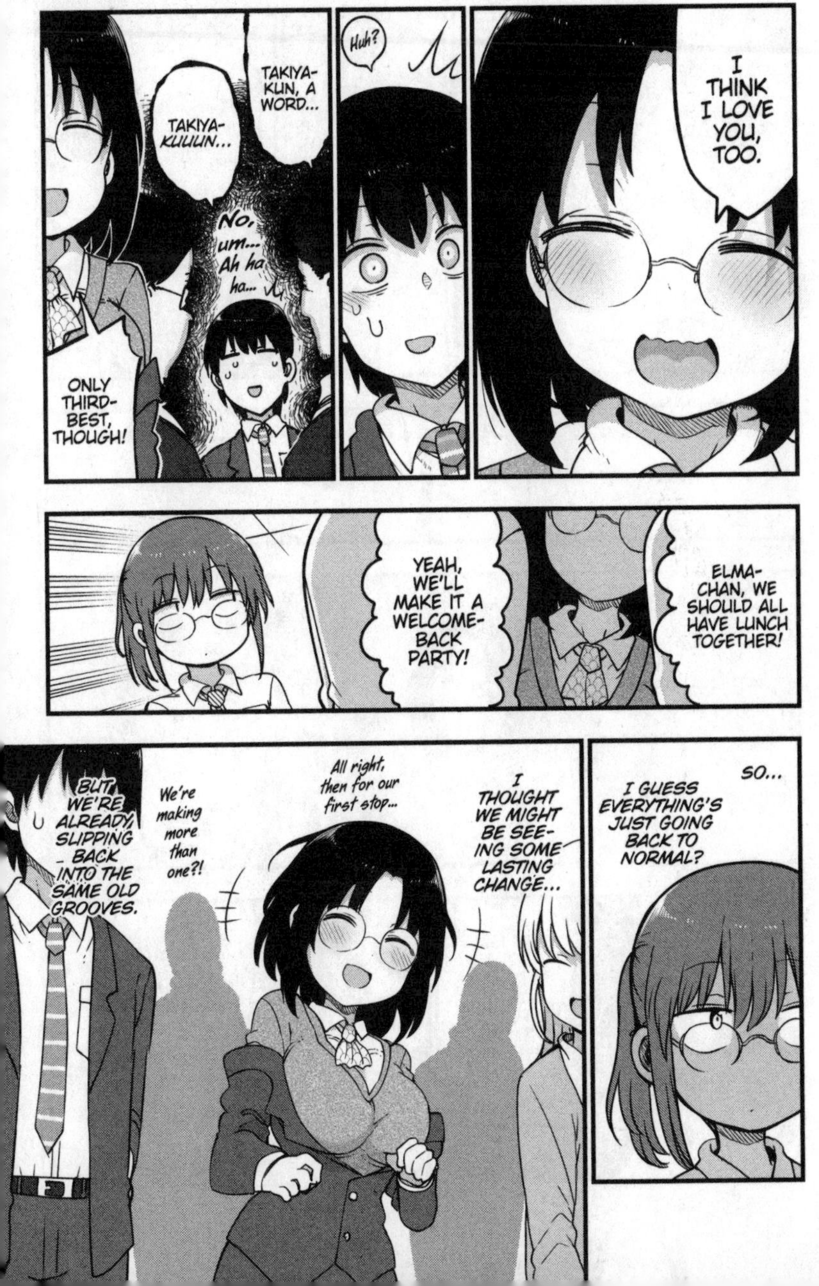
I THINK I LOVE YOU, TOO.
Huh?
TAKIYA-KUN, A WORD...
TAKIYA-KUUUN...
No, um... Ah ha ha...
ONLY THIRD-BEST, THOUGH!
ELMA-CHAN, WE SHOULD ALL HAVE LUNCH TOGETHER!
YEAH, WE'LL MAKE IT A WELCOME-BACK PARTY!
SO...
I GUESS EVERYTHING'S JUST GOING BACK TO NORMAL?
I THOUGHT WE MIGHT BE SEEING SOME LASTING CHANGE...
All right, then for our first stop...
We're making more than one?!
BUT WE'RE ALREADY SLIPPING BACK INTO THE SAME OLD GROOVES.

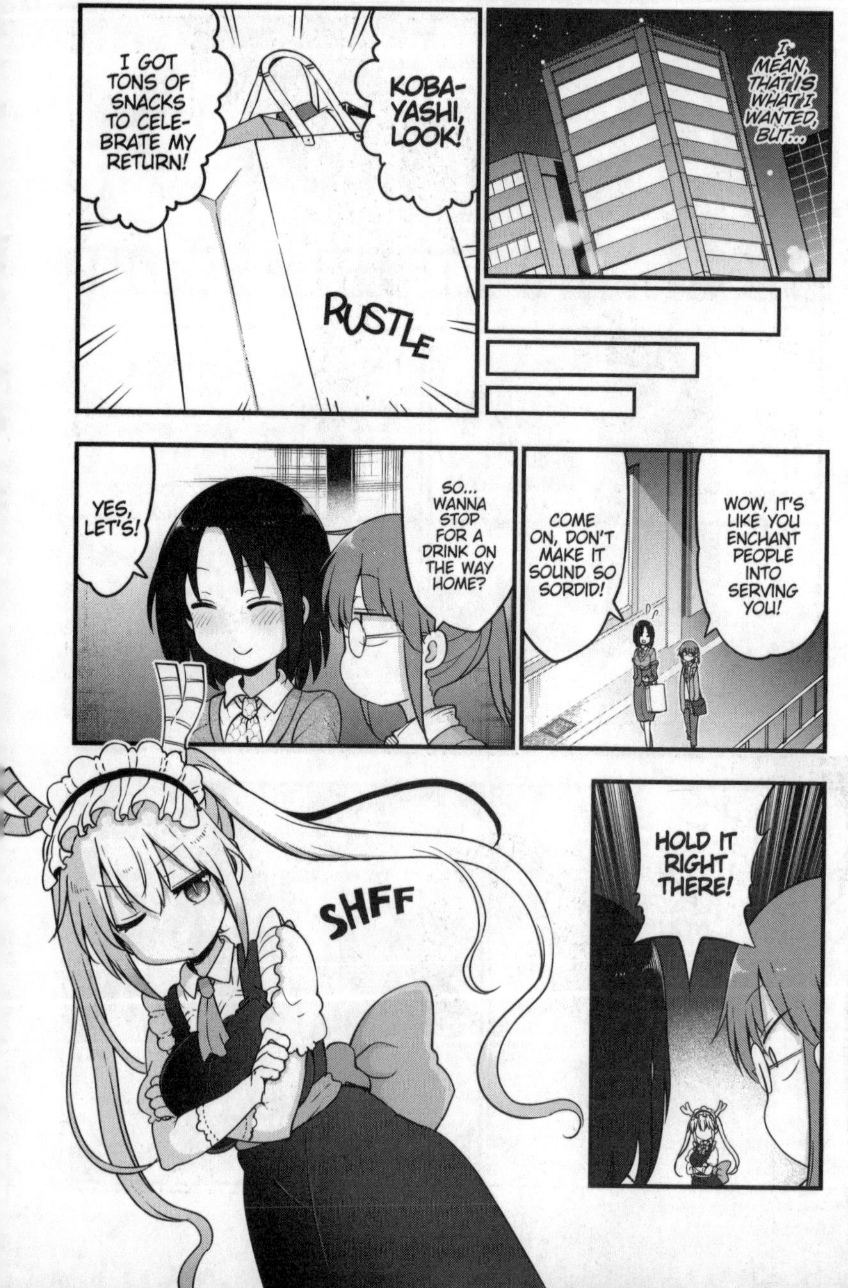
I MEAN, THAT IS WHAT I WANTED, BUT...
KOBA-YASHI, LOOK!
I GOT TONS OF SNACKS TO CELEBRATE MY RETURN!
RUSTLE
WOW, IT'S LIKE YOU ENCHANT PEOPLE INTO SERVING YOU!
COME ON, DON'T MAKE IT SOUND SO SORDID!
SO... WANNA STOP FOR A DRINK ON THE WAY HOME?
YES, LET'S!
HOLD IT RIGHT THERE!
SHFF

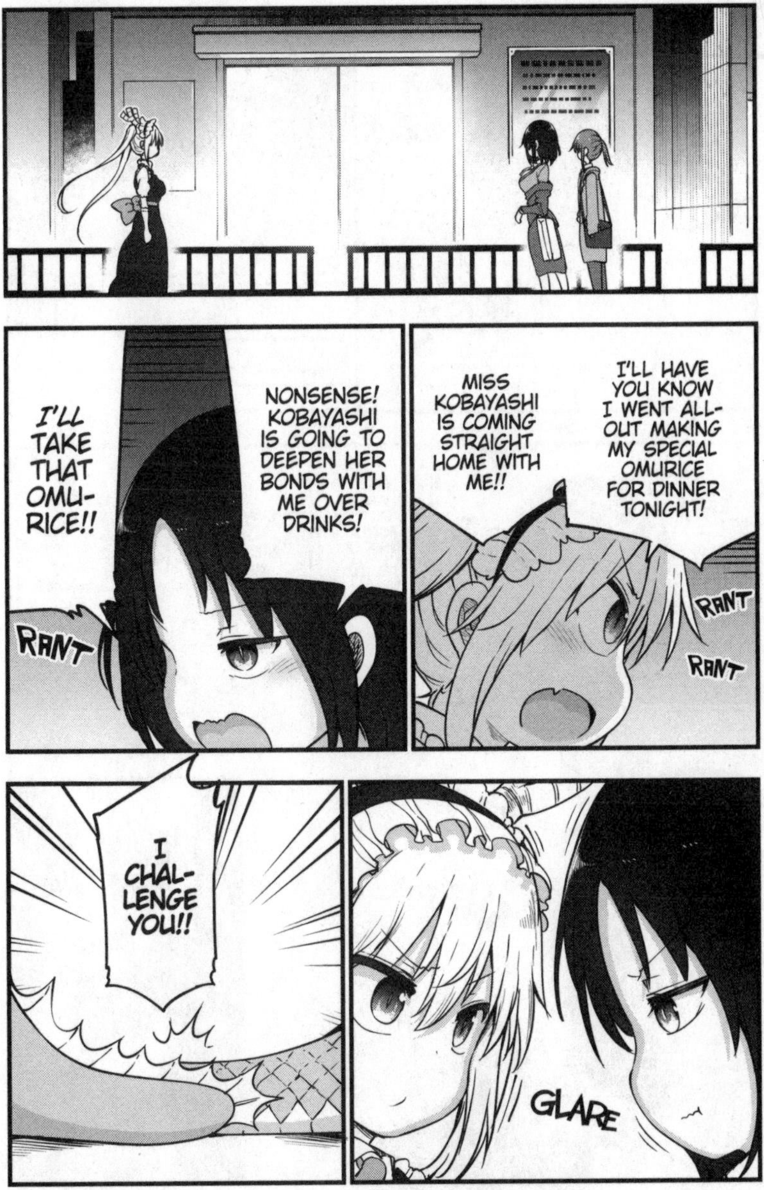
I'LL HAVE YOU KNOW I WENT ALL-OUT MAKING MY SPECIAL OMURICE FOR DINNER TONIGHT!
MISS KOBAYASHI IS COMING STRAIGHT HOME WITH ME!!
RANT
RANT
NONSENSE! KOBAYASHI IS GOING TO DEEPEN HER BONDS WITH ME OVER DRINKS!
I'LL TAKE THAT OMU-RICE!!
RANT
GLARE
I CHAL-LENGE YOU!!

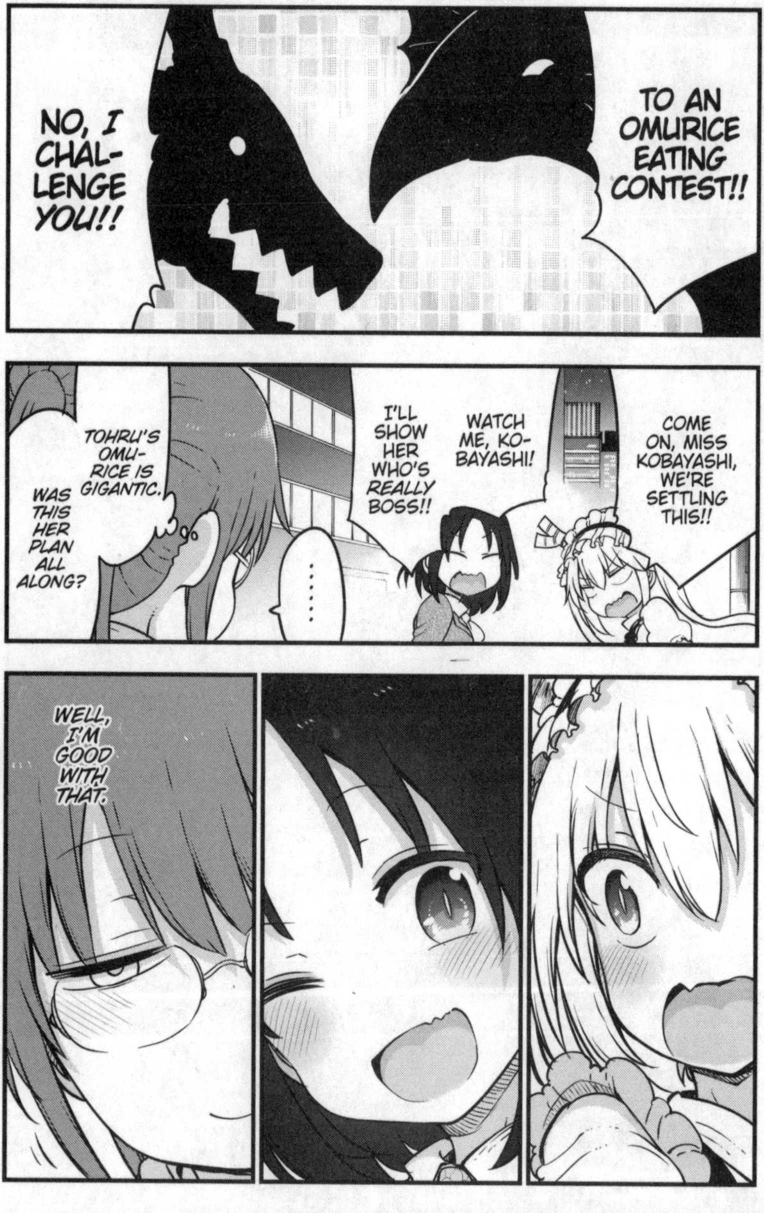
NO, I CHALLENGE YOU!!
TO AN OMURICE EATING CONTEST!!
COME ON, MISS KOBAYASHI, WE'RE SETTLING THIS!!
WATCH ME, KOBAYASHI!
I'LL SHOW HER WHO'S REALLY BOSS!!
......
TOHRU'S OMURICE IS GIGANTIC.
WAS THIS HER PLAN ALL ALONG?
WELL, I'M GOOD WITH THAT.

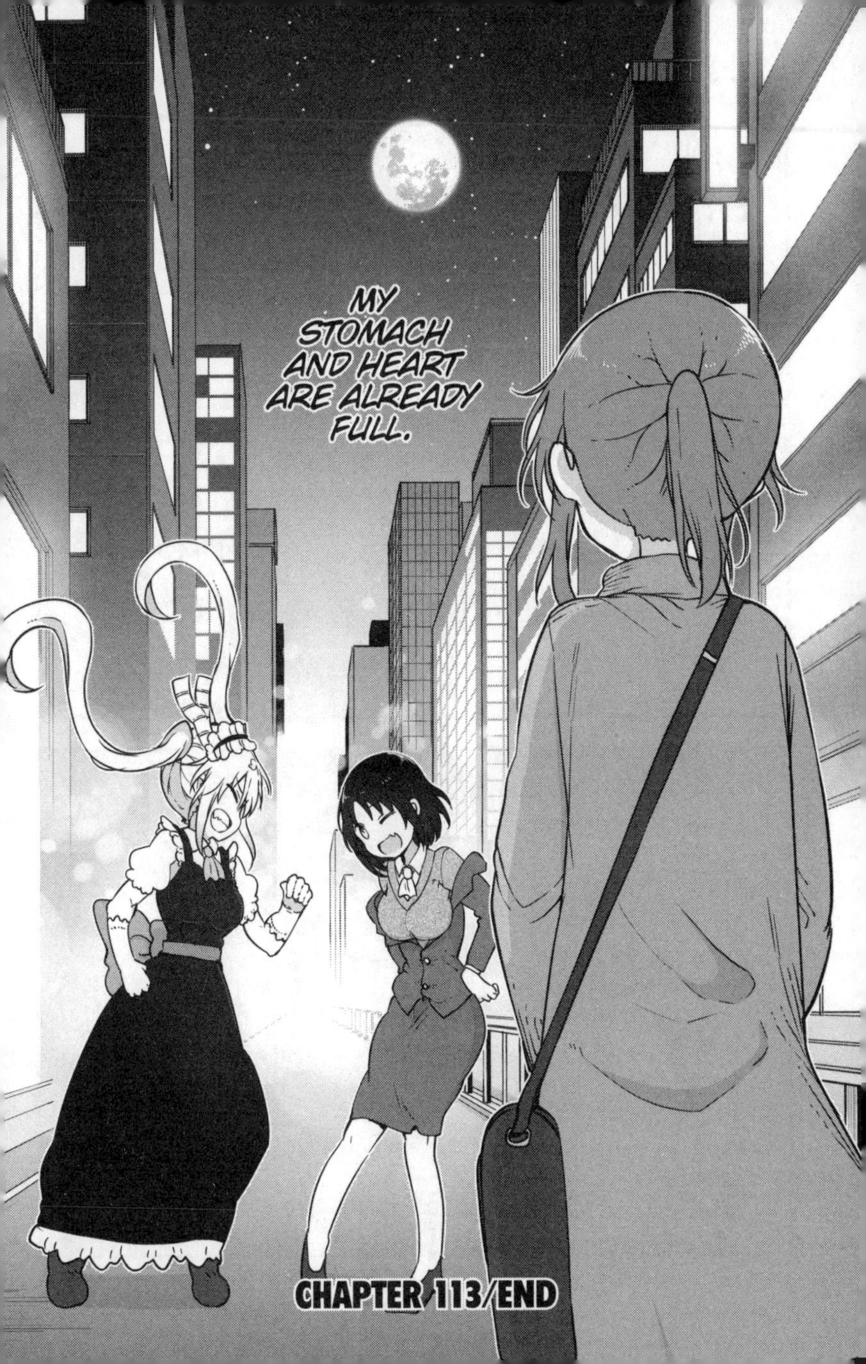
MY STOMACH AND HEART ARE ALREADY FULL.
CHAPTER 113/END

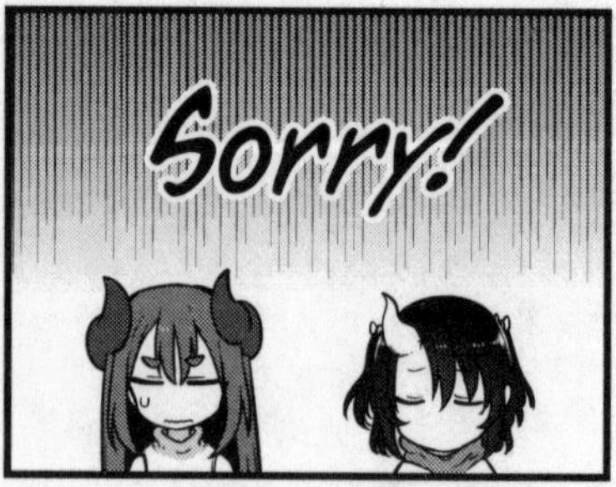
Sorry!

Miss Kobayashi's
DRAGON MAID

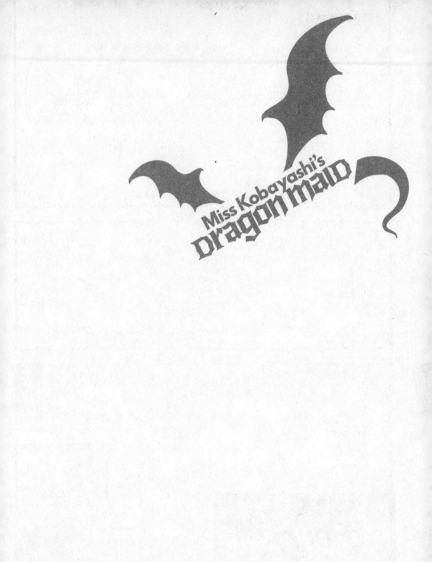

CHAPTER 114

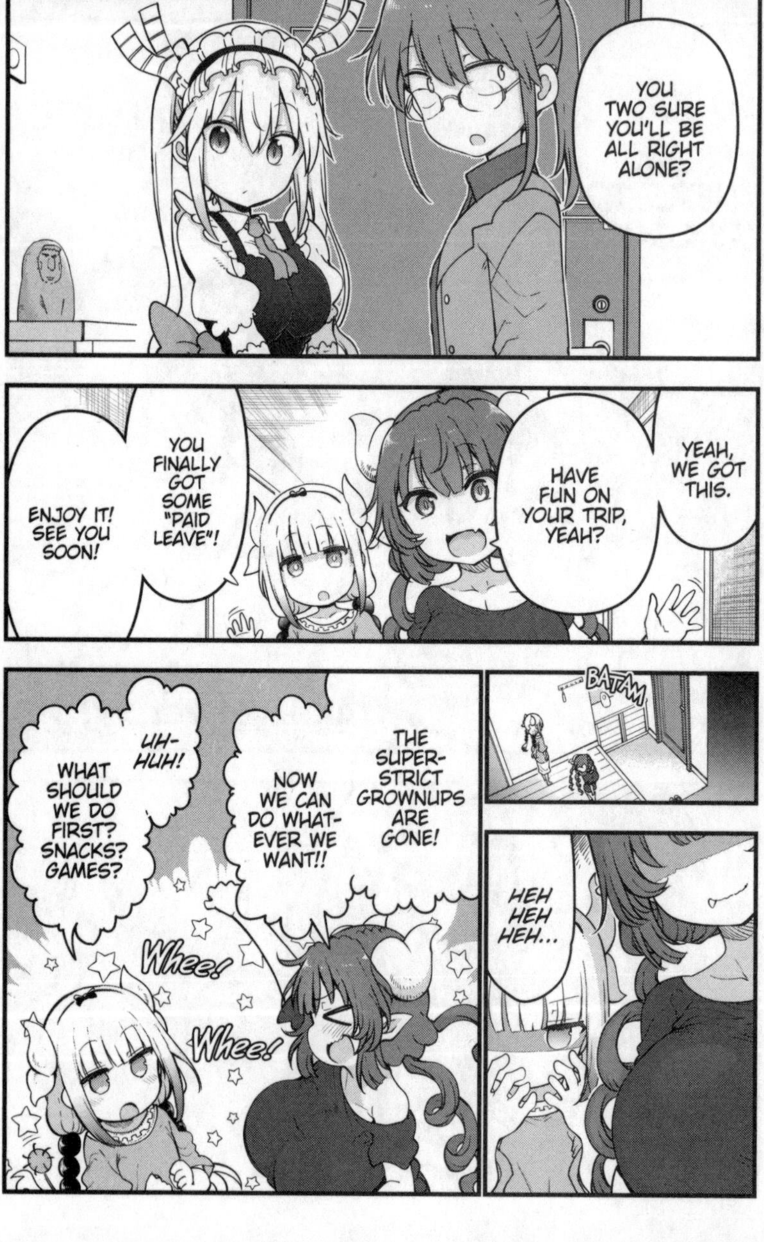
YOU TWO SURE YOU'LL BE ALL RIGHT ALONE?
YEAH, WE GOT THIS.
HAVE FUN ON YOUR TRIP, YEAH?
YOU FINALLY GOT SOME "PAID LEAVE"!
ENJOY IT! SEE YOU SOON!
BATAM
HEH HEH HEH...
THE SUPER-STRICT GROWNUPS ARE GONE!
NOW WE CAN DO WHAT-EVER WE WANT!!
UH-HUH!
WHAT SHOULD WE DO FIRST? SNACKS? GAMES?
Whee!
Whee!

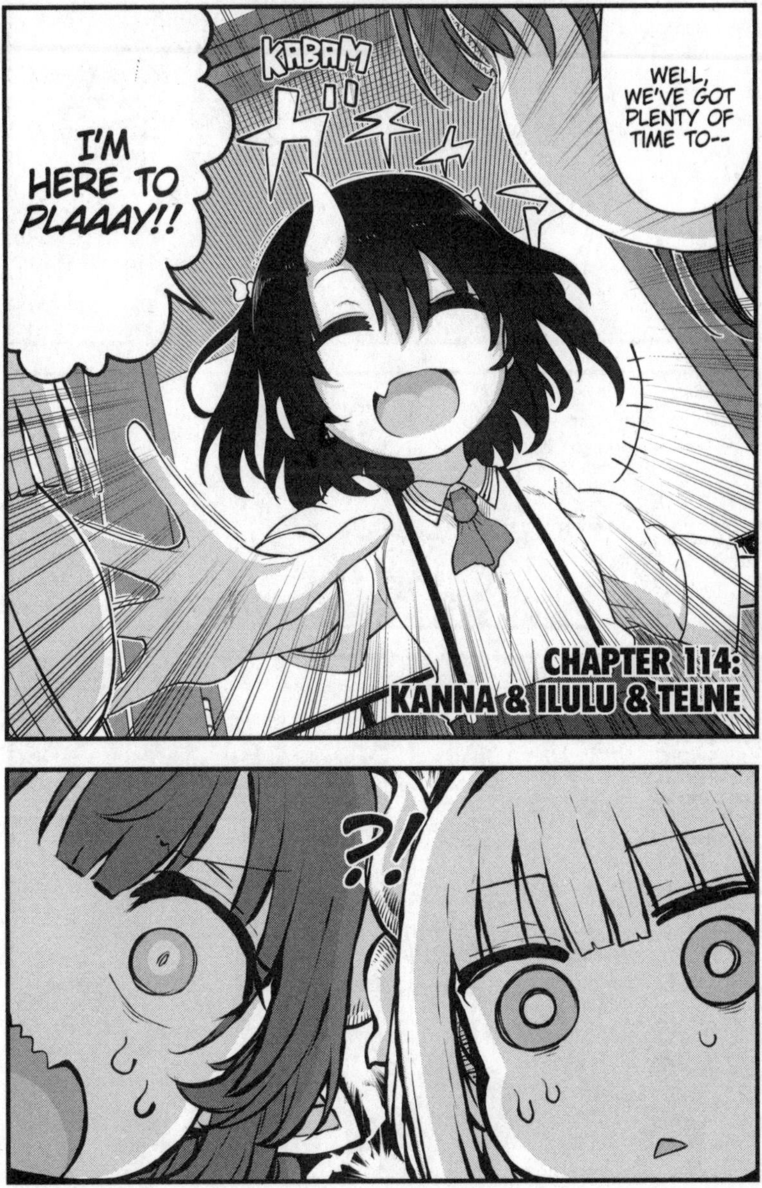
WELL, WE'VE GOT PLENTY OF TIME TO--
KABAM
I'M HERE TO PLAAAY!!
CHAPTER 114:
KANNA & ILULU & TELNE
?!

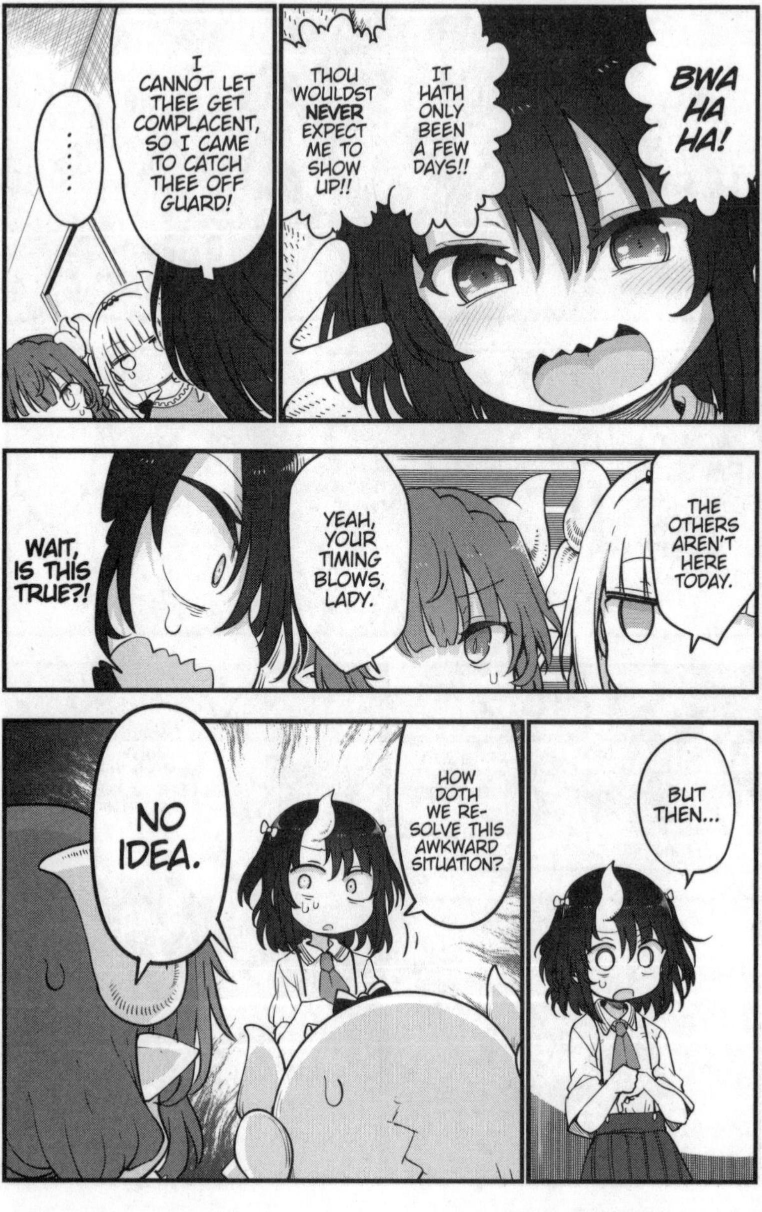
BWA HA HA!
IT HATH ONLY BEEN A FEW DAYS!!
THOU WOULDST **NEVER** EXPECT ME TO SHOW UP!!
I CANNOT LET THEE GET COMPLACENT, SO I CAME TO CATCH THEE OFF GUARD!
……
THE OTHERS AREN'T HERE TODAY.
YEAH, YOUR TIMING BLOWS, LADY.
WAIT, IS THIS TRUE?!
BUT THEN...
HOW DOTH WE RESOLVE THIS AWKWARD SITUATION?
NO IDEA.

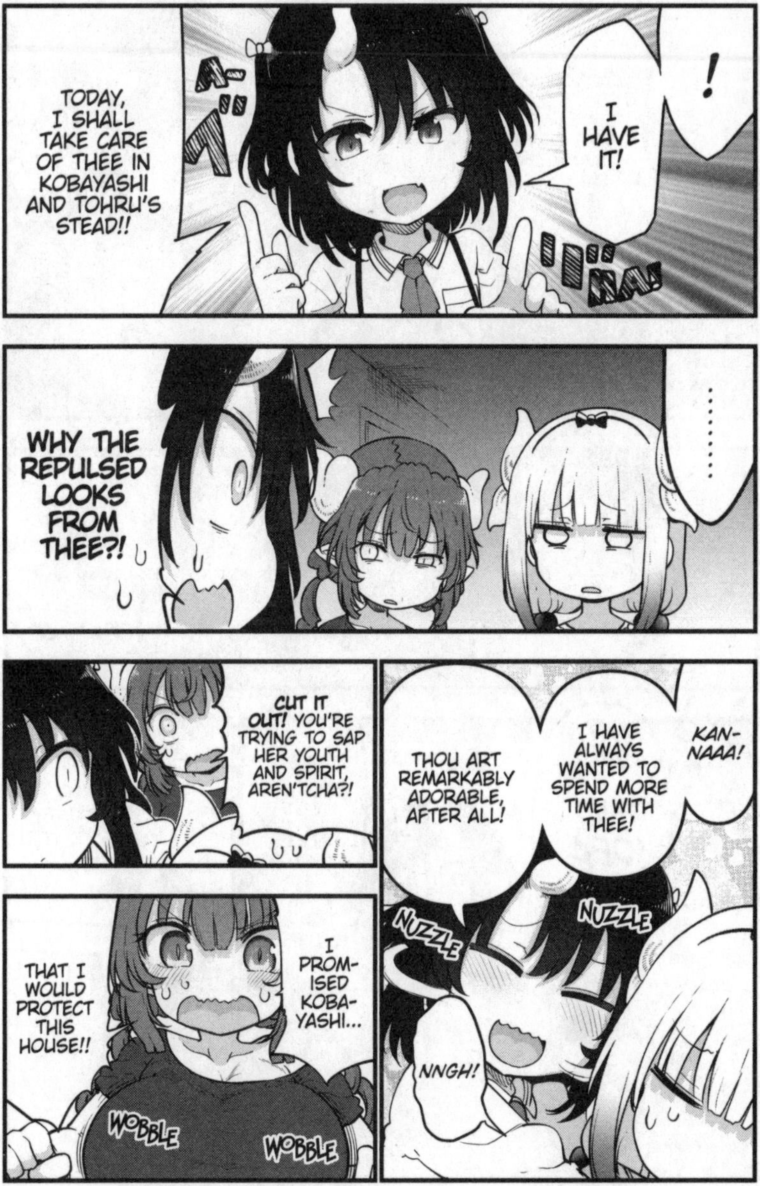
!
I HAVE IT!
NA!
A-
TODAY, I SHALL TAKE CARE OF THEE IN KOBAYASHI AND TOHRU'S STEAD!!
......
WHY THE REPULSED LOOKS FROM THEE?!
KAN-NAAA!
I HAVE ALWAYS WANTED TO SPEND MORE TIME WITH THEE!
THOU ART REMARKABLY ADORABLE, AFTER ALL!
NUZZLE
NUZZLE
NNGH!
CUT IT OUT! YOU'RE TRYING TO SAP HER YOUTH AND SPIRIT, AREN'TCHA?!
I PROMISED KOBAYASHI...
THAT I WOULD PROTECT THIS HOUSE!!
WOBBLE
WOBBLE

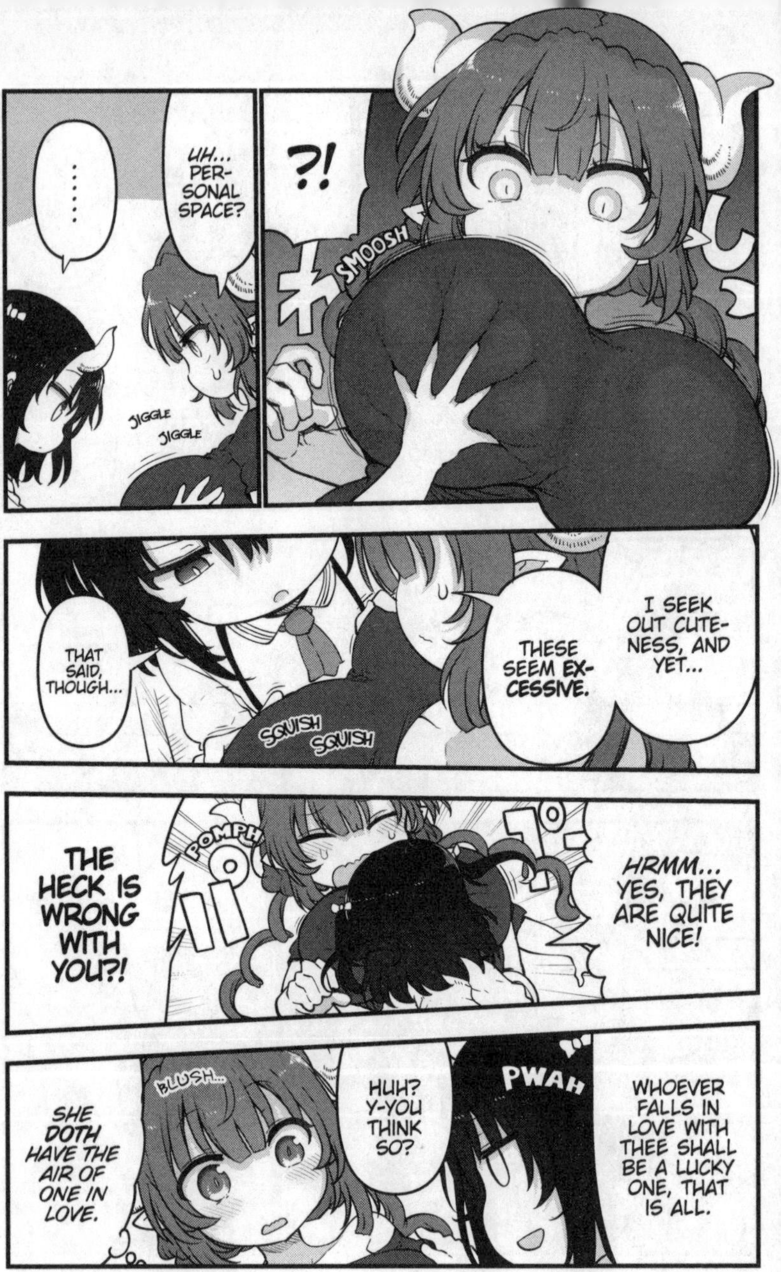
?!
SMOOSH
UH... PERSONAL SPACE?
......
JIGGLE JIGGLE
I SEEK OUT CUTENESS, AND YET...
THESE SEEM EXCESSIVE.
SQUISH SQUISH
THAT SAID, THOUGH...
HRMM... YES, THEY ARE QUITE NICE!
POMPH
THE HECK IS WRONG WITH YOU?!
WHOEVER FALLS IN LOVE WITH THEE SHALL BE A LUCKY ONE, THAT IS ALL.
PWAH
HUH? Y-YOU THINK SO?
BLUSH...
SHE DOTH HAVE THE AIR OF ONE IN LOVE.

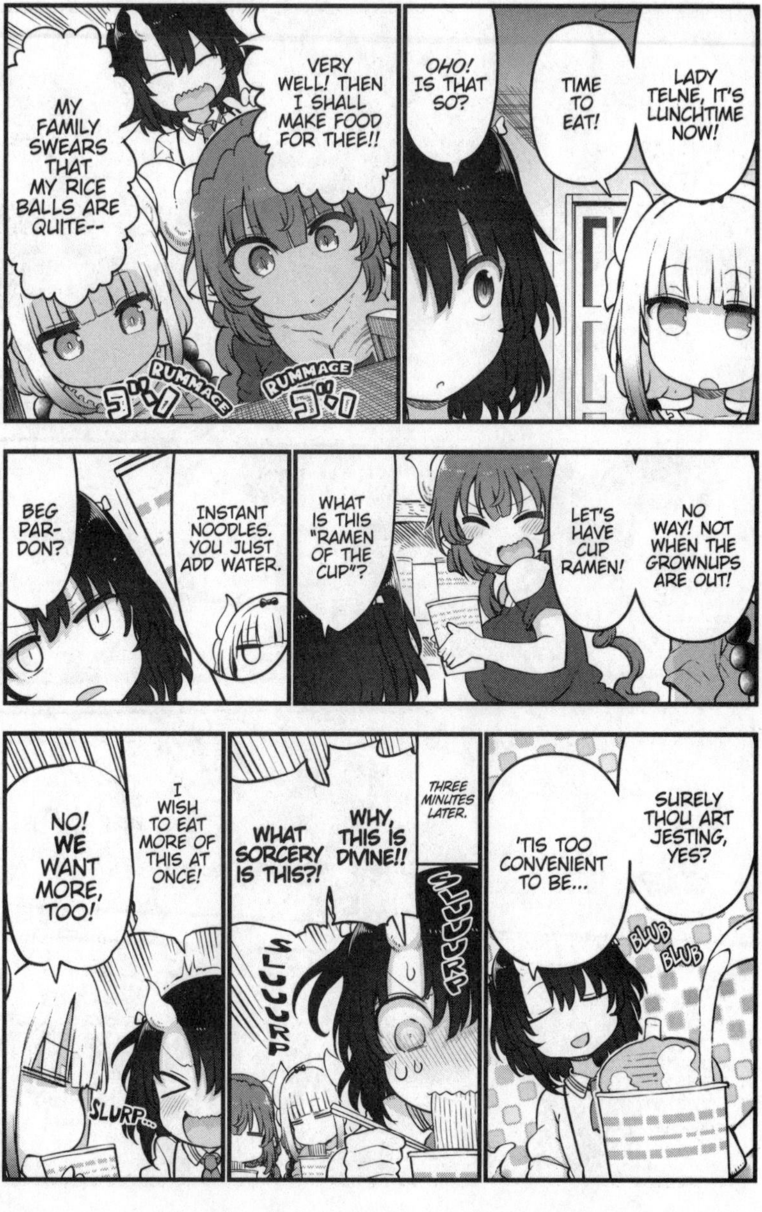
LADY TELNE, IT'S LUNCHTIME NOW!
TIME TO EAT!
OHO! IS THAT SO?
VERY WELL! THEN I SHALL MAKE FOOD FOR THEE!!
MY FAMILY SWEARS THAT MY RICE BALLS ARE QUITE--
RUMMAGE
RUMMAGE
NO WAY! NOT WHEN THE GROWNUPS ARE OUT!
LET'S HAVE CUP RAMEN!
WHAT IS THIS "RAMEN OF THE CUP"?
INSTANT NOODLES. YOU JUST ADD WATER.
BEG PARDON?
SURELY THOU ART JESTING, YES?
'TIS TOO CONVENIENT TO BE...
BLUB BLUB
THREE MINUTES LATER.
WHY, THIS IS DIVINE!!
WHAT SORCERY IS THIS?!
SLUUURP
SLUUURP
I WISH TO EAT MORE OF THIS AT ONCE!
NO! WE WANT MORE, TOO!
SLURP...

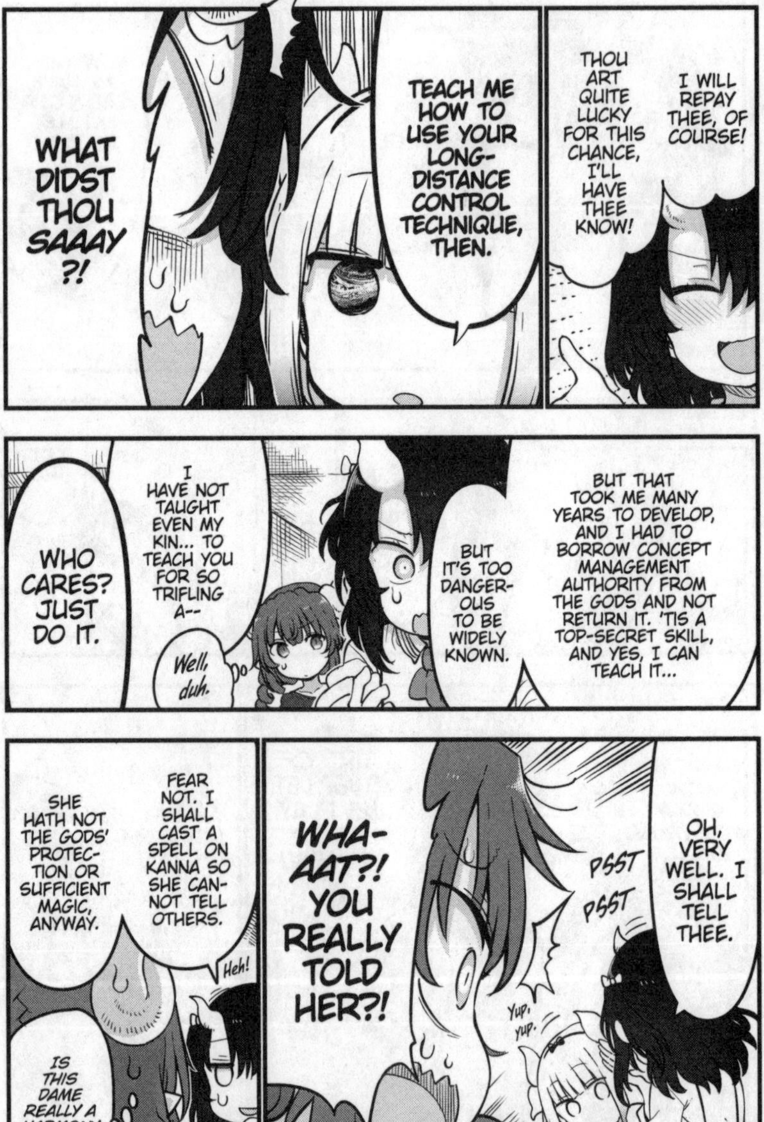
I WILL REPAY THEE, OF COURSE!
THOU ART QUITE LUCKY FOR THIS CHANCE, I'LL HAVE THEE KNOW!
TEACH ME HOW TO USE YOUR LONG-DISTANCE CONTROL TECHNIQUE, THEN.
WHAT DIDST THOU SAAAY?!
BUT THAT TOOK ME MANY YEARS TO DEVELOP, AND I HAD TO BORROW CONCEPT MANAGEMENT AUTHORITY FROM THE GODS AND NOT RETURN IT. 'TIS A TOP-SECRET SKILL, AND YES, I CAN TEACH IT...
BUT IT'S TOO DANGER-OUS TO BE WIDELY KNOWN.
I HAVE NOT TAUGHT EVEN MY KIN... TO TEACH YOU FOR SO TRIFLING A--
Well, duh.
WHO CARES? JUST DO IT.
OH, VERY WELL. I SHALL TELL THEE.
PSST
PSST
Yup, yup.
WHA-AAT?! YOU REALLY TOLD HER?!
FEAR NOT. I SHALL CAST A SPELL ON KANNA SO SHE CAN-NOT TELL OTHERS.
SHE HATH NOT THE GODS' PROTEC-TION OR SUFFICIENT MAGIC, ANYWAY.
Heh!
IS THIS DAME REALLY A HARMONY DRAGON?

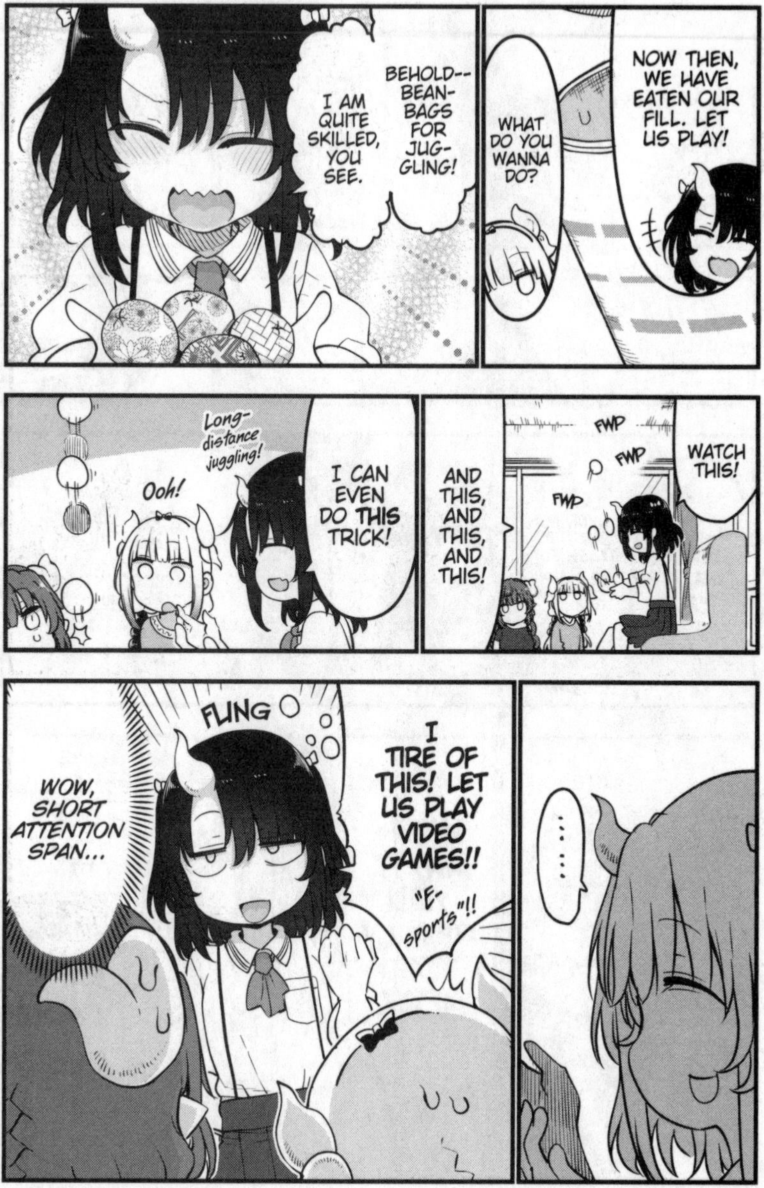
NOW THEN, WE HAVE EATEN OUR FILL. LET US PLAY!
WHAT DO YOU WANNA DO?
BEHOLD-- BEAN-BAGS FOR JUG-GLING!
I AM QUITE SKILLED, YOU SEE.
WATCH THIS!
FWP
FWP
FWP
AND THIS, AND THIS, AND THIS!
I CAN EVEN DO THIS TRICK!
Long-distance juggling!
Ooh!
......
I TIRE OF THIS! LET US PLAY VIDEO GAMES!!
FLING
"E-sports"!!
WOW, SHORT ATTENTION SPAN...

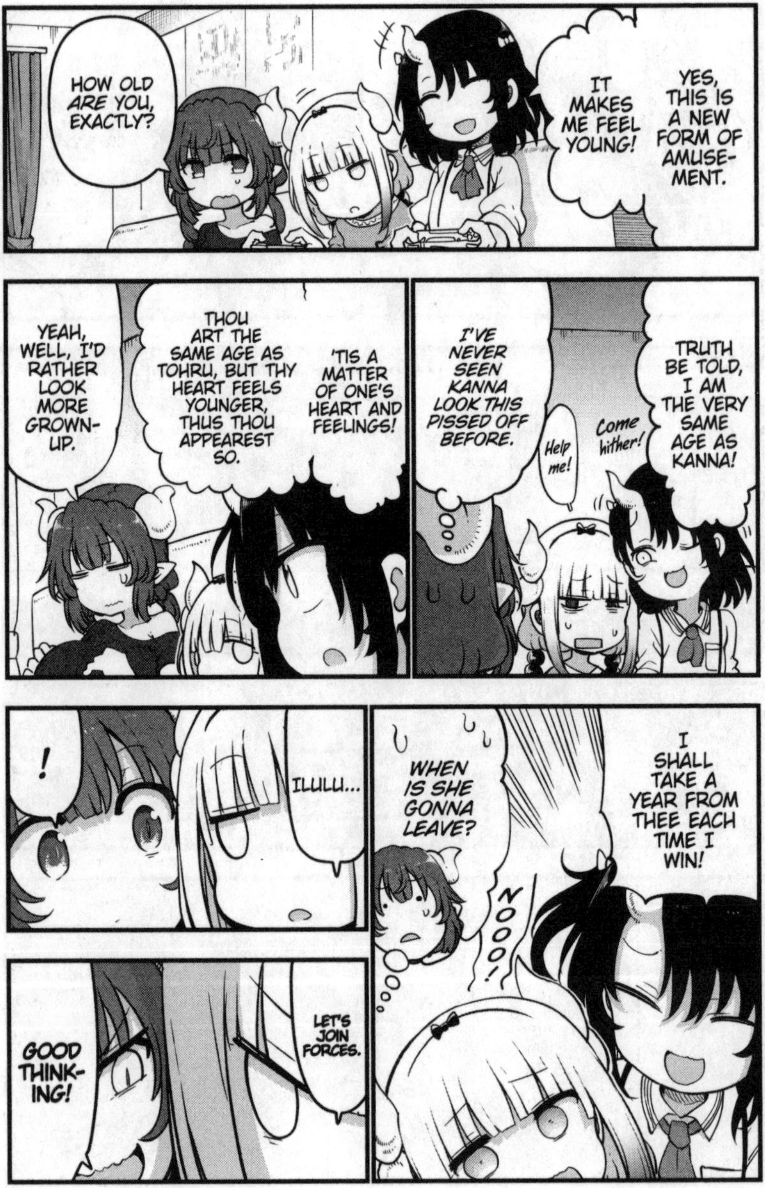
YES, THIS IS A NEW FORM OF AMUSEMENT.
IT MAKES ME FEEL YOUNG!
HOW OLD ARE YOU, EXACTLY?
TRUTH BE TOLD, I AM THE VERY SAME AGE AS KANNA!
Come hither!
Help me!
I'VE NEVER SEEN KANNA LOOK THIS PISSED OFF BEFORE.
'TIS A MATTER OF ONE'S HEART AND FEELINGS!
THOU ART THE SAME AGE AS TOHRU, BUT THY HEART FEELS YOUNGER, THUS THOU APPEAREST SO.
YEAH, WELL, I'D RATHER LOOK MORE GROWN-UP.
I SHALL TAKE A YEAR FROM THEE EACH TIME I WIN!
WHEN IS SHE GONNA LEAVE?
NOOOO!
ILULU...
!
LET'S JOIN FORCES.
GOOD THINKING!

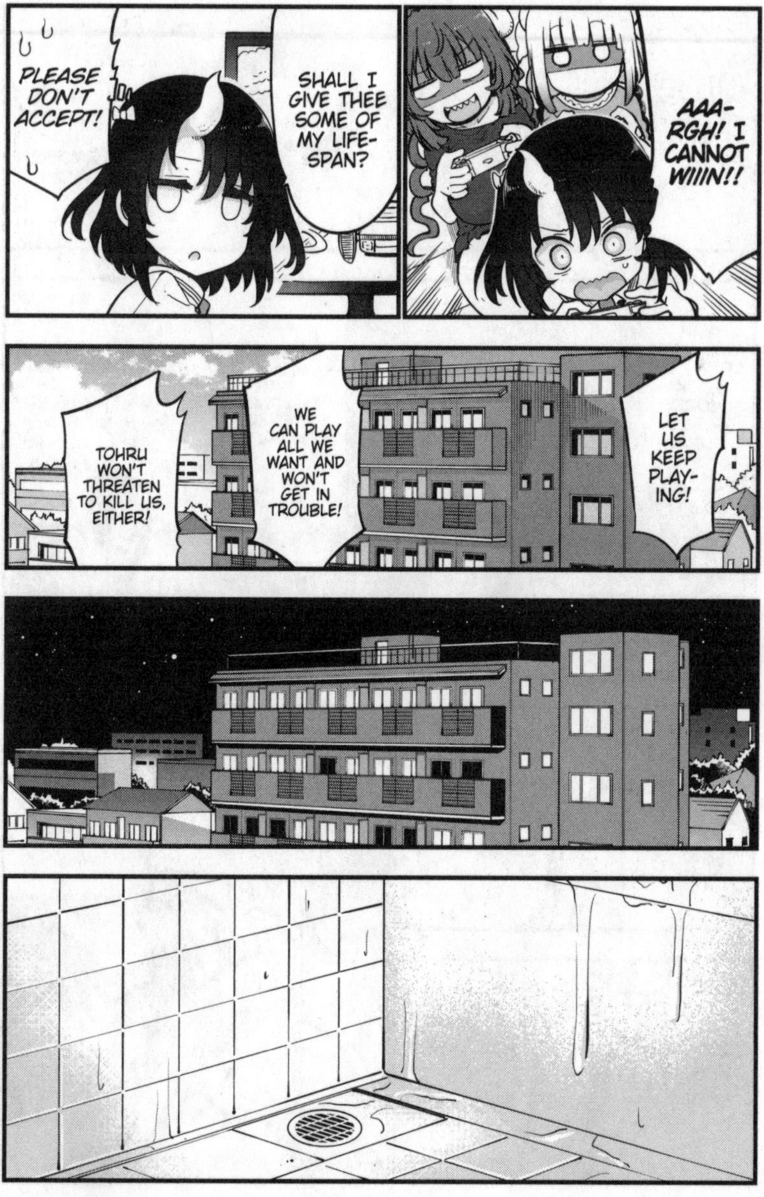
AAA-RGH! I CANNOT WIIIN!!
SHALL I GIVE THEE SOME OF MY LIFE-SPAN?
PLEASE DON'T ACCEPT!
LET US KEEP PLAY-ING!
WE CAN PLAY ALL WE WANT AND WON'T GET IN TROUBLE!
TOHRU WON'T THREATEN TO KILL US, EITHER!

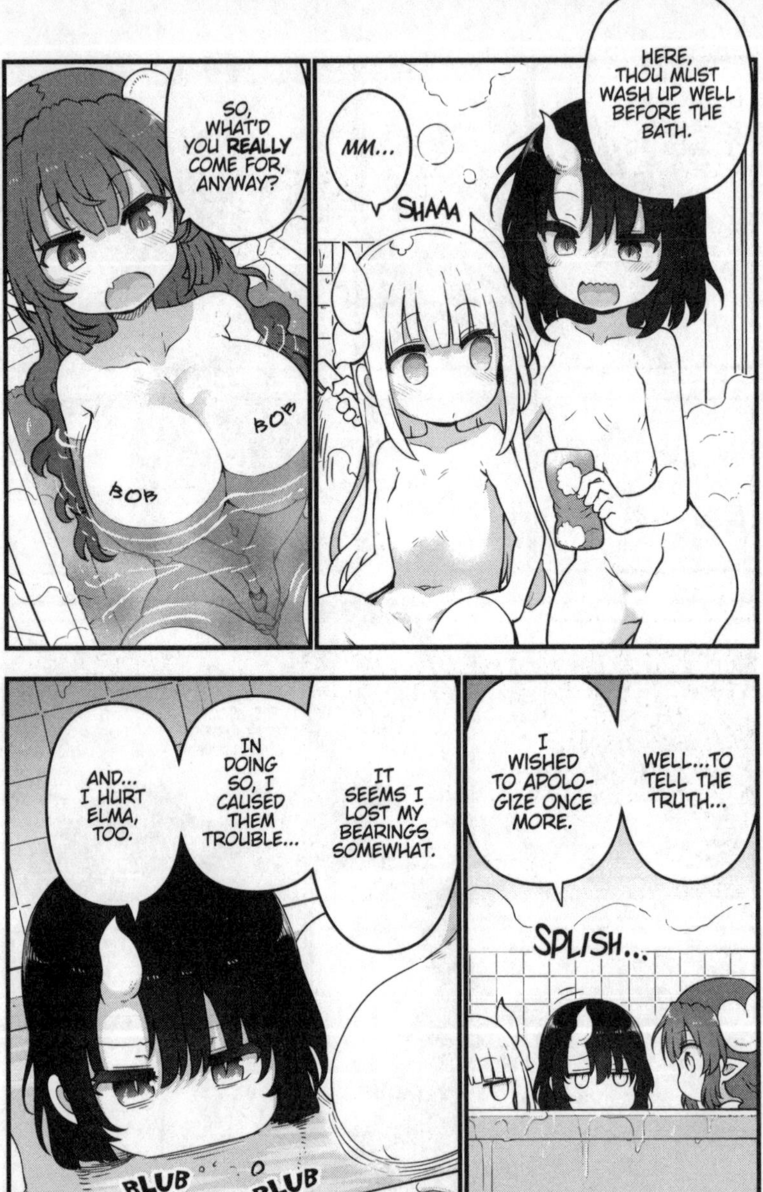

HERE, THOU MUST WASH UP WELL BEFORE THE BATH.
MM...
SHAAA
SO, WHAT'D YOU **REALLY** COME FOR, ANYWAY?
BOB
BOB
WELL...TO TELL THE TRUTH...
I WISHED TO APOLO-GIZE ONCE MORE.
SPLISH...
IT SEEMS I LOST MY BEARINGS SOMEWHAT.
IN DOING SO, I CAUSED THEM TROUBLE...
AND... I HURT ELMA, TOO.
BLUB
BLUB

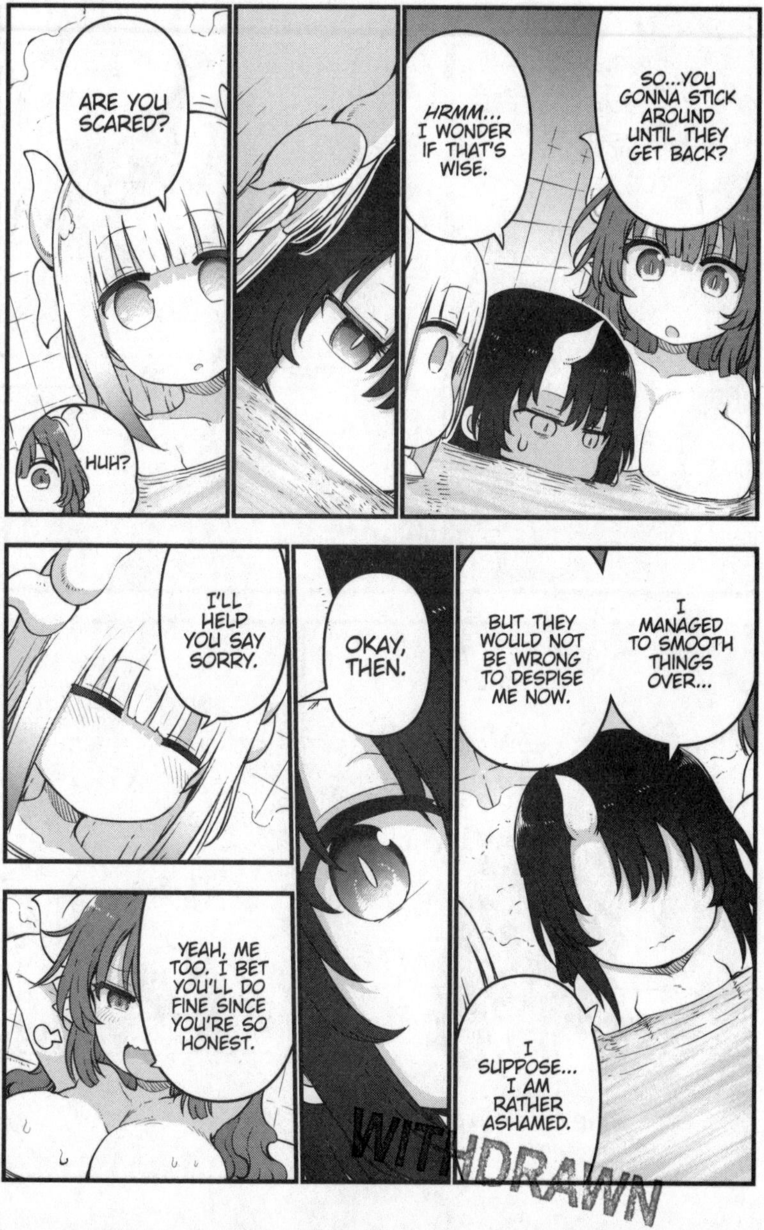
SO...YOU GONNA STICK AROUND UNTIL THEY GET BACK?
HRMM... I WONDER IF THAT'S WISE.
ARE YOU SCARED?
HUH?
I MANAGED TO SMOOTH THINGS OVER...
BUT THEY WOULD NOT BE WRONG TO DESPISE ME NOW.
I SUPPOSE... I AM RATHER ASHAMED.
OKAY, THEN.
I'LL HELP YOU SAY SORRY.
YEAH, ME TOO. I BET YOU'LL DO FINE SINCE YOU'RE SO HONEST.

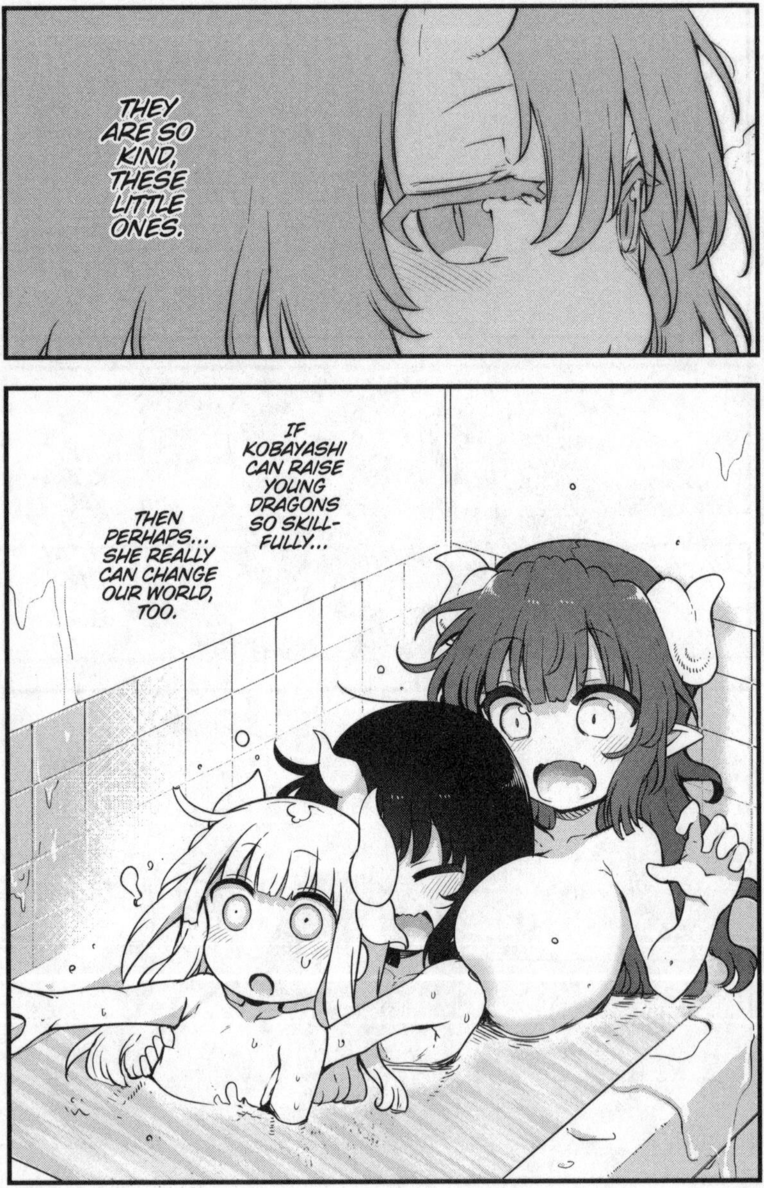
THEY ARE SO KIND, THESE LITTLE ONES.
IF KOBAYASHI CAN RAISE YOUNG DRAGONS SO SKILL-FULLY...
THEN PERHAPS... SHE REALLY CAN CHANGE OUR WORLD, TOO.

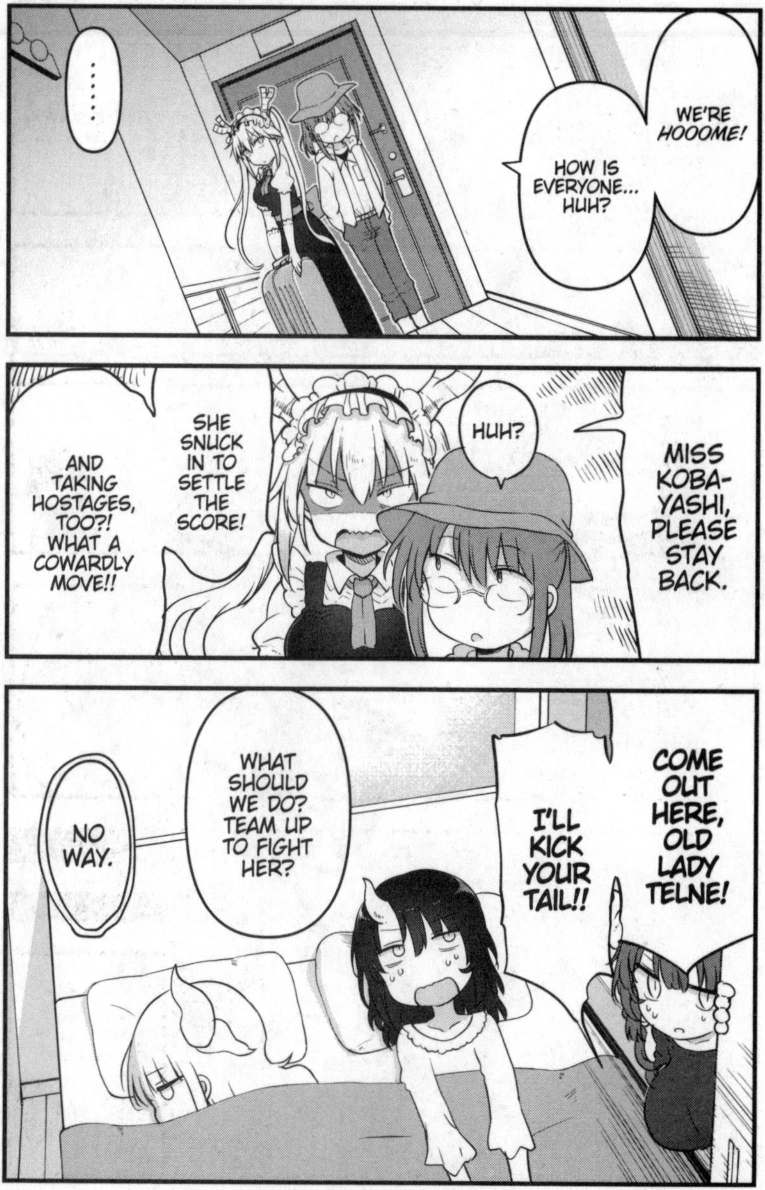
WE'RE HOOOME!
HOW IS EVERYONE... HUH?
......
MISS KOBA-YASHI, PLEASE STAY BACK.
HUH?
SHE SNUCK IN TO SETTLE THE SCORE!
AND TAKING HOSTAGES, TOO?! WHAT A COWARDLY MOVE!!
COME OUT HERE, OLD LADY TELNE!
I'LL KICK YOUR TAIL!!
WHAT SHOULD WE DO? TEAM UP TO FIGHT HER?
NO WAY.

CHAPTER 114/END

AFTERWORD

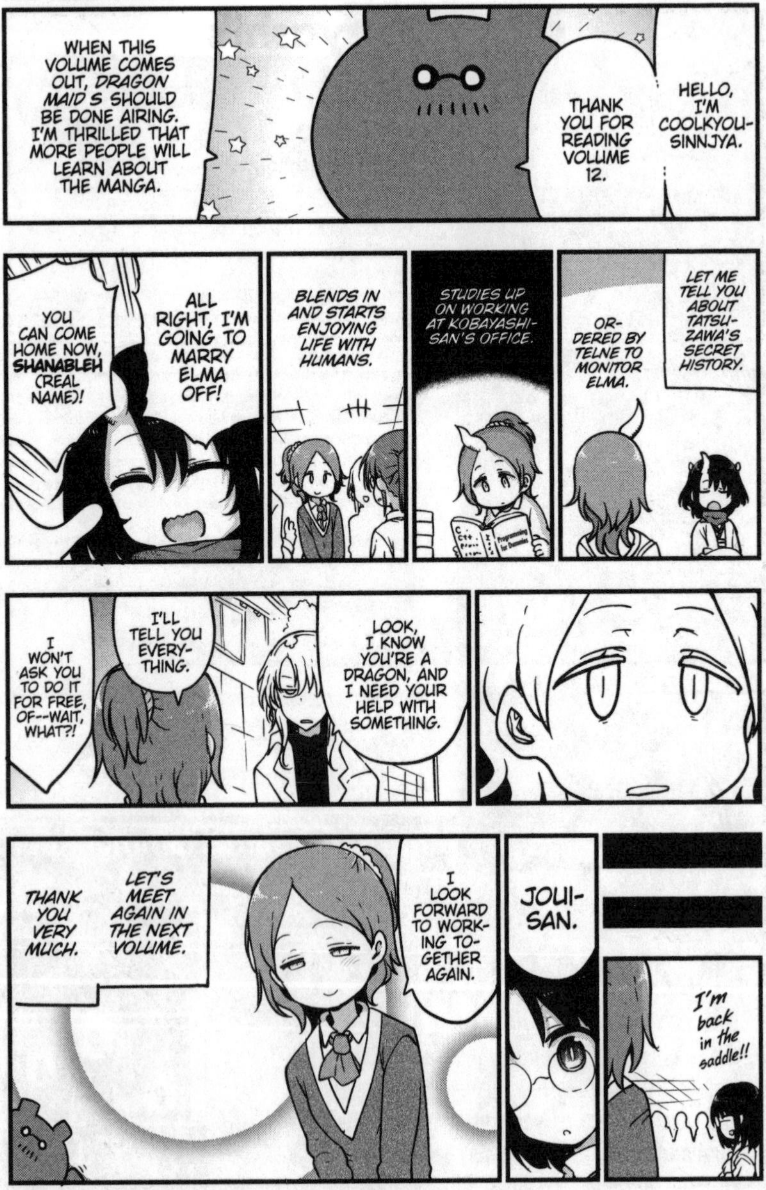
HELLO, I'M COOLKYOU-SINNJYA.
THANK YOU FOR READING VOLUME 12.
WHEN THIS VOLUME COMES OUT, *DRAGON MAID S* SHOULD BE DONE AIRING. I'M THRILLED THAT MORE PEOPLE WILL LEARN ABOUT THE MANGA.
LET ME TELL YOU ABOUT TATSUZAWA'S SECRET HISTORY.
ORDERED BY TELNE TO MONITOR ELMA.
STUDIES UP ON WORKING AT KOBAYASHI-SAN'S OFFICE.
BLENDS IN AND STARTS ENJOYING LIFE WITH HUMANS.
ALL RIGHT, I'M GOING TO MARRY ELMA OFF!
YOU CAN COME HOME NOW, **SHANABLEH** (REAL NAME)!
LOOK, I KNOW YOU'RE A DRAGON, AND I NEED YOUR HELP WITH SOMETHING.
I'LL TELL YOU EVERYTHING.
I WON'T ASK YOU TO DO IT FOR FREE, OF--WAIT, WHAT?!
I'm back in the saddle!!
JOUI-SAN.
I LOOK FORWARD TO WORKING TOGETHER AGAIN.
LET'S MEET AGAIN IN THE NEXT VOLUME.
THANK YOU VERY MUCH.

Assistants: Namazenmai-sama, Giovanni Works-sama

SEVEN SEAS ENTERTAIN

Miss Koba
Dragon Maid
VOL. 12

story and art by **coolkyousinnjya**

TRANSLATION
Jenny McKeon

ADAPTATION
Shanti Whitesides

LETTERING
Jennifer Skarupa

LOGO DESIGN
H. Qi

COVER DESIGN
Nicky Lim

PROOFREADING
Krista Grandy

PRINT MANAGER
Rhiannon Rasmussen-Silverstein

PRODUCTION MANAGER
Lissa Pattillo

EDITOR-IN-CHIEF
Julie Davis

ASSOCIATE PUBLISHER
Adam Arnold

PUBLISHER
Jason DeAngelis

MISS KOBAYASHI'S DRAGON MAID VOL. 12

First published in Japan in 2021 by Futabasha Publishers Ltd., Tokyo.
English version published by Seven Seas Entertainment.
Under license from Futabasha Publishers Ltd.

Seven Seas press and purchase enquiries can be sent to Marketing Manager Lianne Sentar at press@gomanga.com. Information regarding the distribution and purchase of digital editions is available from Digital Manager CK Russell at digital@gomanga.com.

ISBN: 978-1-63858-607-4
Printed in Canada
First Printing: August 2022
10 9 8 7 6 5 4 3 2 1

FOLLOW US ONLINE: ***www.sevenseasentertainment.com***

READING DIRECTIONS

This book reads from ***right to left***, Japanese style. If this is your first time reading manga, you start reading from the top right panel on each page and take it from there. If you get lost, just follow the numbered diagram here. It may seem backwards at first, but you'll get the hang of it! Have fun!!

1
2
3
4
5
6
7
8
9

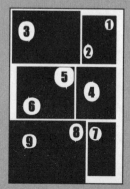